Problem Solving with Python

Peter D. Kazarinoff, PhD

3.7 Edition

Problem Solving with Python 3.7 Edition
by Peter D. Kazarinoff

ISBN: 9781693405419

Copywrite © 2018 - 2019 Peter D. Kazarinoff

Revision History

2018-01-09 Initial Release

2019-02-01 3.6.2 Edition
Reformat Table of Contents
Revision to end of chapter questions

2019-03-15 3.7.0 Edition
Re-ordered chapters: Jupyter Notebooks chapter after Orientation chapter
Re-ordered chapters: Arrays and Matricies chapter after Data Types and Variables chapter
Re-ordered chapters: Functions chapter after Plotting with Matplotlib chapter

2019-09-15 3.7.4 Edition
Revision of Orientation chapter: Images and text for Python 3.7 installation
Revision of Plotting with Matplotlib chapter: New table of object-oriented plotting commands
New end of chapter questions: Arrays and Matricies chapter, Loops chapter

This book is dedicated to my wonderful and loving wife, Sophie and our two inquisitive daughters. I love you very much. Thank-you for helping make this text a reality.

4

Contents

Preface — **11**
    Motivation 11
    Acknowledgments 11
    Supporting Materials. 11
    Formatting Conventions 12
    Errata 14

1 Orientation — **15**
    1.1 Introduction 15
    1.2 Why Python? 16
    1.3 The Anaconda Distribution of Python 17
    1.4 Installing Anaconda on Windows 18
    1.5 Installing Anaconda on MacOS 23
    1.6 Installing Anaconda on Linux 27
    1.7 Installing Python from Python.org 30
    1.8 Summary 33
    1.9 Review Questions 33

2 Jupyter Notebooks — **37**
    2.1 Introduction 37
    2.2 What is a Jupyter Notebook? 38
    2.3 Why Jupyter Notebooks? 38
    2.4 Installing Juypter 39
    2.5 Opening a Jupyter Notebook 40
    2.6 The Jupyter Notebook Interface 45
    2.7 Magic Commands 58
    2.8 Getting Help in a Jupyter Notebook. 61

	2.9	Summary	64
	2.10	Review Questions	65
3	**The Python REPL**		**69**
	3.1	Introduction	69
	3.2	Python as a Calculator	70
	3.3	Variables	75
	3.4	String Operations	76
	3.5	Print Statements	77
	3.6	Summary	79
	3.7	Review Questions	80
4	**Data Types and Variables**		**87**
	4.1	Introduction	87
	4.2	Numeric Data Types	88
	4.3	Boolean Data Type	90
	4.4	Strings	92
	4.5	Lists	95
	4.6	Dictionaries and Tuples	96
	4.7	Summary	99
	4.8	Review Questions	100
5	**NumPy and Arrays**		**107**
	5.1	Introduction	107
	5.2	NumPy	108
	5.3	Installing NumPy	108
	5.4	Python Lists and NumPy Arrays	109
	5.5	Array Creation	111
	5.6	Array Indexing	118
	5.7	Array Slicing	121
	5.8	Array Operations	123
	5.9	Systems of Linear Equations	127
	5.10	Summary	129
	5.11	Review Questions	129
6	**Plotting with Matplotlib**		**135**
	6.1	Introduction	135

CONTENTS

6.2	What is Matplotlib?	136
6.3	Installing Matplotlib	136
6.4	Line Plots	137
6.5	Saving plots	144
6.6	Multi Line Plots	146
6.7	Bar Charts and Pie Charts	149
6.8	Error Bars	154
6.9	Histograms	158
6.10	Box Plots and Violin Plots	159
6.11	Scatter Plots	162
6.12	Plot annotations	165
6.13	Subplots	168
6.14	Plot Styles	170
6.15	Contour Plots	174
6.16	Quiver and Stream Plots	180
6.17	3D Surface Plots	196
6.18	Summary	203
6.19	Review Questions	204

7 Functions and Modules — 211

7.1	Introduction	211
7.2	Why Functions?	212
7.3	First Function	212
7.4	Functions with Multiple Arguments	214
7.5	Functions with Default Arguments	216
7.6	Calling Functions from Other Files	217
7.7	Docstrings in Functions	218
7.8	Positional and Keyword Arguments	221
7.9	Summary	224
7.10	Review Questions	224

8 If Else Try Except — 231

8.1	Introduction	231
8.2	User Input	232
8.3	Selection Statements	233
8.4	If statements	234

8.5	If Else Statements	236
8.6	Try-Except Statements	237
8.7	Flowcharts	240
8.8	Summary	247
8.9	Review Questions	247

9 Loops — 251

9.1	Introduction	251
9.2	For Loops	252
9.3	While Loops	254
9.4	Break and Continue	255
9.5	Flowcharts Describing Loops	256
9.6	Summary	261
9.7	Review Questions	261

10 Symbolic Math — 267

10.1	Introduction	267
10.2	SymPy	268
10.3	Installing SymPy	268
10.4	Defining Variables	269
10.5	Expressions and Substitutions	269
10.6	Equations	273
10.7	Solving Equations	274
10.8	Solving Two Equations for Two Unknowns	275
10.9	Summary	280
10.10	Review Questions	280

11 Python and External Hardware — 285

11.1	Introduction	285
11.2	PySerial	286
11.3	Bytes and Unicode Strings	286
11.4	Controlling an LED with Python	288
11.5	Reading a Sensor with Python	294
11.6	Summary	302
11.7	Project Ideas	303

12 MicroPython — 305

12.1	Introduction	305
12.2	What is MicroPython?	306
12.3	Installing MicroPython	307
12.4	The MicroPython REPL	316
12.5	Blinking a LED	321
12.6	Reading a Sensor	324
12.7	Uploading Code	328
12.8	Summary	332
12.9	Project Ideas	332

Appendix 335

Appendix A	Contents	335
Appendix B	Reserved and Keywords in Python	336
Appendix C	ASCII Character Codes	337
Appendix D	Virtual Environments	339
Appendix E	NumPy Math Functions	342
Appendix F	Git and GitHub	343
Appendix G	LaTeX Math	345
Appendix H	Problem Solving with Python Book Construction	345
Appendix I	Contributions	347
Appendix J	Cover Artwork	347
Appendix K	About the Author	347

Preface

Motivation

The motivation for writing this book is that many undergraduate engineering students have to take a programming course based on MATLAB. MATLAB is a great piece of software, but it currently costs $49.00 for a student license and requires a site license to be used on school computers. Subsequently, it is costly for a student to use MATLAB and it is costly for a college to support a course that uses MATLAB. In addition, this site license eventually expires and students need to purchase another copy often before they finish their degree.

The Python programming language, on the other hand, is open source and free. To download and use Python, the cost to both the student and the college is zero (minus time spent). By moving an undergraduate engineering programming class to Python, students save money and gain greater access to the software they use in class. Later on in their engineering education, students can continue to use Python for free.

Acknowledgments

The creation of this book and supporting material would not be possible without the gracious support of my wife and family. Students at Portland Community College continue to give me hope that the next generation of engineers will be a diverse group of team problem solvers.

The Python Data Science Handbook and *Machine Learning in Python* as well as *Reiman Equations in Python* served as inspiration and examples of using Jupyter notebooks to construct a book. The *bookbook* repository on GitHub provided a starting point for the tooling used to convert this book from Jupyter notebooks into a website and into LaTeX for printing.

Supporting Materials

Supporting materials for this text can be found on the textbook website:

> problemsolvingwithpython.com

The textbook website contains all of the text in web format. Code examples and Jupyter notebooks for the text can be found in the GitHub repository for the book:

github.com/ProfessorKazarinoff/Problem-Solving-with-Python-37-Edition

Live notebooks, where code examples found in the text can be run without installing any software, are available at:

mybinder.org/v2/gh/ProfessorKazarinoff/Problem-Solving-with-Python-37-Edition/master

If you are an instructor and using this book in a course with students- please send me an email using your school email address. In the email, include the course you are teaching and the term, approximate enrollment, and a link to the course listing on your school website.

peter.kazarinoff@problemsolvingwithpython.com

I am happy to reply with a solution key for the end of chapter review problems as well as quiz and exam question banks.

Formatting Conventions

This book and supporting materials use the following formatting conventions.

Web Address

Web address will be shown as:

```
https://github.com/professorkazarinoff/Problem-Solving-with-Python
```

Important terms and vocabulary

Important terms and vocabulary are shown in *italic text*.

There is a difference between *local variables* and *global variables* in Python code.

File Names

File names are shown in ***bold and italic text***.

After completing the code, save the file as ***hello.py*** in the current directory.

Module and Package Names

Module and Package names will be shown in **bold text**.

NumPy and **Matplotlib** are two useful packages for problem solvers.

Inline code

Inline code, including variable names, is shown in `monospace font`.

> To compare a variable use `var == 'string'` and make sure to include `==`, the double equals sign.

Separate code blocks

Separate code blocks appear in their own sections in `monospaced font`.

```
import numpy as np
import pandas as pd
import matplotlib.pyplot as plt
```

Anaconda Prompt Commands

Commands typed into the **Anaconda Prompt** are shown in separate sections which contain the prompt symbol > before each line. Note the prompt > should not be typed. The prompt symbol is included to indicate **Anaconda Prompt**, not a character for the user to enter.

```
> conda create -n env python=3.7
> conda activate env
```

Terminal Commands

Commands typed into the MacOS or Linux terminal appear in separate sections which contain the dollar symbol $ before each line. Note the dollar symbol $ should not be typed. The dollar symbol is included to indicate a terminal prompt, not a character for the user to enter.

```
$ pip install pint
$ cd pint_srcipts
```

Python REPL Commands

Commands typed into the **Python REPL** (the Python Interpreter) appears in separate code sections, which contain the triple arrow prompt >>> . Note the triple arrow >>> prompt should not be typed. Triple arrows are included to indicate the Python REPL prompt, not a character for the user to enter. The output from the Python REPL is shown on a separate line below the command, without the >>> prompt.

```
>>> 2 + 2
4
>>> print('Problem Solving with Python')
Problem Solving with Python
```

Jupyter Notebook cells

Commands typed into Jupyter notebook cells appear with the label In [#]: to the left of the code section. The output from Jupyter notebook cells is shown below the input cell. Only code in the input cells needs to be typed. Output cell are be produced automatically by clicking the run button or typing [shift]+[Enter].

```
In [1]:  A = 2
         B = 3
         C = A + B
         print(C)
```

5

Keystrokes and Buttons

Keystrokes directly entered by the keyboard or buttons that are indicated on programs or web pages are shown inside square brackets in [monospaced font].

In order to delete a line use the [Backspace] key. To exit the shell type [shift]+[c]

Errata

Errata including any typos, code errors and formatting inconsistencies can be submitted to:

errata@problemsolvingwithpython.com

Please include the chapter number and section number in your email. Thank-you in advance for helping improve this text for future readers.

Chapter 1

Orientation

1.1 Introduction

Welcome to the world of problem solving with Python! This first Orientation chapter will help you get started by guiding you through the process of installing Python on your computer.

By the end of this chapter, you will be able to:

- Describe why Python is a useful computer language for problem solvers
- Describe applications where Python is used
- Detail advantages of Python over other programming languages
- Know the cost of Python
- Know the difference between Python and Anaconda
- Install Python on your computer
- Install Anaconda on your computer

1.2 Why Python?

You might be wondering "Why should I solve problems with Python?" There are other programming languages in the world such as MATLAB, LabView, C++ and Java. What makes Python useful for solving problems?

Python is a powerful programming language

Python defines the types of objects you build into your code. Unlike some other languages such as C, you do not need to declare the object type. The object type is also mutable, you can change the type of object easily and on the fly. There is a wide array of object types built into Python. Objects can change in size. Python objects can also contain mixed data types. Strings and floating point numbers can be part of the same list.

Python has an extensive Standard Library. A huge number of object types, functions and methods are available for use without importing any external modules. These include math functions, list methods, and calls to a computer's system. There is a lot that can be done with the Python Standard Library. The first couple of chapters of this book will just use the standard library. It can do a lot.

Python has over 100,000 external packages available for download and use. They are easy to install off of the Python Package Index, commonly called PyPI ("pie pee eye"). There is a Python package for just about everything. There are packages which can help you: interact with the web, make complex computations, calculate unit conversions, plot data, work with .csv, .xls, and .pdf files, manipulate images and video, read data from sensors and test equipment, train machine learning algorithms, design web apps, work with GIS data, work with astronautical data. There are and many more Python packages added to PyPI every day. In this book, we will use some of the more useful Python packages for problem solvers such as NumPy, Matplotlib, and SymPy.

Python is easy to learn and use

One way Problem solvers code solutions faster in Python faster than coding solutions in other programming languages is that Python is easy to learn and use. Python programs tend to be shorter and quicker to write than a program which completes a similar function in another languages. In the rapid design, prototype, test, iterate cycle programming solutions in Python can be written and tested quickly. Python is also an easy language for fellow problem solvers on your team to learn. Python's language syntax is also quite human readable. While programmers can become preoccupied with a program's runtime, it is development time that takes the longest.

Python is transportable

Python can be installed and run on each of the three major operating systems: Windows, Mac and Linux. On Mac and Linux Python comes installed out of the box. Just open up a terminal in on a MacOS or Linux machine and type `python`. That's it, you are now using Python. On Windows, I recommend downloading and installing the Anaconda distribution of Python. The Anaconda distribution of Python is free and can be installed on all three major operating systems.

Python is free

Some computer languages used for problem solving such as MATLAB and LabView cost money to download and install. Python is free to download and use. Python is also open source and individuals are free to modify, contribute to, and propose improvements to Python. All of the packages available on the Python Package Index are free to download and install. Many more packages, scripts and utilities can be found in open source code repositories on GitHub and BitBucket.

Python is growing

Python is growing in popularity. Python is particularly growing in the data sciences and in use with GIS systems, physical modeling, machine learning and computer vision. These are growing team problem-solving areas for engineers.

1.3 The Anaconda Distribution of Python

I recommend problem solvers install the *Anaconda distribution of Python*. The following section details the differences between the Anaconda distribution of Python and the version of Python you can download from Python.org

How is Anaconda different from Python?

When you download Python from Python.org, you get the *Python Interpreter*, a little text editing program called **IDLE** and all of the Python Standard Library modules.

The Python Interpreter is an application or program that runs your Python code. A program written in the Python programming language is run with the Python Interpreter. So Python corresponds to both the language that a program is written in as well as the application that runs the program.

When you download the Anaconda distribution of Python from Anaconda.com, you get a Python Interpreter, the **Anaconda Prompt** (a command line program), **Spyder** (a code editor) and about 600 extra Python modules that aren't included in the Python Standard Library. The Anaconda distribution of Python also includes a program called Anaconda Navigator that allows you to launch Jupyter notebooks quickly.

Why download Anaconda, if I want to use is Python?

Regardless if you download Python from Python.org or if you download Anaconda (with all the extra stuff it comes with) from Anaconda.com, you will be able to write and execute Python code. However, there are a couple of advantages to using the Anaconda distribution of Python.

Anaconda includes Python plus about 600 additional Python packages

The Anaconda distribution of Python is advantageous because it includes Python as well as about 600 additional Python packages. These additional packages are all free to install. The packages that come with Anaconda includes many of the most common Python packages use to solve problems.

If you download Anaconda, you get Python including the Python Standard Library plus about 600 extra packages. If you download Python from Python.org, you just get Python and The Standard Library but no additional modules. You could install the extra modules that come with Anaconda (that don't come with plain old Python), but why not save a step (or about 600 steps) and just install Anaconda instead of installing about 600 different modules?

Anaconda installs without administrator privileges

Even if you don't have the ability to install programs on a computer, like a computer in a school computer lab, you can still download and use Anaconda. The Anaconda distribution of Python will also allow you to install additional modules from the Python package index (PyPI.org) and conda-forge (conda-forge.org), the conda package index.

Anaconda works on MacOS

If you use MacOS, you probably already have Python installed on your computer. Most MacOS installations come with Python included. The problem is that the version of Python that comes with MacOS is old (usually legacy Python, Python 2) and the version of Python that comes with MacOS is locked up behind a set of administrator privileges. Because the pre-installed version of Python included with MacOS can require administrator privileges, you can have trouble with installation and run-time problems. Some things will seem to work fine, and then other things won't run at all, or you will keep getting asked for an administrator password over and over.

Downloading and installing Anaconda (separate from the version of Python that came with MacOS) prevents most of the problems on MacOS caused by using the pre-installed version of Python.

Anaconda makes package management and virtual environments easier

Another advantage of Anaconda is that package management and virtual environments are a lot easier when you have Anaconda. Virtual environments and package handling might not seem to make a huge difference right now. If you just downloaded Anaconda for the first time, you are probably not dealing with package management and virtual environments yet. (It's OK if you don't even know what those two things are yet). After you write a couple of Python programs and start downloading a couple of extra modules from PyPI or conda-forge, dealing with package management and virtual environments becomes more critical.

1.4 Installing Anaconda on Windows

For problem solvers, I recommend installing and using the Anaconda distribution of Python.

This section details the installation of the Anaconda distribution of Python on Windows 10. I think the Anaconda distribution of Python is the best option for problem solvers who want to use Python. Anaconda is free (although the download is large which can take time) and can be installed on school or work computers where you don't have administrator access or the ability to install new programs. Anaconda comes bundled with about 600 packages pre-installed including **NumPy**, **Matplotlib** and **SymPy**. These three packages are very useful for problem solvers and will be discussed in subsequent chapters.

1.4. INSTALLING ANACONDA ON WINDOWS

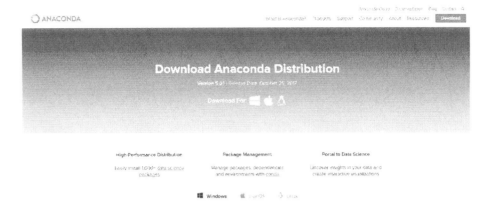

Figure 1.1. The Anaconda distribution of Python download page

Figure 1.2. Anaconda downloads page. Windows download option is selected

Follow the steps below to install the Anaconda distribution of Python on Windows.

Steps:

1. Visit Anaconda.com/downloads
2. Select Windows
3. Download the *.exe* installer
4. Open and run the *.exe* installer
5. Open the **Anaconda Prompt** and run some Python code

1. Visit the Anaconda downloads page

Go to the following link: Anaconda.com/downloads
The Anaconda Downloads Page will look something like this:

2. Select Windows

Select Windows where the three operating systems are listed.

3. Download

Download the most recent Python 3 release. At the time of writing, the most recent release was the Python 3.6 Version. Python 2.7 is legacy Python. For problem solvers, select the Python 3.6 version.

Figure 1.3. Anaconda downloads page. Select Python 3.6 version or higher. Python 2 is legacy Python.

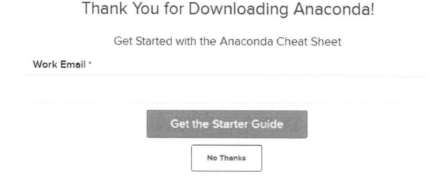

Figure 1.4. Part of Anaconda installation. You don't have to enter your work email to proceed.

If you are unsure if your computer is running a 64-bit or 32-bit version of Windows, select 64-bit as 64-bit Windows is most common.

You may be prompted to enter your email. You can still download Anaconda if you click [No Thanks] and don't enter your Work Email address.

The download is quite large (over 500 MB) so it may take a while to for Anaconda to download.

4. Open and run the installer

Once the download completes, open and run the *.exe* installer

At the beginning of the install, you need to click **Next** to confirm the installation.

Figure 1.5. Anaconda downloading.Note the file size and amount of time remaining

1.4. INSTALLING ANACONDA ON WINDOWS

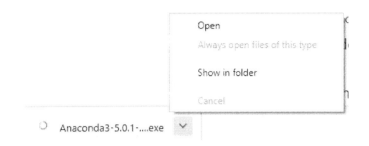

Figure 1.6. Once the download is complete, open the .exe file

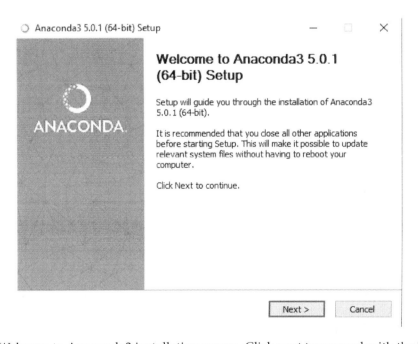

Figure 1.7. Welcome to Anaconda3 installation screen. Click next to proceed with the installation.

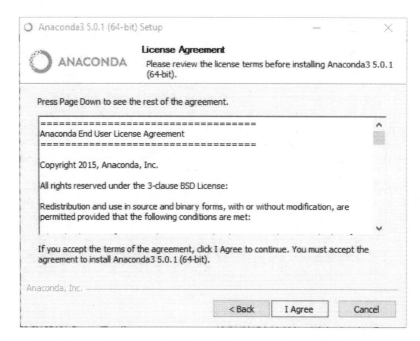

Figure 1.8. Anaconda End User License Agreement. Click I Agree to proceed

Then agree to the license.

At the Advanced Installation Options screen, I recommend that you **do not check** "Add Anaconda to my PATH environment variable"

5. Open the Anaconda Prompt from the Windows start menu

After the installation of Anaconda is complete, you can go to the Windows start menu and select the Anaconda Prompt.

This opens the **Anaconda Prompt**. **Anaconda** is the Python distribution and the **Anaconda Prompt** is a command line shell (a program where you type in commands instead of using a mouse). The black screen and text that makes up the **Anaconda Prompt** doesn't look like much, but it is really helpful for problem solvers using Python.

At the Anaconda prompt, type python and hit [Enter]. The python command starts the Python interpreter, also called the Python REPL (for Read Evaluate Print Loop).

```
> python
```

Note the Python version. You should see something like Python 3.6.1. With the interpreter running, you will see a set of greater-than symbols >>> before the cursor.

Now you can type Python commands. Try typing import this. You should see the *Zen of Python* by Tim Peters

To close the Python interpreter, type exit() at the prompt >>>. Note the double parenthesis at the end of the exit() command. The () is needed to stop the Python interpreter and get back out to the **Anaconda Prompt**.

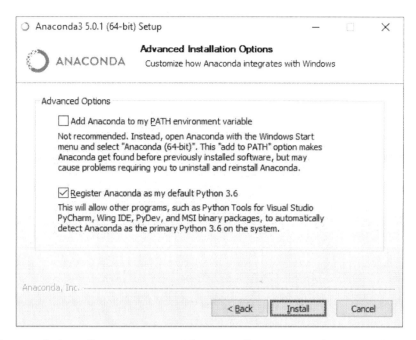

Figure 1.9. Anaconda installation options. When installing Anaconda on Windows, do not check Add Anaconda to my PATH environment variable

To close the **Anaconda Prompt**, you can either close the window with the mouse, or type `exit`, no parenthesis necessary.

When you want to use the Python interpreter again, just click the Windows Start button and select the **Anaconda Prompt** and type `python`.

1.5 Installing Anaconda on MacOS

This section details the installation of the Anaconda Distribution of Python on MacOS. Most versions of MacOS come pre-installed with legacy Python (Version 2.7). You can confirm the legacy version of Python is installed on MacOS by opening and running a command at the MacOS **terminal**. To open the MacOS terminal use `[command]+[Space Bar]` and type `terminal` in the Spotlight Search bar.

In the MacOS Terminal type (note: the dollar sign $ is used to indicate the terminal prompt. The dollar sign $ does not need to be typed):

```
$ python
```

You will most likely see Python version 2.7 is installed. An issue for MacOS users is that the installed system version of Python has a set of permissions that may always allow Python to run and may not allow users to install external packages. Therefore, I recommend the Anaconda distribution of Python is installed alongside the system version of Python that comes pre-installed with MacOS. You will be able to run Python code using the Anaconda distribution of Python, and you will be able to install external packages using the Anaconda distribution of Python.

Follow the steps below to install the Anaconda distribution of Python on MacOS.

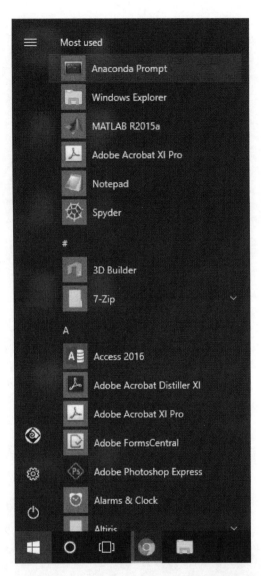

Figure 1.10. The Anaconda Prompt in the Windows Start Menu

Figure 1.11. The Anaconda Prompt: What you see when you open the Anaconda Prompt. Note the word "python" was typed at the > prompt

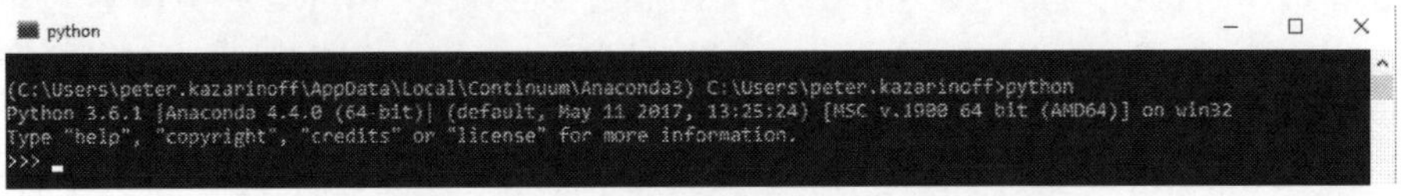

Figure 1.12. The Anaconda Prompt: The result of typing python is the Python REPL opens. Note the >>> prompt which denotes the Python interpreter is running

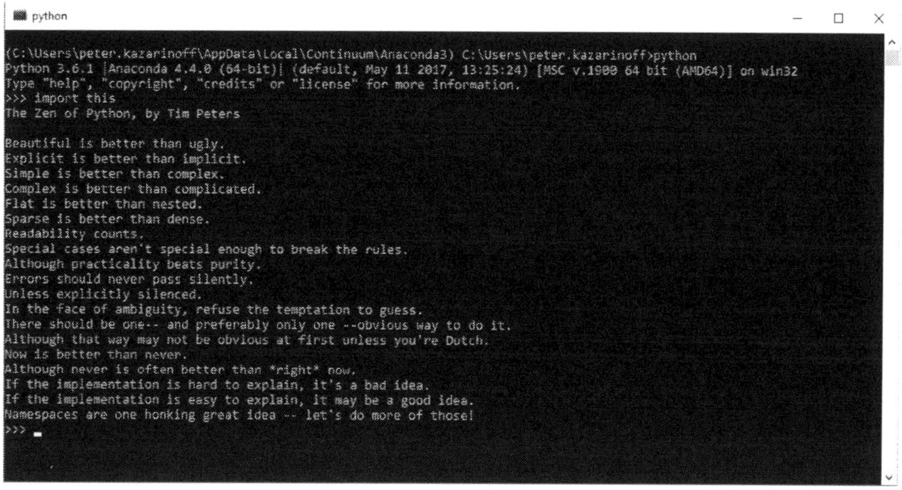

1.5. INSTALLING ANACONDA ON MACOS

Figure 1.13. Anaconda Prompt: Results of entering import this is The Zen of Python, by Tim Peters

Steps:

1. Visit Anaconda.com/downloads
2. Select MacOS and Download the *.pkg* installer
3. Open the *.pkg* installer
4. Follow the installation instructions
5. Source your *.bash-rc* file
6. Open a terminal and type `python` and run some code.

1. Visit the Anaconda downloads page

Go to the following link: Anaconda.com/downloads

2. Select MacOS and download the .pkg installer

In the operating systems box, select [MacOS]. Then download the most recent Python 3 distribution (at the time of this writing the most recent version is Python 3.6) graphical installer by clicking the Download link. Python 2.7 is legacy Python. For problem solvers, select the most recent Python 3 version.

You may be prompted to enter your email. You can still download Anaconda if you click [No Thanks] or [x] and don't enter your Work Email address.

3. Open the .pkg installer

Navigate to the Downloads folder and double-click the *.pkg* installer file you just downloaded. It may be helpful to order the contents of the Downloads folder by date to find the *.pkg* file.

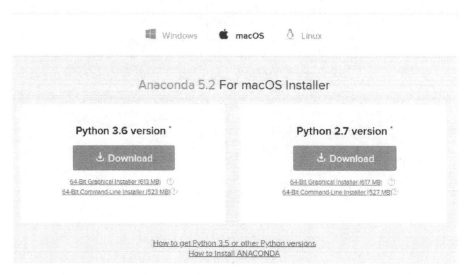

Figure 1.14. Anaconda distribution of Python downloads page. Notice the macOS operating system is selection. Download Python 3.6 verion or higher

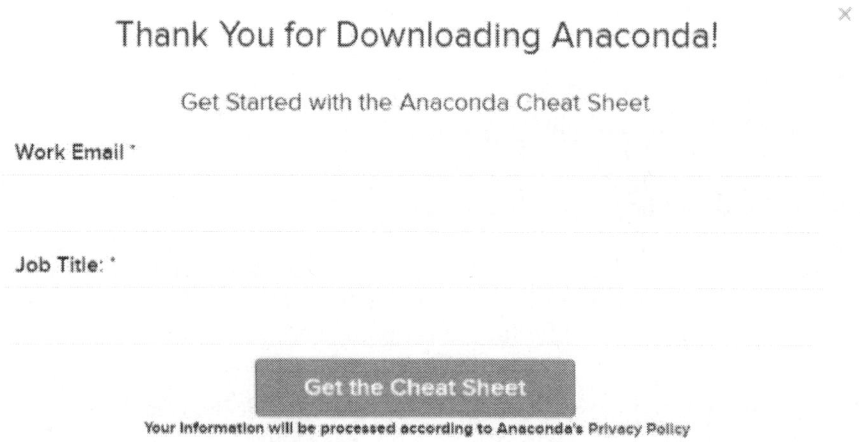

Figure 1.15. Anaconda downloads page. You do not have to enter your Work Email

4. Follow the installation instructions

Follow the installation instructions. It is advised that you install **Anaconda** for the current user and that **Anaconda is added to your PATH**.

5. Source your .bash-rc file

Once Anaconda is installed, you need to load the changes to your PATH environment variable in the current terminal session.

Open the MacOS Terminal and type:

```
$ cd ~
$ source .bashrc
```

6. Open a terminal and type python and run some code.

Open the MacOS Terminal and type:

```
$ python
```

You should see something like

```
Python 3.6.3 | Anaconda Inc. |
```

At the Python REPL (the Python >>> prompt) try:

```
>>> import this
```

If you see the Zen of Python, the installation was successful. Exit out of the Python REPL using the command `exit()`. Make sure to include the double parenthesis () after the `exit` command.

```
>>> exit()
```

1.6 Installing Anaconda on Linux

This section details the installation of the Anaconda distribution of Python on Linux, specifically Ubuntu 18.04, but the instructions should work for other Debian-based Linux distributions as well.

Ubuntu 18.04 comes pre-installed with Python (Version 3.6) and legacy Python (Version 2.7). You can confirm the legacy version of Python is installed by opening up a terminal.

In the terminal type:

```
$ python
```

You will most likely see Python Version 2.7 is installed. If you enter:

```
$ python3
```

Figure 1.16. Anaconda downloads page operating systems option. Notice Linux is selected

You will most likely see Python Version 3.6 is also installed. You can use the 3.6 Version of Python, but each time a new package needs to be downloaded, the `$ pip3 install` command must be used.

Install the Anaconda distribution of Python to follow the examples in the book without the need to install additional third-party packages.

Steps:

1. Visit Anaconda.com/downloads
2. Select Linux
3. Copy the bash (.sh file) installer link
4. Use `wget` to download the bash installer
5. Run the bash script to install **Anaconda3**
6. `source` the `.bash-rc` file to add Anaconda to your PATH
7. Start the Python REPL

1. Visit the Anaconda downloads page

Go to the following link: Anaconda.com/downloads

2. Select Linux

On the downloads page, select the Linux operating system

3. Copy the bash (.sh file) installer link

In the **Python 3.6 Version*** box, right-click on the [64-Bit(x86) Installer] link. Select [copy link address].

4. Use `wget` to download the bash installer

Now that the bash installer (.sh file) link is stored on the clipboard, use `wget` to download the installer script. In a terminal, `cd` into the home directory and make a new directory called `tmp`. `cd` into `tmp` and use `wget` to download the installer. Although the installer is a bash script, it is still quite large and the download will not be immediate (Note the link below includes `<release>`. the specific release depends on when you download the installer).

1.6. INSTALLING ANACONDA ON LINUX

Figure 1.17. Anaconda installation on Linux, Copy the download link address.

```
$ cd ~
$ mkdir tmp
$ cd tmp
$ https://repo.continuum.io/archive/Anaconda3<release>.sh
```

5. Run the bash script to install Anaconda3

With the bash installer script downloaded, run the *.sh* script to install **Anaconda3**. Ensure you are in the directory where the installer script downloaded:

```
$ ls
Anaconda3-5.2.0-Linux-x86_64.sh
```

Run the installer script with bash.

```
$ bash Anaconda3-5.2.0-Linux-x86_64.sh
```

Accept the Licence Agreement and allow Anaconda to be added to your PATH. By adding Anaconda to your PATH, the Anaconda distribution of Python will be called when you type $ python in a terminal.

6. source the .bash-rc file to add Anaconda to your PATH

Now that **Anaconda3** is installed and **Anaconda3** is added to our PATH, source the .bashrc file to load the new PATH environment variable into the current terminal session. Note the .bashrc file is in the home directory. You can see it with $ ls -a.

```
$ cd ~
$ source .bashrc
```

Figure 1.18. Python.org downloads page showing download for Windows button

7. Start the Python REPL

To verify the installation is complete, open Python from the command line:

```
$ python

Python 3.6.5 |Anaconda, Inc.| (default, Mar 29 2018, 18:21:58)
[GCC 7.2.0] on linux
Type "help", "copyright", "credits" or "license" for more information.
>>>
```

If you see Python 3.6 from Anaconda listed, your installation is complete. To exit the Python REPL, type:

```
>>> exit()
```

1.7 Installing Python from Python.org

Below is the recommended way to install a new version of Python from Python.org on each of the three major operating systems: Windows, MacOS and Linux.

This book is based on Python version 3.6. Some of the examples in the book may not work properly on legacy Python (version 2.7). I recommend installing the Anaconda Distribution of Python on Windows and MacOSX. The installation of Anaconda on these operating systems was detailed in previous sections.

Installing Python on Windows

Go to `https://www.python.org/downloads/` and download the latest release. Make sure to select the box [add Python to my path] during the installation.

1.7. INSTALLING PYTHON FROM PYTHON.ORG

Figure 1.19. Python.org downloads page showing download for MacOS link button

Installing Python on MacOS

Go to `https://www.python.org/downloads/mac-osx/` and download the latest release.

Installing Python on Linux

Open a terminal and enter $ python to see if a version of Python is already installed on the system.

```
$ python
Python 2.7.12 (default, Dec  4 2017, 14:50:18)
[GCC 5.4.0 20160609] on linux2
Type "help", "copyright", "credits" or "license" for more information.
>>> exit()
```

In the code block above, the version of Python is Python 2.7.12. If the Python version is 2.7 or below, try the command $ python3.

```
$ python3
Python 3.6.7 (default, Oct 22 2018, 11:32:17)
[GCC 8.2.0] on linux
Type "help", "copyright", "credits" or "license" for more information.
>>> exit()
```

If no version of Python is shown, you can download a release of Python 3.6 from the deadsnakes package repository.

```
$ sudo add-apt-repository ppa:deadsnakes/ppa
[Enter]
$ sudo apt-get update
$ sudo apt-get install python3.6
```

After installation, you may need to append your PATH environment variable to ensure the newly installed Python 3.6 version is the version of Python called when using the terminal. The commands below will add /usr/bin to your PATH, and add an alias in *.bashrc* so that the command $ python3.6 produces the Python 3.6 REPL. Take care to ensure the double chevron >> is used, as a single chevron > will overwrite the *.bashrc* file.

```
$ cd ~
$ echo  "PATH=/usr/bin:$PATH" >>  ~/.bashrc
$ echo "alias python3.6='/usr/bin/python3.6'" >> ~/.bashrc
$ source .bashrc
$ python3.6
Python 3.6.6 (default, Jun 28 2018, 04:42:43)
[GCC 5.4.0 20160609] on linux
Type "help", "copyright", "credits" or "license" for more information.
>>> exit()
```

1.8 Summary

In this chapter, you learned about the Anaconda distribution of Python and how the Anaconda distribution of Python compares the version of Python at Python.org. The Anaconda distribution of Python comes with about 600 packages pre-installed as well as Jupyter notebooks and the Anaconda Prompt. Jupyter notebooks and some of the pre-installed packages that come with Anaconda will be used later chapters. This text recommends that problem solvers install the Anaconda distribution of Python.

This chapter showed how to install the Anaconda distribution of Python on Windows, MacOS, and Linux.

At the end of the chapter, a description of how to download and install Python from Python.org was shown.

Key Terms and Concepts

Anaconda	Legacy Python	Windows
Anaconda Prompt	Python Interpreter	MacOS
download	Python REPL	Linux
install	package	terminal
Python	operating system	PATH

1.9 Review Questions

Q01.01 What is Python? How is the Python language different than the Python Interpreter?

Q01.02 What is the difference between the version of Python at python.org and the version of Python at Anaconda.com?

Q01.03 What are the advantages and disadvantages of using the Anaconda distribution of Python compared to using the version of Python at python.org?

Q01.04 There are many different applications to edit Python code. Some examples include: JupyterLab, Sublime Text, Visual Studio Code, and PyCharm. Pick two Python code editors and explain a feature of each code editor.

Q01.05 What are some advantages of Python compared to other computer programming languages?

Q01.06 What is PyPI? How many packages are currently available for download on PyPI?

Q01.07 Find three modules that are part of the Python Standard Library. Write a short description of what each of the modules you choose is used for.

Q01.08 Which computer operating systems can Python be installed on?

Q01.09 How much does Python cost to download and install?

Q01.10 What are three subject areas that have seen a growth in the use of Python?

Q01.11 Besides PyPI where else can problem solvers go to find Python packages, scripts, and utilities?

Q01.12 Name three packages that come pre-installed with the Anaconda distribution of Python

Q01.13 How much does the Anaconda distribution of Python cost to download and install?

Q01.14 Which operating systems can the Anaconda distribution of Python be installed on?

Q01.15 What type of program is the Anaconda Prompt?

Q01.16 What is another name for the Python interpreter?

Q01.17 How can you bring up the Python interpreter (the Python REPL) using the Anaconda Prompt?

Q01.18 What prompt is shown in the Python interpreter (the Python REPL)?

Q01.19 What command do you type to close the Python interpreter (the Python REPL)?

Q01.20 What are the first three lines in *The Zen of Python* by Tim Peters?

Q01.21 How do you open the Anaconda Prompt?

Installing Python on MacOS

Q01.30 What web address do you go to download the Anaconda distribution of Python for MacOS?

Q01.31 What file extension does the installer for MacOS of the Anaconda distribution of Python use?

Q01.32 When you install the Anaconda distribution of Python on MacOS, what is advised to do for the installation options?

Q01.33 Why do you need to `source` the *.bashrc* file after you install the Anaconda distribution of Python for MacOS?

Q01.34 How can you bring up the Python interpreter (the Python REPL) using the MacOS terminal?

Q01.35 Which version of Python is it advisable to download and install on MacOS?

Q01.36 Python can be installed on MacOS using a terminal program called **Homebrew**. What command is issued to the MacOS terminal to install Python using **Homebrew**?

Q01.37 What version of Python comes pre-installed on MacOS?

Installing Python on Linux

Q01.40 What version(s) of Python comes pre-installed on most Linux distributions?

Q01.41 In Linux, what happens when you type `python` at the terminal compared to when you type `python3` at the terminal?

Q01.42 If you use the system version of Python 3 installed on Linux, what command must you enter to install Python packages to the Python 3 version that comes pre-installed?

Q01.43 What kind of file type (what is the file extension) is downloaded from Anaconda.com to install the Anaconda distribution of Python on Linux?

Q01.44 Why do you need to `source` the *.bashrc* file after you install the Anaconda distribution of Python for Linux?

1.9. REVIEW QUESTIONS 35

Q01.45 How can you bring up the Python interpreter (the Python REPL) using a Linux terminal?

Q01.46 Which version of Python is it advisable to download and install on Linux?

Q01.47 What is a disadvantage of using the version of Python that comes pre-installed on Linux, compared to using the Anaconda distribution of Python on Linux?

Q01.48 Before you install the Anaconda distribution of Python on Linux, what version of Python are you most likely to see when you enter the command $ python in a Linux terminal?

Q01.49 Before you install the Anaconda distribution of Python on Linux, what version of Python are you most likely to see when you enter the command $ python3 in a Linux terminal?

Installing Python from Python.org

Q01.50 What web address do you go to download Python from Python.org?

Q01.51 What option is advised to select when downloading and installing Python from Python.org on Windows?

Q01.52 If Python 3 is not available on Linux, what package repository can Python 3.6 be downloaded from?

Q01.53 Go to Python.org. What is the current version of Python available for download?

Errors, Explanations, and Solutions

For each of the problems below, run the line of code. Copy the output, then suggest and run a line of code that fixes the error.

Q01.91 Open the Python Interpreter (the Python REPL). Try to close the Python Interpreter with the command:

```
>>> exit
```

Q02.92 Open the Python Interpreter (the Python REPL). Try to view *The Zen of Python* by Tim Peters with the command:

```
>>> Zen of Python
```

Q01.93 Open the Anaconda Prompt. Try to open the Python Interpreter (the Python REPL) with the command:

```
> python3
```

Q01.94 Open the Anaconda Prompt. Try to open the Python Interpreter (the Python REPL) with the command:

```
> Python
```

Q02.95 Open the Python Interpreter (the Python REPL). Try to view *The Zen of Python* by Tim Peters with the command:

```
>>> import this()
```

Chapter 2

Jupyter Notebooks

2.1 Introduction

In this chapter, you will be introduced to Jupyter notebooks. A Jupyter notebook is an application that can run Python code, display plots, show equations and contain formatted text. Jupyter notebooks are a great tool for problem solvers to write, run, document and share Python code with others.

By the end of this chapter you will be able to:

- Explain what a Jupyter notebook is
- Open a Jupyter notebook
- Write Python code in a Jupyter notebook
- Run Python code in a Jupyter notebook
- Write and render markdown text in a Jupyter notebook
- Save and close a Jupyter notebook
- Download Jupyter notebooks in different file formats

2.2 What is a Jupyter Notebook?

A *Jupyter notebook* is an electronic file that contains both programming code and text descriptions. Jupyter notebooks can also contain embedded charts, plots, images, videos, and links. Jupyter notebooks run in a web browser like Firefox or Google Chrome.

Although Jupyter notebooks can contain the code of many different programming languages, many Jupyter notebooks contain Python code. The Python code in a Jupyter notebook is the same type of Python code found in a *.py* file.

The text description sections of Jupyter notebooks contain explanations and clarifications of the programming code in the *markdown* format. *Markdown* files have the extension *.md*. Markdown sections of a Jupyter notebook can include formatting to make text bold, italic, form tables and lists, show code listings and render images.

One way to think of a Jupyter notebook is as a combination of the Python REPL and a Python module *.py* file with a markdown *.md* file thrown in between code sections.

In the Python REPL, only one command can be typed at a time, and only one line of output is shown at a time. In a *.py* file, the entire file is run at one time, line by line. The output of the entire file is produced all at once. Markdown *.md* files contain text in markdown format, but that text is not rendered. In a Jupyter notebook, chunks of code one line or many lines long can be run individually and in any order without running all of the code in the Jupyter notebook. Jupyter notebooks render the markdown sections and display rich text with headings, formatting, and images.

Jupyter notebooks contain three types of cells: *code cells*, *output cells*, and *markdown cells*.

- Code cells: Lines of Python code are run in code cells.

- Output cells: The output from running the code cells is also shown in output cells. Charts, plots, command line output, and images can all be shown in Jupyter notebooks as well.

- Markdown cells: Contain text-like descriptions of what will happens in subsequent code cells. Markdown cells can also contain images and links.

2.3 Why Jupyter Notebooks?

There is a vast array of editors and IDE's (Integrated Development Environments) which can be used to edit and run Python code. Why should problem solvers learn to use Jupyter notebooks?

Below is a table of simple text editors and IDE's which can edit and run Python code:

Python Text Editor or IDE	Description
Notepad	Simple text editor - included with Windows
Idle	Included with Python from Python.org
Sublime Text	Full-featured editor with long-time no-cost license
Spyder	IDE included with the Anaconda Distribution of Python
Visual Studio Code	An multi-language open source IDE
PyCharm	Professional Developer-friendly Python IDE

2.4. INSTALLING JUYPTER

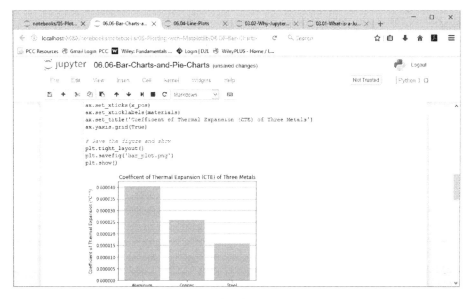

Figure 2.1. A Jupyter notebook open showing a bar graph

A Jupyter notebook is neither a simple text editor nor a full-featured IDE. Jupyter notebooks provide a quick and streamlined way for problem-solvers to prototype code and quickly share code.

Jupyter notebooks also provide a way for problem-solvers to share programming solutions with team members, supervisors, and customers.

In a way, Jupyter notebooks strike a balance between simple text editors, which are fast to start and simple and easy to manipulate, and IDE's which tend to start slower and be feature-rich and complex. Simple text editors typically can only edit code, and cannot run the code. A full IDE can edit code, run the code, debug code, provide syntax highlighting and context help.

In the context of problem-solving, Jupyter notebooks are quite handy. Jupyter notebooks open quickly and quickly produce output. Data exploration, data cleaning, and plot building are accomplished in Jupyter notebooks easier and quicker than in a text editor or an IDE.

In the context of sharing solutions to problems, Jupyter notebooks are also useful. Markdown cells render text in different sizes, bold and italic. Tables and images, plots and code can all be shown together in the same Jupyter notebook. Notebooks can be exported to a variety of formats including *.html* and *.pdf*.

2.4 Installing Juypter

The simplest way to install **Jupyter notebooks** is to download and install the Anaconda distribution of Python. The Anaconda distribution of Python comes with Jupyter notebook included and no further installation steps are necessary.

Below are additional methods to install Jupyter notebooks if you are not using the Anaconda distribution of Python.

Installing Jupyter on Windows using the Anaconda Prompt

To install Jupyter on Windows, open the **Anaconda Prompt** and type:

```
> conda install jupyter
```

Type y for yes when prompted. Once Jupyter is installed, type the command below into the **Anaconda Prompt** to open the Jupyter notebook file browser and start using Jupyter notebooks.

```
> jupyter notebook
```

Installing Jupyter on MacOS

To install Jupyter on MacOS, open the MacOS terminal and type:

```
$ conda install jupyter
```

Type y for yes when prompted.

If **conda** is not installed, the Anaconda distribution of Python can be installed, which will install **conda** for use in the MacOS terminal.

Problems can crop up on MacOS when using the MacOS provided system version of Python. Python packages may not install on the system version of Python properly. Moreover, packages which do install on the system version of Python may not run correctly. It is therefore recommended that MacOS users install the **Anaconda** distribution of Python or use **homebrew** to install a separate non-system version of Python.

To install a non-system version of Python with **homebrew**, key the following into the MacOS terminal. See the **homebrew** documentation at https://brew.sh.

```
$ brew install Python
```

After **homebrew** installs a non-system version of Python, **pip** can be used to install Jupyter.

```
$ pip install jupyter
```

Installing Jupyter on Linux

To install Jupyter on Linux, open a terminal and type:

```
$ conda install jupyter
```

Type y for yes when prompted.

Alternatively, if the Anaconda distribution of Python is not installed, one can use **pip**.

```
$ pip3 install jupyter
```

2.5 Opening a Jupyter Notebook

In this section, you will learn how to open a Jupyter notebook on Windows and MacOS.

2.5. OPENING A JUPYTER NOTEBOOK

One way problem solvers can write and execute Python code is in Jupyter notebooks. Jupyter notebooks contain Python code, the output that code produces and markdown cells usually used to explain what the code means.

On Windows, a Jupyter notebook can be started from the **Anaconda Prompt**, the Windows start menu and **Anaconda Navigator**.

3 ways to open a Jupyter notebook:

- Windows Start Menu
- **Anaconda Prompt**
- Anaconda Navigator

Open a Jupyter notebook with the Windows Start Menu

One way to open a Jupyter notebook is to use the Windows Start Menu. Note that the Anaconda distribution of Python must be installed to use the Windows Start Menu to open a Jupyter notebook. Download **Anaconda** at the following link: Anaconda.com/distribution

Open the Windows start menu and select [**Anaconda3(64 bit)**] –> [**Jupyter Notebook**]

This action opens the **Jupyter file browser** in a web browser tab.

In the upper right select [**New**] –> [**Python 3**]

A new **notebook** will open as a new tab in your web browser.

Try typing the code below in the first cell in the notebook to the right of the In [ ]: prompt:

```
import this
```

Then click the run button in the middle of the menu at the top of the notebook.

Open a Jupyter Notebook with the Anaconda Prompt

Another method to open a Jupyter notebook is to use the **Anaconda Prompt**.

Go to the Windows start menu and select [**Anaconda Prompt**] under [**Anaconda3**].

If you don't see the **Anaconda Prompt** in the Windows Start Menu, then you need to install the Anaconda distribution of Python. Download **Anaconda** at the following link: Anaconda.com/distribution

The **Anaconda Prompt** window should look something like the image below.

At the **Anaconda Prompt** type:

```
> jupyter notebook
```

This command starts the **Jupyter notebook** server. The output in the **Anaconda Prompt** will look something like the output shown below:

```
Copy/paste this URL into your browser when you connect ...
```

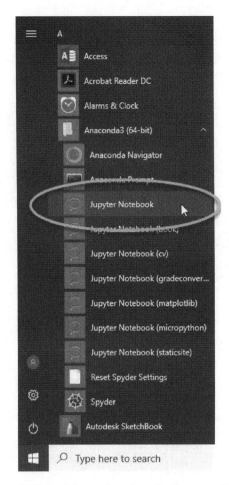

Figure 2.2. Windows 10 Start Menu showing the Jupyter Notebook application

Figure 2.3. Jupyter notebook file browser. Note a new Python 3 notebook is selected

2.5. OPENING A JUPYTER NOTEBOOK

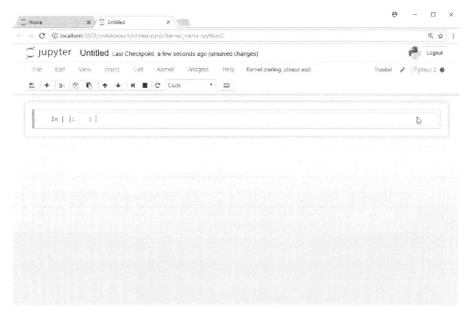

Figure 2.4. A newly opened Jupyter notebook

Figure 2.5. A Jupyter notebook running "import this". Note the run button is selected

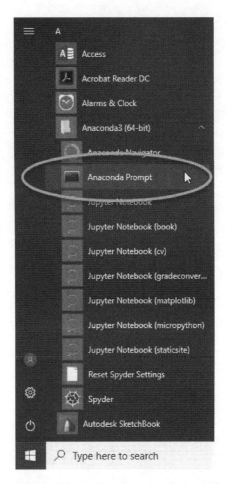

Figure 2.6. Windows 10 Start Menu showing the Anaconda Prompt application

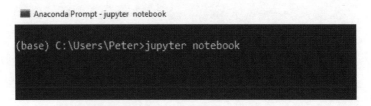

Figure 2.7. The Anaconda Prompt. Note the command jupyter noteooks is entered

2.6. THE JUPYTER NOTEBOOK INTERFACE
45

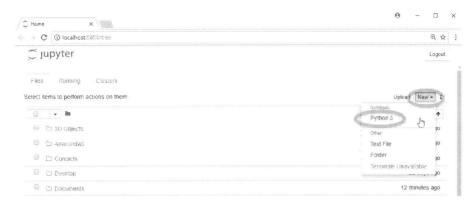

Figure 2.8. Jupyter notebook file browser: create new Python 3 notebook

```
   to login with a token:

      http://localhost:8888/?token=6bdef677d3503fbb2 ...

[I 16:14:12.661 NotebookApp] Accepting one-time-token ...
```

A web browser should open, and you should be able to see the **Jupyter file browser**. If a web browser doesn't open automatically, you can copy the web address from the **Anaconda Prompt** and paste it into a web browser's address bar.

In the upper right select [**New**] –> [**Python 3**]

You will see a new tab open in your web browser. This web browser page is a **Jupyter notebook**.

Open a Jupyter Notebook with Anaconda Navigator

One additional way to open a Jupyter notebook is to use **Anaconda Navigator**. Anaconda Navigator comes with the Anaconda distribution of Python. Open **Anaconda Navigator** using the Windows start menu and select [**Anaconda3(64-bit)**] –> [**Anaconda Navigator**].

An **Anaconda Navigator** window will open. In the middle of the page, in the **Jupyter notebook** tile, click [**Launch**]

A **Jupyter file browser** will open in a web browser tab.

In the upper right select [**New**] –> [**Python 3**]

A new notebook will open as a new tab in your web browser.

2.6 The Jupyter Notebook Interface

When a new Jupyter notebook opens, you will see the Jupyter notebook interface. Across the top of the notebook you see the Jupyter icon and the notebook name. You can click on the notebook name field and change the name of the notebook. Note that the file extension .ipynb is not printed

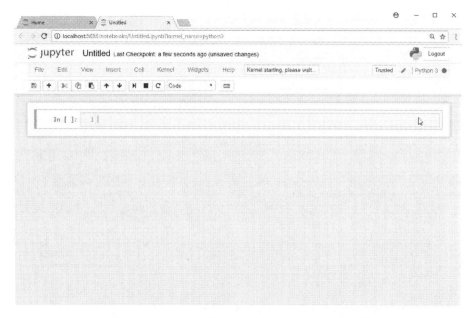

Figure 2.9. A newly opened Jupyter notebook

in the file name field, but if you look in the Home tab, you will see that the notebook is saved with the .ipynb extension.

Menus and Buttons

A Jupyter notebook is comprised of a bunch of *cells* which are arrayed one after another in boxes below the menu items and buttons. There are three main types of cells: code cells, output cells, and markdown cells.

Code Cells

In code cells, you can write Python code, then execute the Python code and see the resulting output. An example of a code cell is shown below.

You can tell you are typing in a code cell because In [ ]: is shown to the left of the cell and the cell-type drop-down menu shows **Code**.

To run the Python code in a code cell push the [Run] button or type [Shift]+[Enter]. Hitting [Enter] when the cursor is inside a code cell brings the cursor down to a new line.

Output Cells

After a code cell is run, an output cell can be produced below the code cell. The output cell contains the output from the code cell above it. Not all code produces output, so not all code cells produce output cells. The results in output cells can't be edited. If a code cell produces plots, charts or images, these outputs are shown in output cells.

2.6. THE JUPYTER NOTEBOOK INTERFACE

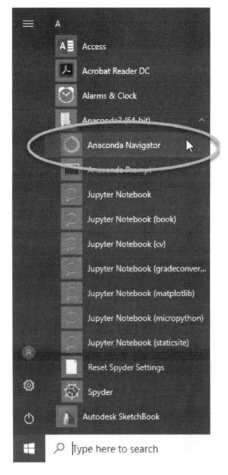

Figure 2.10. Windows 10 Start Menu showing the Anaconda Navigator application

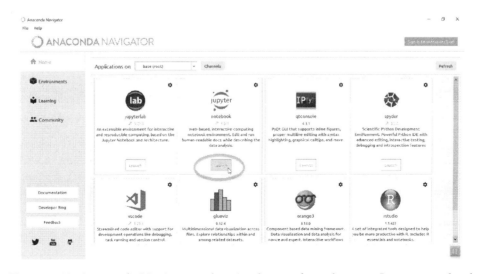

Figure 2.11. Anaconda Navigator- showing how to launch a new Jupyter notebook

Figure 2.12. Jupyter notebook file browser - create new Python 3 notebook

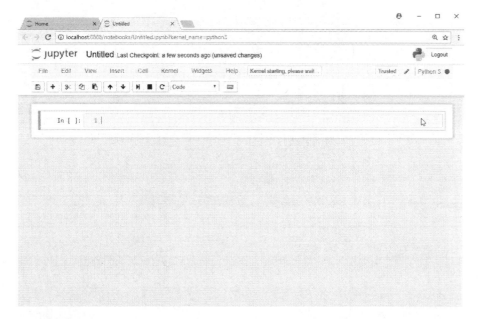

Figure 2.13. A newly opened Jupyter notebook showing a blank code cell

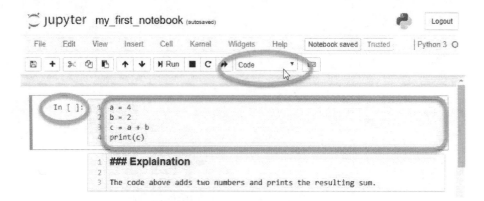

Figure 2.14. A Jupyter notebook code cell

2.6. THE JUPYTER NOTEBOOK INTERFACE

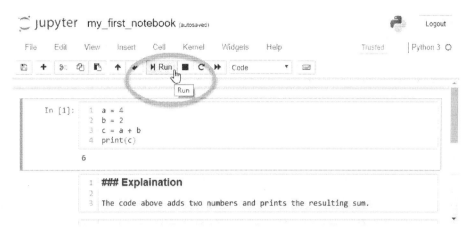

Figure 2.15. The Jupyter notebook run cell button

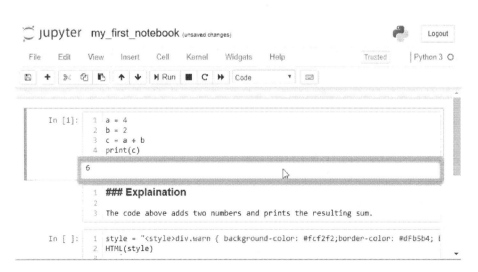

Figure 2.16. A Jupyter notebook output cell

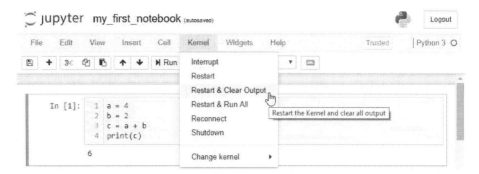

Figure 2.17. The Jupyter notebook Kernal menu showing Restart and Clear Output selected

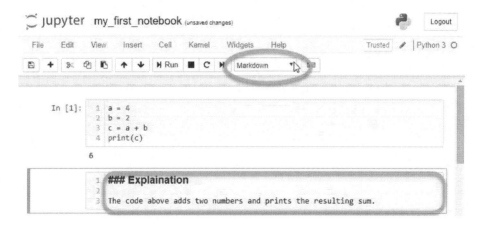

Figure 2.18. A Jupyter notebook markdown cell. Note Markdown is selected in the cell type menu

You can clear all the output cells and re-run code cells by selecting [**Kernal**] –> [**Restart Kernal and Clear Output**].

Markdown Cells

Markdown cells don't contain Python code. Markdown cells contain text written in Markdown format. Text in markdown cells can be formatted to show **bold** or *italic* text. Tables, images, and lists can also be included in markdown cells.

Markdown cells are used for documentation and explaining your code. The text in a markdown cell is not executed. Markdown cells can be formatted with a few special characters.

Markdown cells are run like code cells. The difference is that when markdown cells are run, the text is formatted (when code cells run, code is executed). Markdown cells are run by clicking the [Run] button or by pressing [Shift] + [Enter].

Text in markdown cells can be formatted using *markdown syntax*. An example of markdown syntax is putting an underscore before and after a word to cause the word to be formatted in *italics*.

2.6. THE JUPYTER NOTEBOOK INTERFACE

Headings

Headings are created in markdown cells using the hash symbol #. One # is the largest heading. Four hashes #### is the smallest heading.

```
# H1 Heading

## H2 Heading

### H3 Heading

#### H4 Heading
```

Code Blocks

Code blocks can be inserted in Jupyter notebook markdown cells. For inline code blocks use the ' left quote character, the character to the left of the number [1] and above [Tab] on most keyboards.

This is inline code: ' ' ' Inline code block ' ' ' within a paragraph

For a separated code block use three ' left quote characters on one line, followed by the code block on separate lines. Terminate the separate code block with a line of three ' left quote characters.

```
'''
```

Separated code block

```
'''
```

The code in markdown cell code blocks do not execute when the markdown cell is run. A code block in a markdown cell is formatted when the markdown cell executes.

Bold and Italics

Bold and *italic font* is displayed by surrounding text with a double asterisk for **bold** and a single underscore for _italics_

bold produces **bold**

italics produces *italics*

bold and italic produces ***bold and italic***

Tables

Tables are displayed using the pipe | character, which is [Shift] + [\] on most keyboards. Columns are separated by pipes | and rows are separated by lines. After the header row, a row of pipes and dashes --- are needed to define the table.

```
| header1 | header 2 | header 3 |
| --- | --- | --- |
| col 1 | col 2 | col 3 |
| col 1 | col 2 | col 3 |
```

produces:

header1	header 2	header 3
col 1	col 2	col 3
col 1	col 2	col 3

Bullet Points and Lists

Bullet points are produced using the asterisk character *

```
* item 1
* item 2
* item 3
```

produces

- item 1
- item 2
- item 3

Numbered lists are produced using sequential numbers followed by a dot. Indent sub-items with two spaces.

```
1. First item
2. Second item
3. Third item
  1. sub item
  2. sub item
    1. sub-sub item
    2. sub-sub item
```

produces

1. First item
2. Second item
3. Third item
   (a) sub item
   (b) sub item
      i. sub-sub item
      ii. sub-sub item

Horizontal Rule

A horizontal rule is specified with three asterisks *** on a single line.

```
***
```

produces

2.6. THE JUPYTER NOTEBOOK INTERFACE

Figure 2.19. Image displayed in a Jupyter notebook markdown cell

Links

Hyperlinks are specified using a set of square brackets [ ] followed by a pair of parenthesis ( ) The text inside the square brackets will be the link, the link address goes in the parenthesis.

    [Python.org](https://python.org/)

produces

Python.org

Images

Images are embedded in Jupyter Notebook markdown using the exclamation point and square brackets ![ ], followed by the image file path in parenthesis ( ). If the image can not be displayed, the text in square brackets will be shown. The image can be in the same directory as the notebook, or a relative path can be specified. In this case, the image engineering.png is stored in the images directory, which is a subdirectory of the directory the notebook is saved in.

    ![Engineering Image](images/engineering.png)

displays the image

LaTeX Math

LaTeX Math equations and symbols are rendered by markdown cells. A more extensive list of LaTeX commands can be found in the appendix.

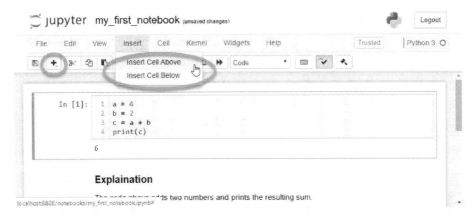

Figure 2.20. Jupyter notebook New Cell Button and Insert Cell Above option shown

$$ \int_{a}^{b} \frac{1}{x^2} dx $$

produces

$$\int_a^b \frac{1}{x^2} dx$$

html

Because Jupyter notebooks are rendered by web browsers, just about any HTML tag can be included in the markdown portion of a notebook. An example of an HTML tag is the `<sup> </sup>` tags that surround superscript text.

    x²

produces
x^2

Text can be colored using html `<font> </font>` tags

    <font color=red>Red Text</font>

produces
Red Text

Creating a new cell

You can create a new cell in a Jupyter Notebook by clicking the [+] button in the upper menu. Clicking the [+] button produces a new code cell below the active cell.

You can also create a new cell using **Insert** –> **Insert Cell Above** or **Insert Cell Below**. You can choose to insert a cell above or below the active cell.

2.6. THE JUPYTER NOTEBOOK INTERFACE

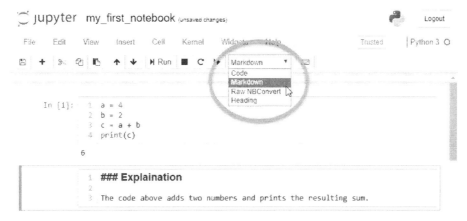

Figure 2.21. Jupyter notebook cell type drop down menu. Note the Markdown cell type is selected

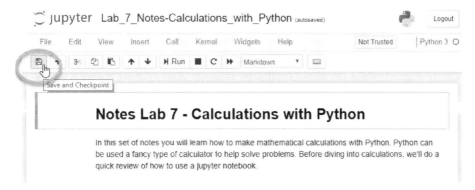

Figure 2.22. Jupyter notebook Save button

Changing the cell type

The type of cell: code cell or markdown cell, is changed by clicking on a cell and selecting the cell type from the drop-down menu. Typing [Esc] + [m] changes the cell type to a markdown cell. Typing [Esc] + [y] changes the cell type to a code cell.

Saving a Jupyter Notebook

Jupyter notebooks can be saved using the save icon in the upper menu or by pressing [Ctrl] + [s].

Jupyter notebooks can also be saved as a copy, similar to the Save As command common in many programs. To save a copy of a Jupyter notebook use **File –> Make a Copy...**

Renaming a Jupyter Notebook

Jupyter notebooks are renamed by clicking on the notebook name above the upper menu and typing a new name into the dialog box.

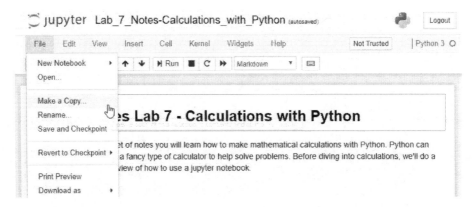

Figure 2.23. Jupyter notebook File menu. Make a Copy... is selected

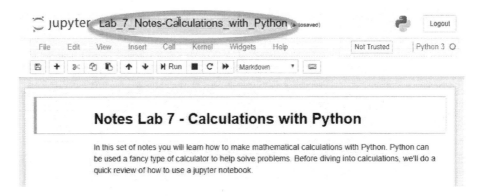

Figure 2.24. Jupyter notebook rename notebook

Figure 2.25. Jupyter notebook Rename Notebook dialog box

2.6. THE JUPYTER NOTEBOOK INTERFACE

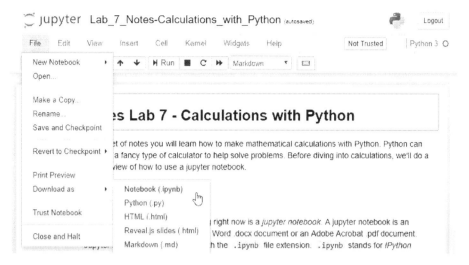

Figure 2.26. Jupyter notebook downloaded as .ipynb file

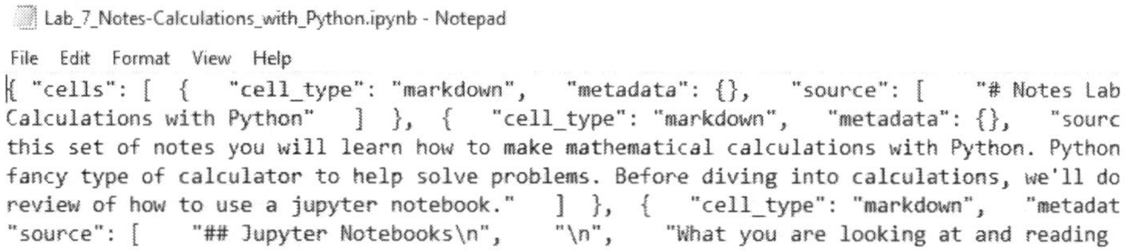

Figure 2.27. Jupyter notebook JSON in notepad

Downloading a Jupyter Notebook

Jupyter notebooks can be downloaded and saved using **File –> Download As –> Notebook (.ipynb)**. Selecting this menu option will download the notebook as a `.ipynb` file.

Note that when a `.ipynb` file is viewed in a text editor like notepad, the notebook is unformatted and looks like a confusing jumble of text. The notebook needs to be opened in a Jupyter notebook file browser in order for the code in the notebook to run and the markdown text to render.

Saving Jupyter Notebooks in Other Formats

Jupyter notebooks can be saved in other formats besides the native `.ipynb` format. These formats can be accessed using the **[File] –> [Download As]** menu.

The available file download types are:

- Notebook (.ipynb) - The native jupyter notebook format
- Python (.py) - The native Python code file type.
- HTML (.html) - A web page
- Markdown (.md) - Markdown format
- reST (.rst) - Restructured text format
- LaTeX (.tex) - LaTeX Article format

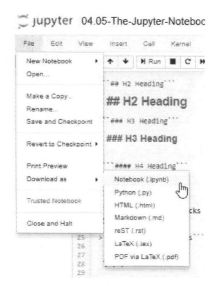

Figure 2.28. Jupyter notebook Download As file-type options

- PDF via LaTeX (.pdf) - a pdf exported from LaTeX, requires a converter

When a notebook is saved as a .py file, all text in markdown cells is converted to comments, and any code cells stay intact as Python code.

2.7 Magic Commands

Jupyter notebook code cells can contain special commands which are not valid Python code but affect the behavior of the notebook. These special commands are called *magic commands*.

%matplotlib inline

One of the most popular magic commands is:

```
%matplotlib inline
```

Entering the `%matplotlib inline` command at the top of a Jupyter notebook renders Matplotlib plots in cells of the notebook. Without `%matplotlib inline`, plots may jump out as external windows. A typical start to a Jupyter notebook using **Matplotlib** might start as:

```
import numpy as np
import pandas as pd
import matplotlib.pyplot as plt
%matplotlib inline
```

2.7. MAGIC COMMANDS

Figure 2.29. Markdown cells as comments seen in a downloaded .py file

%load

The %load command loads a Python module, webpage or file into a Jupyter notebook. If there is a file called *hello.py* in the same directory as the notebook with some Python code written in it, we can load that same code into a Jupyter notebook code cell with the %load command.

Within a Jupyter notebook code cell type the command:

    %load hello.py

The result is the code from the file *hello.py* is copied into the current notebook.

```
In [1]: # %load hello.py
        # hello.py

        print('This code was run from a seperate Python file')
        print('Hello from the file hello.py')

This code was run from a seperate Python file
Hello from the file hello.py
```

%run

If the %run magic command followed by the name of a valid Python file, the Python file runs as a script. Suppose the file *hello.py* is created in the same directory as the running Jupyter notebook. The directory structure will look something like this:

```
| folder
---| notebook.ipynb
---| hello.py
```

In the file *hello.py* is the code:

```
# hello.py

print('This code was run from a separate Python file')
print('Hello from the file hello.py')
```

Within our Jupyter notebook, if we %run this file, we get the output of the *hello.py* script in a Jupyter notebook output cell.

```
In [2]: %run hello.py

This code was run from a separate Python file
Hello from the file hello.py
```

Other useful magic commands

Below is a table of other useful Jupyter notebook magic commands

Magic command	Result
%pwd	Print the current working directory
%cd	Change the current working directory
%ls	List the contents of the current directory
%history	Show the history of the In [ ]: commands

You can list all of the available magic commands by typing and running %lsmagic in a Jupyter notebook code cell:

```
%lsmagic
```

The output shows all the available line magic commands that begin with the percent sign %.

```
Available line magics:
%alias   %alias_magic   %autocall   %automagic   %autosave ...
%dhist   %dirs   %doctest_mode   %ed   %edit   %env   %gui ...
dir   %more   %mv   %notebook   %page   %pastebin   %pdb   %pdef ...
...

Available cell magics:
%%!   %%HTML   %%SVG   %%bash   %%capture   %%debug   %%file   %%html ...
%%python   %%python2   %%python3   %%ruby   %%script   %%sh   %%svg ...
```

2.8 Getting Help in a Jupyter Notebook

There are a couple of different ways to get help when using a Jupyter notebook.

Get help using `dir`

Typing `dir()` and passing in a function, method, variable or object shows the possible object, method and function calls available to that object. For example, we can investigate the different functions in the **glob** module, part of Python's Standard Library, by importing `glob`, then calling `dir(glob)`.

```
In [1]: import glob
        dir(glob)

Out[1]: ['__all__',
         '__builtins__',
         '__cached__',
         '__doc__',
         '__file__',
         '__loader__',
         '__name__',
         '__package__',
         '__spec__',
         '_glob0',
         '_glob1',
         '_glob2',
         '_iglob',
         '_ishidden',
         '_isrecursive',
         '_iterdir',
         '_rlistdir',
         'escape',
         'fnmatch',
         'glob',
         'glob0',
         'glob1',
         'has_magic',
         'iglob',
         'magic_check',
         'magic_check_bytes',
         'os',
         're']
```

Get help using Tab

After typing the name of a variable, object or function following the . character hit the [Tab] key. Typing [Tab] brings up a list of available options. Scroll through the list or type a letter to filter the list to certain starting letters. Use [Enter] to select the option you want.

Tab completion can also be used during module import. Hit [Tab] after typing the module name to see which functions and classes are available in that module.

```
from math import <tab>
```

Get help using the `help()` function

After importing a module, you can use the `help()` function to see documentation about the command if it is available.

```
In [2]: import math
        help(math.sin)
```

```
Help on built-in function sin in module math:

sin(...)
    sin(x)

    Return the sine of x (measured in radians).
```

After importing a module, you can view help on the imported module by typing the module name followed by a question mark ?

```
In [3]: import statistics
        statistics.mean?
```

```
Signature: statistics.mean(data)
Docstring:
Return the sample arithmetic mean of data.

>>> mean([1, 2, 3, 4, 4])
2.8

>>> from fractions import Fraction as F
>>> mean([F(3, 7), F(1, 21), F(5, 3), F(1, 3)])
Fraction(13, 21)

>>> from decimal import Decimal as D
>>> mean([D("0.5"), D("0.75"), D("0.625"), D("0.375")])
Decimal('0.5625')

If ``data`` is empty, StatisticsError will be raised.
File:      ~/anaconda3/envs/book/lib/python3.6/statistics.py
Type:      function
```

You can view the source code where a particular function is defined using a double question mark ??

2.8. GETTING HELP IN A JUPYTER NOTEBOOK

```
In [4]: import statistics
        statistics.mean??

Signature: statistics.mean(data)
Source:
def mean(data):
    """Return the sample arithmetic mean of data.

    >>> mean([1, 2, 3, 4, 4])
    2.8

    >>> from fractions import Fraction as F
    >>> mean([F(3, 7), F(1, 21), F(5, 3), F(1, 3)])
    Fraction(13, 21)

    >>> from decimal import Decimal as D
    >>> mean([D("0.5"), D("0.75"), D("0.625"), D("0.375")])
    Decimal('0.5625')

    If ``data`` is empty, StatisticsError will be raised.
    """
    if iter(data) is data:
        data = list(data)
```

Help online

Help is also available online at in the offical Jupyter documentation:

http://jupyter.readthedocs.io/en/latest/

You can always try to find help by typing something into Google. The site Stack Overflow is devoted to programming questions and answers. The highest rated answers on Stack Overflow are at the top of each question page.

2.9 Summary

In this chapter, you learned about Jupyter notebooks. You learned what a Jupyter notebook is and why Jupyter notebooks are useful for problem solvers. This chapter showed how to install Jupyter notebooks on Windows, MacOS, and Linux.

Some specific operations with Jupiter notebooks were introduced:

- Open a Jupyter Notebook
- Rename a Jupyter Notebook
- Write Python code in a Jupyter notebook code cells
- Run Python code in a Jupyter notebook code cell
- Write text in Jupyter notebook markdown cells
- Use markdown syntax to produce formatted text, headings, lists, and tables
- Save a Jupyter notebook
- Download a Jupyter notebook in different file types

You also learned about special "magic" commands that can be used in a Jupyter notebook. The final section of the chapter detailed a couple of ways to get help when working with Jupyter notebooks.

Key Terms and Concepts

Jupyter	execute	hyperlink
notebook	Anaconda Prompt	LaTeX
Jupyter notebook	file browser	HTML tag
kernel	code cell	.ipynb-file
iPython	markdown cell	.py-file
IDE	code block	.md-file
text editor	inline code block	magic commands
markdown	pipe character	

Python Commands and Functions

Jupyter Notebook Magic Commands

Command	Description
`%matplotlib inline`	Display plots in output cells
`%run file.py`	Run file.py and displays output
`%pwd`	Print the working directory file path
`%ls`	List contents of the current working directory
`%precision`	Set float point precision for pretty printing
`%whos`	List variables and types in the running kernel session
`function?`	Display help on a function
`function??`	Display source code of a function

2.10 Review Questions

Code cells and markdown cells

Q02.01 Run the following code in two different Jupyter notebook cells. Run one cell as a code cell. Run the other cell as a Markdown cell. Why is the output different?

```
# Problem Solving with Python
```

Q02.02 Run the following code in two different Jupyter notebook cells. Run one cell as a code cell. Run the other cell as a Markdown cell. Why is the output different?

```
print('Problem Solving with Python')
```

Markdown cells

Q02.10 Recreate the following headings in one Jupyter notebook markdown cell:

```
# BIG heading

## Big heading

### SMALL heading

#### small heading
```

Q02.11 Recreate the following table in one Jupyter notebook markdown cell:

Python Package	Use
Jupyter	Jupyter notebooks
NumPy	arrays
Matplotlib	plots
PySerial	serial communication

Q02.12 Recreate the following code block in one Jupyter notebook markdown cell:

```
import numpy as np
import matplotlib.pyplot as plt
%matplotlib inline
```

Q02.12 Recreate the following bullet points in one Jupyter notebook markdown cell:

- markdown cell : markdown
- code cell: Python code
- raw NBConvert: LaTeX

Q02.13 Recreate the following list in one Jupyter notebook markdown cell:

1. Open Jupyter notebook

2. Write code
3. Restart Kernel & run all
4. Download notebook

Q02.14 Recreate two horizontal rules in a Jupyter notebook markdown cell. In between the horizontal rules write the text *In between the lines* like below:

In between the lines

Q02.15 Inside a Jupyter notebook markdown cell, make the word Red the color red, make the word Green, the color green, make the word Blue the color blue.

Q02.16 Create a warning box on the inside of a Jupyter notebook markdown cell that says:

Warning! Python counting starts at 0 and ends at n-1

LaTeX Math

Q02.20 Write the Pythagorean Theorem in a Jupyter notebook markdown cell using LaTeX math.

$$a^2 + b^2 = c^2$$

Q02.21 Write the formula for the area of a circle in a Jupyter notebook markdown cell using LaTeX math.

$$A = \pi r^2$$

Q02.22 Write the formula below in a Jupyter notebook Markdown cell using LaTeX math.

$$\int_0^1 \frac{1}{y^3} dy$$

Code cells

Q02.31 Run the following code in a Jupyter notebook code cell:

```
import this
```

Q02.32 Run the following code in a Jupyter notebook code cell:

```
import sys
print(sys.version)
```

Q02.33 Run the following code in a Jupyter notebook code cell:

2.10. REVIEW QUESTIONS

```
import matplotlib.pyplot as plt
%matplotlib inline

plt.plot([1,3,6,10])
plt.show()
```

Q02.34 Run the following code in a Jupyter notebook code cell. Move the slider back and forth and observe the results.

```
from ipywidgets import interact
import ipywidgets as widgets

def func(x):
    return x

interact(func, x=10);
```

Cell Magic

Q02.50 Create a file called *hello.py* in the same directory as your Jupyter notebook. Inside the file *hello.py* write the code below:

```
# hello.py

print("hello from the file")
```

Use the Jupyter notebook magic command %load to load the code from *hello.py* into your Jupyter notebook.

Q02.51 Create a file called *hello.py* in the same directory as your Jupyter notebook. Inside the file *hello.py* write the code below:

```
# hello.py

print("hello from the file")
```

Use the Jupyter notebook magic command %run to run the code from *hello.py* into your Jupyter notebook.

Q02.52 Run the code below in a Jupyter notebook code cell:

```
import os

print(os.getcwd())

%pwd
```

Why is the output of these two commands similar?

Getting Help

Q02.60 Use Python's `dir()` function in a Jupyter notebook code cell to find all the functions available in Python's `math` module. Remember to `import math` at the start of the code cell.

Q02.61 In a Jupyter notebook code cell, `import math` and run `math.sqrt?`. Copy the contents of the help you receive in a Jupyter notebook markdown cell.

Q02.62 In a Jupyter notebook code cell, `import statistics` and run `statistics.mode?`. Copy the examples from the help you receive in a Jupyter notebook code cell. Run the code cell.

Chapter 3

The Python REPL

3.1 Introduction

In this chapter, you will learn how to write and run your first lines of Python code at the Python REPL also called the Python prompt. You will learn how to use Python as a calculator and be introduced to Python variables and Python's `print()` function.

By the end of this chapter, you will be able to:

- Open and close the Python REPL
- Compute mathematical calculations using the Python REPL
- Use the output from the Python REPL as input in another problem
- Import the math and statistics modules from the Python Standard Library and use their functions
- Assign values to variables
- Use variables in calculations
- Create strings
- Combine and compare strings

3.2 Python as a Calculator

Python can be used as a calculator to compute arithmetic operations like addition, subtraction, multiplication and division. Python can also be used for trigonometric calculations and statistical calculations.

Arithmetic

Python can be used as a calculator to make simple arithmetic calculations.

Simple arithmetic calculations can be completed at the Python Prompt, also called the *Python REPL*. REPL stands for Read Evaluate Print Loop. The Python REPL shows three arrow symbols >>> followed by a blinking cursor. Programmers type commands at the >>> prompt then hit [ENTER] to see the results.

Commands typed into the Python REPL are *read* by the interpreter, results of running the commands are *evaluated*, then *printed* to the command window. After the output is printed, the >>> prompt appears on a new line. This process repeats over and over again in a continuous *loop*.

Try the following commands at the Python REPL:

Suppose the mass of a battery is 5 kg and the mass of the battery cables is 3 kg. What is the mass of the battery cable assembly?

```
>>> 5 + 3
8
```

Suppose one of the cables above is removed and it has a mass of 1.5 kg. What is the mass of the leftover assembly?

```
>>> 8 - 1.5
6.5
```

If the battery has a mass of 5000 g and a volume of 2500 cm^3 What is the density of the battery? The formula for density is below, where D is density, m is mass and v is volume.

$$D = \frac{m}{v}$$

In the problem above $m = 5000$ and $v = 2500$

Let's solve this with Python.

```
>>> 5000 / 2500
2.0
```

What is the total mass if we have 2 batteries, and each battery weighs 5 kg?

```
>>> 5 * 2
10
```

The length, width, and height of each battery is 3 cm. What is the area of the base of the battery? To complete this problem, use the double asterisk symbol ** to raise a number to a power.

3.2. PYTHON AS A CALCULATOR

```
>>> 3 ** 2
9
```

What is the volume of the battery if each the length, width, and height of the battery are all 3 cm?

```
>>> 3 ** 3
27
```

Find the mass of the two batteries and two cables.

We can use Python to find the mass of the batteries and then use the answer, which Python saves as an underscore _ to use in our next operation. (The underscore _ in Python is comparable to the ans variable in MATLAB)

```
>>> 2 * 5
10
>>> _ + 1.5 + 1
12.5
```

Section Summary

A summary of the arithmetic operations in Python is below:

Operator	Description	Example	Result
+	addition	2 + 3	5
-	subtraction	8 - 6	2
-	negative number	-4	-4
*	multiplication	5 * 2	10
/	division	6 / 3	2
**	raises a number to a power	10**2	100
_	returns last saved value	_ + 7	107

Trigonometry: sine, cosine, and tangent

Trigonometry functions such as sine, cosine, and tangent can also be calculated using the Python REPL.

To use Python's trig functions, we need to introduce a new concept: *importing modules*.

In Python, there are many operations built into the language when the REPL starts. These include +, -, *, / like we saw in the previous section. However, not all functions will work right away when Python starts. Say we want to find the sine of an angle. Try the following:

```
>>> sin(60)
Traceback (most recent call last):
  File "<stdin>", line 1, in <module>
NameError: name 'sin' is not defined
```

This error results because we have not told Python to include the sin function. The sin function is part of the *Python Standard Library*. The Python Standard Library comes with every Python installation and includes many functions, but not all of these functions are available to us when we start a new Python REPL session. To use Python's `sin` function, first import the `sin` function from the `math` *module* which is part of the Python Standard Library.

Importing modules and functions is easy. Use the following syntax:

```
from module import function
```

To import the `sin()` function from the `math` module try:

```
>>> from math import sin
>>> sin(60)
-0.3048106211022167
```

Success! Multiple modules can be imported at the same time. Say we want to use a bunch of different trig functions to solve the following problem.

An angle has a value of $\pi/6$ radians. What is the sine, cos, and tangent of the angle?

To solve this problem we need to import the `sin()`, `cos()`, and `tan()` functions. It is also useful to have the value of π, rather than having to write `3.14...`. We can import all of these functions at the same time using the syntax:

```
from module import function1, function2, function3
```

Note the commas in between the function names.

Try:

```
>>> from math import sin, cos, tan, pi
>>> pi
3.141592653589793
>>> sin(pi/6)
0.49999999999999994
>>> cos(pi/6)
0.8660254037844387
>>> tan(pi/6)
0.5773502691896257
```

Section Summary

The following trig functions are part of Python's **math** module:

Trig function	Name	Description	Example	Result
`math.pi`	pi	mathematical constant π	`math.pi`	3.14
`math.sin()`	sine	sine in radians	`math.sin(4)`	9.025
`math.cos()`	cosine	cosine in radians	`cos(3.1)`	400
`math.tan()`	tangent	tangent in radians	`tan(100)`	2.0
`math.asin()`	arc sine	inverse sine in radians	`math.sin(4)`	9.025
`math.acos()`	arc cosine	inverse cosine in radians	`log(3.1)`	400
`math.atan()`	arc tangent	inverse tangent in radians	`atan(100)`	2.0
`math.radians()`	radians conversion	degrees to radians	`math.radians(90)`	1.57
`math.degrees()`	degree conversion	radians to degrees	`math.degrees(2)`	114.59

3.2. PYTHON AS A CALCULATOR

Exponents and Logarithms

Calculating exponents and logarithms with Python is easy. Note the exponent and logarithm functions are imported from the **math** module just like the trig functions were imported from the **math** module above.

The following exponents and logarithms functions can be imported from Python's math module:

- `log`
- `log10`
- `exp`
- `e`
- `pow(x,y)`
- `sqrt`

Let's try a couple of examples:

```
>>> from math import log, log10, exp, e, pow, sqrt
>>> log(3.0*e**3.4)         # note: natural log
4.4986122886681095
```

A right triangle has side lengths 3 and 4. What is the length of the hypotenuse?

```
>>> sqrt(3**2 + 4**2)
5.0
```

The power function `pow()` works like the `**` operator. `pow()` raises a number to a power.

```
>>> 5**2
25

>>> pow(5,2)
25.0
```

Section Summary

The following exponent and logarithm functions are part of Python's **math** module:

Math function	Name	Description	Example	Result
math.e	Euler's number	mathematical constant e	math.e	2.718
math.exp()	exponent	e raised to a power	math.exp(2.2)	9.025
math.log()	natural logarithm	log base e	math.log(3.1)	400
math.log10()	base 10 logarithm	log base 10	math.log10(100)	2.0
math.pow()	power	raises a number to a power	math.pow(2,3)	8.0
math.sqrt()	square root	square root of a number	math.sqrt(16)	4.0

Statistics

To round out this section, we will look at a couple of statistics functions. These functions are part of the Python Standard Library, but not part of the **math** module. To access Python's statistics functions, we need to import them from the **statistics** module using the statement `from statistics import mean, median, mode, stdev`. Then the functions `mean`, `median`, `mode` and `stdev` (standard deviation) can be used.

```
>>> from statistics import mean, median, mode, stdev

>>> test_scores = [60, 83, 83, 91, 100]

>>> mean(test_scores)
83.4

>>> median(test_scores)
83

>>> mode(test_scores)
83

>>> stdev(test_scores)
14.842506526863986
```

Alternatively, we can import the entire **statistics** module using the statement `import statistics`. Then to use the functions, we need to use the names `statistics.mean`, `statistics.median`, `statistics.mode`, and `statistics.stdev`. See below:

```
>>> import statistics

>>> test_scores = [60, 83, 83, 91, 100 ]

>>> statistics.mean(test_scores)
83.4

>>> statistics.median(test_scores)
83

>>> statistics.mode(test_scores)
83

>>> statistics.stdev(test_scores)
14.842506526863986
```

Section Summary

The following functions are part of Python's **statistics** module. These functions need to be imported from the `statistics` module before they are used.

Statistics function	Name	Description	Example	Result
`mean()`	mean	mean or average	`mean([1,4,5,5])`	3.75
`median()`	median	middle value	`median([1,4,5,5])`	4.5
`mode()`	mode	most often	`mode([1,4,5,5])`	5
`stdev()`	standard deviation	spread of data	`stdev([1,4,5,5])`	1.892
`variance()`	variance	variance of data	`variance([1,4,5,5])`	3.583

3.3 Variables

Variables are assigned in Python using the = equals sign also called the *assignment operator*. The statement:

```
a = 2
```

Assigns the integer 2 to the variable a.

```
>>> a = 2
>>> a
2
```

Note the assignment operator =(equals), is different from the logical comparison operator == (equivalent to).

```
>>> a == 2
True
```

Variable names in Python must conform to the following rules:

- variable names must start with a letter
- variable names can only contain letters, numbers, and the underscore character _
- variable names can not contain spaces
- variable names can not include punctuation
- variable names are not enclosed in quotes or brackets

The following code lines show valid variable names:

```
constant = 4

new_variable = 'var'

my2rules = ['rule1','rule2']

SQUARES = 4
```

The following code lines show invalid variable names:

```
a constant = 4

3newVariables = [1, 2, 3]

&sum = 4 + 4
```

Let's solve the problem below at the Python REPL using variables.

Problem

The Arrhenius relationship states:

$$n = n_v e^{-Q_v/(RT)}$$

In a system where $n_v = 2.0 \times 10^{-3}$, $Q_v = 5$, $R = 3.18$, and $T = 293$, calculate n.

Solution

Use variables to assign a value to each one of the constants in the problem and calculate n.

```
>>> nv = 2.0e(-0.3)
>>> Qv = 5
>>> R = 3.18
>>> T = 293
>>> from math import exp
>>> n = nv*exp(-1*Qv/(R*T))
>>> n
0.8079052775625613
```

3.4 String Operations

Strings are sequences of letters, numbers, punctuation, and spaces. Strings are defined at the Python REPL by enclosing letters, numbers, punctuation, and spaces in single quotes ' ' or double quotes " ".

```
>>> word = "Solution"
>>> another_word = "another solution"
>>> third_word = "3rd solution!"
```

In Python, string operations include concatenation (combining strings), logical comparisons (comparing strings) and indexing (pulling specific characters out of strings).

String Concatenation

Strings can be *concatenated* or combined using the + operator.

```
>>> word = "Solution"
>>> another_word = "another solution"
>>> third_word = "3rd solution!"
>>> all_words = word+another_word+third_word
>>> all_words
'Solutionanother solution3rd solution!'
```

3.5. PRINT STATEMENTS

To include spaces in the concatenated string, add a string which just contains one space " " in between each string you combine.

```
>>> word = "Solution"
>>> another_word = "another solution"
>>> third_word = "3rd solution!"
>>> all_words = word + " " + another_word + " " + third_word
>>> all_words
'Solution another solution 3rd solution!'
```

String Comparison

Strings can be compared using the comparison operator; the double equals sign ==. Note the comparison operator (double equals ==) is not the same as the assignment operator, a single equals sign =.

```
>>> name1 = 'Gabby'
>>> name2 = 'Gabby'
>>> name1 == name2
True

>>> name1 = 'Gabby'
>>> name2 = 'Maelle'
>>> name1 == name2
False
```

Capital letters and lower case letters are different characters in Python. A string with the same letters, but different capitalization are not equivalent.

```
>>> name1 = 'Maelle'
>>> name2 = 'maelle'
>>> name1 == name2
False
```

3.5 Print Statements

One built-in function in Python is print(). The value or expression inside of the parenthesis of a print() function "prints" out to the REPL when the print() function is called.

An example using the print() function is below:

```
>>> name = "Gabby"
>>> print("Your name is: ")
Your name is:
>>> print(name)
Gabby
```

Remember that strings must be enclosed by quotation marks. The following command produces an error.

```
>>> print(Gabby)

NameError: name 'Gabby' is not defined
```

This error is corrected by surrounding the string Gabby with quotation marks.

```
>>> print("Gabby")
Gabby
```

Expressions passed to the `print()` function are evaluated before they are printed out. For instance, the sum of two numbers can be shown with the `print()` function.

```
>>> print(1+2)
3
```

If you want to see the text 1+2, you need to define "1+2" as a string and print out the string "1+2" instead.

```
>>> print("1+2")
1+2
```

Strings can be concatenated (combined) inside of a `print()` statement.

```
>>> name = Gabby
>>> print('Your name is: ' + name)
Your name is Gabby
```

The `print()` function also prints out individual expressions one after another with a space in between when the expressions are placed inside the `print()` function and separated by a comma.

```
>>> print("Name:","Gabby","Age", 2+7)
Name: Gabby Age 9
```

3.6 Summary

In this chapter, you learned how to use the Python REPL, also called the Python prompt, to solve problems. You learned how to do arithmetic, powers and logarithms, trigonometry and save values to variables. Operations on strings were introduced including concatenation and comparison. In the last section of the chapter, Python's `print()` function was introduced.

Key Terms and Concepts

REPL	import	variable
Python REPL	module	assignment operator
Python Prompt	Python Standard Library	comparison operator
prompt	Standard Library	concatenate
Python Interpreter	syntax	equivalent
interpreter	functions	index
operator	command line	indexing
mathematical operator	error	slicing

Summary of Python Functions and Commands

Below is a summary of the functions and operators used in this chapter:

Arithmetic

Arithmetic Operator	Description
+	addition
-	subtraction
*	multiplication
/	division
**	exponents
_	answer in memory

Trigonometry

Trig Function	Description
`from math import *`	
sin	sine of angle in radians
cos	cosine of angle in radians
tan	tangent of angle in radians
pi	π

Trig Function	Description
degrees	convert radians to degrees
radians	convert degrees to radians
asin	inverse sine
acos	inverse cosine
atan	inverse tangent

Logarithms and Exponents

Logarithms and Exponent Function	Description
from math import *	
log	log base e, natural log
log10	log base 10
exp	e^{power}
e	the math constant e
pow(x,y)	x raised to the y power
sqrt	square root

Statistics

Statistics Function	Description
from statistics import *	
mean	mean (average)
median	median (middle value)
mode	mode (most often)
stdev	standard deviation of a sample
pstdev	standard deviation of a population

3.7 Review Questions

Arithmetic

Q03.01 $2 + \frac{1}{2}$

Q03.02 $4 \times 2 + \frac{2}{4}$

Q03.03 $\frac{5}{2} \times 3 + 4$

Q03.04 $4^2 + 3$

Q03.05 $\sqrt{16}$

Q03.06 3^{4-5}

Q03.07 $\frac{1+3+5}{2+4+6}$

3.7. REVIEW QUESTIONS

Q03.08 $1 - 2 + \frac{9}{6} - 3 + 5$

Q03.09 $(3 + 5 - 2)^{2/3}$

Q03.10 $\frac{5+3}{2\times 5}$

Q03.11 $\sqrt{6^2 + 4}$

Q03.12 $1 + 9 \times \frac{8}{4^2} + 1^{3-4} \times \frac{1}{2.5}$

Strings

Q03.15 Define the string "Problem"

Q03.16 Two strings "Problem" and "Solving with Python". Combine these strings to produce "Problem Solving with Python". Hint: Don't forget the space.

Q03.17 Compare the strings "Problem" and "problem" with the comparison operator ==. Explain the result.

Q03.18 Compare the output of the code 1 + 2 == 3 and '1 + 2' == '3'. Explain why the output is different.

Trigonometry

Q03.30 Find the sine of 0, $\pi/4$, $\pi/2$, $3\pi/4$, and π.

Q03.31 Find the cosine of 0 degrees, 30 degrees, 60 degrees and 90 degrees.

Q03.32 Find the tangent of 3/4, 5/12, and -8/6.

Q03.33 Find the sin of 0.1 radians. Then find the arcsine of the result and see if it equals 0.1 radians.

Q03.34 The U.S. Forest service can use trigonometry to find the height of trees. The height of a tree, h is equal to the distance d between an observer and the base of the tree multiplied by the tangent of the angle θ between looking straight along the ground and looking up at the top of tree according to the formula:

$$h = d \tan(\theta)$$

If a Forest Service ranger is 20 feet away from the base of a douglas fir tree and looks up at a 63 degree angle relative to straight ahead to see the top of the tree, what is the height of the douglas fir tree?

Q03.35 The tangent of an angle is equal to the sine of the angle divided by the cosine of the angle. Make two calculations, one for the tangent of -29 degrees and another calculation for the sine of -29 degrees divided by the cosine of -29 degrees. Do you observe the same output?

Q03.36 A simple model of water level based on tides (assuming high tide is at midnight) is:

$$h = (4.8) \sin(\pi/6)(t + 3) + 5.1$$

Where h is the water height and t is the number of hours since midnight. Using this model, calculate the water level h at 6am ($t = 6$ hours since midnight).

Q03.37 The x-component of a force F_x is equal to the magnitude of the force $|\vec{F}|$ multiplied by the cosine of the angle θ of the force relative to the positive x-axis.

$$F_x = |\vec{F}|\cos(\theta)$$

If the magnitude of a force $|\vec{F}| = 12.4$ and the force acts at $\theta = 110$ degrees relative to the positive x-axis, what is the x-component of the force F_x?

Q03.37 The distance d a free-thrown projectile travels is dependent on the projectile's initial velocity v_0, the acceleration due to gravity $g = 9.81 m/s^2$ and the angle θ at which the project is launched according to:

$$d = \frac{v_0^2}{g}\sin(2\theta)$$

If a projectile is launched at a 12 degree angle with an initial velocity of 150 m/s, how far will the projectile travel?

Logarithms and Exponents

Q03.41 Show that the natural log of Euler's number, $\ln(e)$, is equal to one.

Q03.42 Logarithms turn multiplication into addition. Complete both of the calculations below to see if the expressions are equal to each other:

$$\log(87.1 \times 210 \times 10^3)$$

$$\log(87.1) + \log(210) + \log(10^3)$$

Q03.43 Logarithms turn exponents into multiplication and multiplication into addition. Complete both of the calculations below to see if the expressions are equal. Remember, Python has a couple log functions including `log()` and `log10()`.

$$\log(6.02 \times 10^{23})$$

$$23 + \log(6.02)$$

Q03.44 Python's math module has the natural log (ln) function `math.log()` and the log (base 10) function `math.log10()`. If you want to find the log with an arbitrary base, b, of a number n, you can use a ratio of natural logarithms (log base e) according to:

$$\log_b(n) = \frac{\ln(n)}{\ln(b)}$$

Calculate the base 4 logarithm of 3.9×10^{-9}

$$log_4(3.9 \times 10^{-9})$$

3.7. REVIEW QUESTIONS

Q03.45 The magnitude of a vector $|\vec{v}|$ is equal to the square root of the sum of the squares of the vector's components v_x, v_y, and v_z according to:

$$|\vec{v}| = \sqrt{v_x^2 + v_y^2 + v_z^2}$$

What is the magnitude of a vector $\vec{v}$ that has components $v_x = 76.3$, $v_y = 70.9$, $v_z = 93.6$?

Q03.46 Moore's Law, a relationship that states the number of transistors that fit on a microchip doubles every two years can be modeled as:

$$P_n = P_0 \times 2^n$$

Where P_0 is the original number of transistors on a microchip and P_n is the number of transistors on a microchip after n number of years since the original microchip. If the original microchip has 1000 transistors, how many transistors are projected to be on a microchip 40 years later according to Moore's Law?

Variables in Calculations

Q03.71 $a = 2$, $b = 3$, calculate $\frac{4}{5}(a^2 - b^3)$

Q03.72 The area of a circle, a, is dependent on the circle's radius, r, according to:

$$a = \pi r^2$$

What is the area of a circle with radius $r = 4$?

Q03.73 The area of a circle, a, is dependent on the circle's diameter, d, according to:

$$a = \pi (\frac{d}{2})^2$$

What is the area of a circle with diameter $d = 6$?

Q03.74 The volume of a sphere, v, is dependent on the sphere's radius, r, according to:

$$v = (\frac{4}{3})\pi r^3$$

What is the volume of a sphere with radius $r = 1.5$?

Q03.75 The volume of a cylinder, v, is dependent on the cylinder's radius, r, and height, h, according to:

$$v = \pi r^2 h$$

What is the volume of a cylinder with radius $r = 5$ and height $h = 10$?

Q03.76 The surface area of a sphere, a_s is related to the sphere's radius, r, according to:

$$a_s = 4\pi r^2$$

What is the surface area a_s of a sphere with radius $r = 2.5$?

Q03.77 The general equation for the distance, d, that a free falling body travels (neglecting air resistance) is:

$$d = \frac{1}{2}gt^2$$

g is the acceleration due to gravity and t is the fall time. Assume the acceleration due to gravity $g = 9.81$. How far (what distance) will a ball fall in time $t = 12$?

Q03.78 The general equation for the fall time, t, that a free falling body takes (neglecting air resistance) to cover a distance, d is:

$$t = \sqrt{\frac{d}{0.5g}}$$

g is the acceleration due to gravity. Assume the acceleration due to gravity $g = 9.81$. How long (what time) will it take a base jumper to fall distance $d = 2000$?

Q03.79 The value of an investment v compounded annually at an interest rate of $r\%$ after n years is dependent on the original investment P according to:

$$v = P(1 + r/100)^n$$

If $P = 1000$ dollars at a rate of $r = 7\%$, what will the value v be after $n = 20$ years?

Q03.80 The original principal P needed to produce a total savings of value v at a rate of $r\%$ over n years is calculated by:

$$P = \frac{v}{(1 + r/100)^n}$$

What is the principal P needed to save one million dollars at a rate $r = 10\%$ over $n = 40$ years?

Q03.81 Electrical power P is related to current I and resistance R according to:

$$P = I^2 R$$

An electrical load with a resistance $R = 10,000$ running at a current $I = 0.200$ draws how much power P?

Errors, Explanations, and Solutions

For each of the problems below, run the line of code. Then explain the error in your own words. Give an explanation more specific than `invalid syntax`. Then suggest and run a line of code that fixes the error.

Q03.91

```
>>> 9 x 10
```

Q03.92

3.7. REVIEW QUESTIONS

```
>>> 1 1/2 + 2 2/3
```

Q03.93
```
>>> 3cos(35)
```

Q03.94
```
>>> 8.31 x 10^9
```

Q03.95
```
>>> (2+3)**(2-3e(4)
```

Q03.96
```
>>> 7% + 8% + 9%
```

Q03.97
```
>>> (-)54.2 + 9.2
```

Q03.98
```
>>> '5' / '4'
```

Q03.99
```
>>> ln(e) - log(10)
```

Chapter 4

Data Types and Variables

4.1 Introduction

This chapter is about Python data types. Python has many built-in data types such as integers, floats, booleans, strings, and lists.

By the end of this chapter you will be able to:

- Explain the difference between Python's built-in data types
- Define variables with the assignment operator =
- Create variables with different data types
- Use Python's `type()` function to determine an object's data type
- Compare variables with the comparison operator ==
- Convert variables from one data type to another
- Work with integers, floats and complex numbers
- Understand the boolean data type
- Create and modify lists, dictionaries and tuples
- Index and slice strings, lists and tuples

4.2 Numeric Data Types

Python has many useful built-in *data types*. Python variables can store different types of data based on a variable's data type. A variable's data type is created dynamically, without the need to explicitly define a data type when the variable is created.

It is useful for problem solvers to understand a couple of Python's core data types in order to write well-constructed code.

A review of variable assignment in Python

Recall from the previous chapter that variables in Python are defined with the assignment operator, the equals sign =. To define a variable in Python, the variable name is written first, then the assignment operator = followed by a value or expression.

The general syntax to assign a value to variable name is below:

```
variable_name = value
```

Variable names in Python must adhere to the following rules:

- variable names must start with a letter
- variable names can only contain letters, numbers and the underscore character _
- variable names can not contain spaces or punctuation
- variable names are not enclosed in quotes or brackets

Below is a discussion of a few different built-in data types in Python.

Integers

Integers are one of the Python data types. An integer is a whole number, negative, positive or zero. In Python, integer variables are defined by assigning a whole number to a variable. Python's type() function can be used to determine the data type of a variable.

```
>>> a = 5
>>> type(a)
<class 'int'>
```

The output <class 'int'> indicates the variable a is an integer. Integers can be negative or zero.

```
>>> b = -2
>>> type(b)
<class 'int'>
>>> z = 0
>>> type(z)
<class 'int'>
```

4.2. NUMERIC DATA TYPES

Floating Point Numbers

Floating point numbers or *floats* are another Python data type. Floats are decimals, positive, negative and zero. Floats can also be represented by numbers in scientific notation which contain exponents.

Both a lower case e or an upper case E can be used to define floats in scientific notation. In Python, a float can be defined using a decimal point . when a variable is assigned.

```
>>> c = 6.2
>>> type(c)
<class 'float'>
>>> d = -0.03
>>> type(d)
<class 'float'>
>>> Na = 6.02e23
>>> Na
6.02e+23
>>> type(Na)
<class 'float'>
```

To define a variable as a float instead of an integer, even if the variable is assigned a whole number, a trailing decimal point . is used. Note the difference when a decimal point . comes after a whole number:

```
>>> g = 5
>>> type(g)
<class 'int'>
>>> f = 5.
>>> type(r)
<class 'float'>
```

Complex Numbers

Another useful numeric data type for problem solvers is the *complex number* data type. A complex number is defined in Python using a real component + an imaginary component j. The letter j must be used to denote the imaginary component. Using the letter i to define a complex number returns an error in Python.

```
>>> comp = 4 + 2j
>>> type(comp)
<class 'complex'>

>>> comp2 = 4 + 2i
                ^
SyntaxError: invalid syntax
```

Imaginary numbers can be added to integers and floats.

```
>>> intgr = 3
>>> type(intgr)
```

```
<class 'int'>

>>> comp_sum = comp + intgr
>>> print(comp_sum)
(7+2j)

>>> flt = 2.1
>>> comp_sum = comp + flt
>>> print(comp_sum)
(6.1+2j)
```

4.3 Boolean Data Type

The *boolean* data type is either True or False. In Python, boolean variables are defined by the True and False keywords.

```
>>> a = True
>>> type(a)
<class 'bool'>

>>> b = False
>>> type(b)
<class 'bool'>
```

The output `<class 'bool'>` indicates the variable is a boolean data type.

Note the keywords True and False must have an Upper Case first letter. Using a lowercase true returns an error.

```
>>> c = true
Traceback (most recent call last):
  File "<input>", line 1, in <module>
NameError: name 'true' is not defined

>>> d = false
Traceback (most recent call last):
  File "<input>", line 1, in <module>
NameError: name 'false' is not defined
```

Integers and Floats as Booleans

Integers and floating point numbers can be converted to the boolean data type using Python's bool() function. An int, float or complex number set to zero returns False. An integer, float or complex number set to any other number, positive or negative, returns True.

```
>>> zero_int = 0
>>> bool(zero_int)
False
```

4.3. BOOLEAN DATA TYPE

```
>>> pos_int = 1
>>> bool(pos_int)
True

>>> neg_flt = -5.1
>>> bool(neg_flt)
True
```

Boolean Arithmetic

Boolean arithmetic is the arithmetic of true and false logic. A boolean or logical value can either be True or False. Boolean values can be manipulated and combined with *boolean operators*. Boolean operators in Python include and, or, and not.

The common boolean operators in Python are below:

- or
- and
- not
- == (equivalent)
- != (not equivalent)

In the code section below, two variables are assigned the boolean values True and False. Then these boolean values are combined and manipulated with boolean operators.

```
>>> A = True
>>> B = False

>>> A or B
True

>>> A and B
False

>>> not A
False

>>> not B
True

>>> A == B
False

>>> A != B
True
```

Boolean operators such as and, or, and not can be combined with parenthesis to make compound *boolean expressions*.

```
>>> C = False
>>> A or (C and B)
True
>>> (A and B) or C
False
```

A summary of boolean arithmetic and boolean operators is shown in the table below:

A	B	not A	not B	A == B	A =! B	A or B	A and B
T	F	F	T	F	T	T	F
F	T	T	F	F	T	T	F
T	T	F	F	T	F	T	T
F	F	T	T	T	F	F	F

4.4 Strings

Another built-in Python data type is *strings*. Strings are sequences of letters, numbers, symbols, and spaces. In Python, strings can be almost any length and can contain spaces. Strings are assigned in Python using single quotation marks ' ' or double quotation marks " ".

Python strings can contain blank spaces. A blank space is a valid character in Python string.

```
>>> string = 'z'
>>>> type(string)
<class 'str'>

>>> string = 'Engineers'
>>> type(string)
<class 'str'>
```

The output `<class 'str'>` indicates the variable is a string.

Numbers as Strings

Numbers and decimals can be defined as strings too. If a decimal number is defined using quotes ' ', the number is saved as a string rather than as a float. Integers defined using quotes become strings as well.

```
>>> num = '5.2'
>>> type(num)
<class 'str'>

>>> num = '2'
>>> type(num)
<class 'str'>
```

4.4. STRINGS

Character	S	o	l	u	t	i	o	n
Index	0	1	2	3	4	5	6	7

Figure 4.1. String index assignments

Strings as Boolean Values

Strings can be converted to boolean values (converted to True or False). The empty string "" returns as False. All other strings convert to True.

```
>>> name = "Gabby"
>>> bool(name)
True

>>> empty = ""
>>> bool(empty)
False
```

Note that a string which contains just one space (" ") is not empty. It contains the space character. Therefore a string made up of just one space converts to True.

```
>>> space = " "
>>> bool(space)
True
```

String Indexing

String *indexing* is the process of pulling out specific characters from a string in a particular order. In Python, strings are indexed using square brackets [ ]. An important point to remember:

Python counting starts at 0 and ends at n-1.

Consider the word below.

```
Solution
```

The letter S is at index zero, the letter o is at index one. The last letter of the word Solution is n. n is in the seventh index. Even though the word Solution has eight letters, the last letter is in the seventh index. This is because Python indexing starts at 0 and ends at n-1.

```
>>> word = 'Solution'
>>> word[0]
'S'

>>> word[1]
'o'
```

Negative Index	-8	-7	-6	-5	-4	-3	-2	-1
Character	S	o	l	u	t	i	o	n

Figure 4.2. Negative string index assignments

```
>>> word[7]
'n'
```

If the eighth index of the word Solution is called, an error is returned.

```
>>> word[8]

IndexError: string index out of range
```

Negative Indexing

Placing a negative number inside of the square brackets pulls a character out of a string starting from the end of the string.

```
>>> word[-1]
'n'

>>> word[-2]
'o'
```

String Slicing

String *slicing* is an operation to pull out a sequence of characters from a string. In Python, a colon on the inside of the square brackets between two numbers in a slicing operation indicates *through*. If the index [0:3] is called, the characters at positions 0 through 3 are returned.

Remember Python counting starts at 0 and ends at n-1. So [0:3] indicates the first through third letters, which are indexes 0 to 2.

```
>>> word[0:3]
'Sol'
```

A colon by itself on the inside of square brackets indicates *all*.

```
>>> word[:]
'Solution'
```

When three numbers are separated by two colons inside of square brackets, the numbers represent *start* : *stop* : *step*. Remember that Python counting starts at 0 and ends at n-1.

```
>>> word[0:7:2]    #start:stop:step
'Slto'
```

When two colons are used inside of square brackets, and less than three numbers are specified, the missing numbers are set to their "defaults". The default start is 0, the default stop is n-1, and the default step is 1.

The two code lines below produce the same output since 0 is the default start and 7 (n-1) is the default stop. Both lines of code use a step of 2.

```
>>> word[0:7:2]
'Slto'

>>> word[::2]
'Slto'
```

The characters that make up a string can be reversed by using the default start and stop values and specifying a step of -1.

```
>>> word[::-1]
'noituloS'
```

4.5 Lists

A list is a data structure in Python that can contain multiple elements of any of the other data type. A list is defined with square brackets [ ] and commas , between elements.

```
>>> lst = [ 1, 2, 3 ]
>>> type(lst)
list

>>> lst = [ 1, 5.3, '3rd_Element']
>>> type(lst)
list
```

Indexing Lists

Individual elements of a list can be accessed or *indexed* using bracket [ ] notation. Note that Python lists start with the index zero, not the index 1. For example:

```
>>> lst = ['statics', 'strengths', 'dynamics']
>>> lst[0]
'statics'

>>> lst[1]
'strengths'

>>> lst[2]
'dynamics'
```

Remember! Python lists start indexing at [0] not at [1]. To call the elements in a list with 3 values use: lst[0], lst[1], lst[2].

Slicing Lists

Colons : are used inside the square brackets to denote *all*

```
>>> lst = [2, 4, 6]
>>> lst[:]
[2, 4, 6]
```

Negative numbers can be used as indexes to call the last number of elements in the list

```
>>> lst = [2, 4, 6]
>>> lst[-1]
6
```

The colon operator can also be used to denote *all up to* and *thru end*.

```
>>> lst = [2, 4, 6]
>>> lst[:2]           # all up to 2
[2, 4]

>>> lst = [2, 4, 6]
>>> lst[2:]           # 2 thru end
[6]
```

The colon operator can also be used to denote *start : end + 1*. Note that indexing here in not inclusive. `lst[1:3]` returns the 2nd element, and 3rd element but not the fourth even though 3 is used in the index.

Remember! Python indexing is not inclusive. The last element called in an index will not be returned.

4.6 Dictionaries and Tuples

Besides lists, Python has two additional data structures that can store multiple objects. These data structures are *dictionaries* and *tuples*. Tuples will be discussed first.

Tuples

Tuples are *immutable* lists. Elements of a list can be modified, but elements in a tuple can only be accessed, not modified. The name *tuple* does not mean that only two values can be stored in this data structure.

Tuples are defined in Python by enclosing elements in parenthesis ( ) and separating elements with commas. The command below creates a tuple containing the numbers 3, 4, and 5.

```
>>> t_var = (3,4,5)
>>> t_var
(3, 4, 5)
```

4.6. DICTIONARIES AND TUPLES

Note how the elements of a list can be modified:

```
>>> l_var = [3,4,5]   # a list
>>> l_var[0]= 8
>>> l_var
[8, 4, 5]
```

The elements of a tuple can not be modified. If you try to assign a new value to one of the elements in a tuple, an error is returned.

```
>>> t_var = (3,4,5)   # a tuple
>>> t_var[0]= 8
>>> t_var

TypeError: 'tuple' object does not support item assignment
```

To create a tuple that just contains one numerical value, the number must be followed by a comma. Without a comma, the variable is defined as a number.

```
>>> num = (5)
>>> type(num)
int
```

When a comma is included after the number, the variable is defined as a tuple.

```
>>> t_var = (5,)
>>> type(t_var)
tuple
```

Dictionaries

Dictionaries are made up of key: value pairs. In Python, lists and tuples are organized and accessed based on position. Dictionaries in Python are organized and accessed using keys and values. The location of a pair of keys and values stored in a Python dictionary is irrelevant.

Dictionaries are defined in Python with curly braces { }. Commas separate the key-value pairs that make up the dictionary. Each key-value pair is related by a colon :.

Let's store the ages of two people in a dictionary. The two people are Gabby and Maelle. Gabby is 8 and Maelle is 5. Note the name Gabby is a string and the age 8 is an integer.

```
>>> age_dict = {"Gabby": 8 , "Maelle": 5}
>>> type(age_dict)
dict
```

The values stored in a dictionary are called and assigned using the following syntax:

```
dict_name[key] = value

>>> age_dict = {"Gabby": 8 , "Maelle": 5}
>>> age_dict["Gabby"]
8
```

We can add a new person to our age_dict with the following command:

```
>>> age_dict = {"Gabby": 8 , "Maelle": 5}

>>> age_dict["Peter"]= 40
>>> age_dict
{'Gabby': 8, 'Maelle': 5, 'Peter': 40}
```

Dictionaries can be converted to lists by calling the .items(), .keys(), and .values() methods.

```
>>> age_dict = {"Gabby": 8 , "Maelle": 5}

>>> whole_list = list(age_dict.items())
>>> whole_list
[('Gabby', 8), ('Maelle', 5)]

>>> name_list = list(age_dict.keys())
>>> name_list
['Gabby', 'Maelle']

>>> age_list = list(age_dict.values())
>>> age_list
[8, 5]
```

Items can be removed from dictionaries by calling the .pop() method. The dictionary key (and that key's associated value) supplied to the .pop() method is removed from the dictionary.

```
>>> age_dict = {"Gabby": 8 , "Maelle": 5}
>>> age_dict.pop("Gabby")
>>> age_dict
{'Maelle': 5}
```

4.7 Summary

In this chapter, you learned about a couple of different data types built-in to Python. These data types include the numeric data types: integers, floats, and complex numbers. The string data type is composed of letters, numbers, spaces, and punctuation. Python also has container data types which can store many values. These container data types include lists, tuples, and dictionaries. Strings, lists and tuples can be indexed and sliced using square brackets [ ].

Key Terms and Concepts

data type	complex number	data structure
variable	string	dictionary
assignment operator	boolean	tuple
integer	bool	list
int	boolean arithmetic	index
whole number	boolean operators	indexing
floating point number	or	immutable
float	and	
scientific notation	not	

Summary of Python Functions and Commands

Built-in Data Types

Python Data Type	Description
int	integer
float	floating point number
bool	boolean value: True or False
complex	complex number, real and imaginary components
str	string, sequence of letters, numbers and symbols
list	list, formed with [ ]
dict	dictionary, formed with {'key'=value}
tuple	an immutable list, formed with ( )

Python Functions

Function	Description
type()	output a variable or object data type
len()	return the length of a string, list dictionary or tuple
str()	convert a float or int into a str (string)

Function	Description
int()	convert a float or str into an int (integer)
float()	convert an int or str into an float (floating point number)

Python List Operators

Operator	Description	Example	Result
[ ]	indexing	lst[1]	4
:	start	lst[:2]	[2, 4]
:	end	lst[2:]	[6, 8]
:	through	lst[0:3]	[2, 4, 6]
:	start, step, end+1	lst[0:5:2]	[2, 6]

4.8 Review Questions

Determine the Data Type

Q04.01 Find the data type of a if a=9

Q04.02 Find the data type of a if a=9.

Q04.03 Find the data type of a if a='9.'

Q04.04 Find the data type of a if a=(9)

Q04.05 Find the data type of a if a=False

Q04.06 Find the data type of a if a=[1,2,3]

Q04.07 Find the data type of a if a=(1,2,3)

Q04.08 Find the data type of a if a={'key'=9}

Q04.09 Find the data type of a if a=1 + 9j

Numeric Data Types

Q04.10 Set a=1 and b=2. What data type is a/b?

Q04.11 Set a=1 and b=2. What data type is a*b?

Q04.12 What is 5.1 plus 0 + 3j?

Q04.13 What floating point number converts to the boolean False? Show this in code using the bool() function.

Q04.14 Create the floating point number $0.001 \times 10^{-0.2}$ and assign it to the variable b.

Q04.15 Show that 3e2 is the same as 3E2 with the comparison operator ==

Q04.16 Euler's number, e, can be called in Python using the code below:

```
from math import e
```

4.8. REVIEW QUESTIONS

(a) Round e to the nearest integer. Store the result in a variable called x.

(b) Round e to the nearest 1000ths place (the nearest 0.001). Store the result in a variable called y.

(c) Truncate the decimal portion of e (remove the 0.71828.... portion) so you are left with the integer 2. Store the result in a variable called z. Hint: convert e to a string and use string slicing.

Q04.17 Define the complex number A using the code below:

```
A = 4 + 2j
```

(a) store the real component of A in a variable called `real`.

(b) store the imaginary component of A in a variable called `imaginary`.

(c) store the magnitude of A in a variable called `mag`. The magnitude of an imaginary number is defined as:

$$magnitude = \sqrt{(real)^2 + (imaginary)^2}$$

Booleans

Q04.20 Predict the output if the lines n=5 and (n<3) and (n<7) are run. Then run the the two lines of code.

Q04.21 Predict the output if the lines of code below are run. Then run the code.

```
>>> ans='Yes'
>>> ans=='Yes' or ans=='No'
```

Q04.22 Pick a number n to make the following statement True: (2<n) or (n==2+n) Then run the code to show your number works.

Q04.23 Pick a number n to make the following statement False: not (n<6) and (n<4) Then run the code to show your number works.

Q04.24 Add the integers 1 and 0 and convert the answer to a boolean. Add the boolean values bool(0) + bool(1) and compare the result.

Q04.25 Show that (n>5) and (n<=10) is equivalent to 5 < n <= 10 using the two different numbers for n.

Q04.26 Show that (n<5) or (n>=10) is equivalent to not(5 =< n < 10) using the two different numbers for n.

Strings

Q04.30 Define a string that contains the word *Problem*.

Q04.31 Define one string as the word *Problem* and define another string as the word *Solving*. Combine these two strings to make the statement *Problem Solving*.

Q04.32 (a) Define a string that contains the number 8 and a string that contains the number 5. Combine these two strings with the plus operator +.

(b) Define an integer as the number 8 and an integer as the number 5 and combine these two integers with the plus operator +

(c) Explain why the output from (a) was different from the output of (b)

(d) Multiply the string 8 and the string 5 with the multiplication operator *. Compare the output to multiplying the integers 8 and the integer 5. Why is the output different?

Q03.33 Complete the following index and slicing operations after `word = 'Problem'` is defined.

(a) Pull out the letter *P* from `word`

(b) Pull out the first three letters *Pro* from `word`

(c) Pull out the second through the fourth letters *rob* from `word`

(d) Pull out every other letter from `word` starting with *P*

(e) Use indexing and slicing to ouput `word` backwards to produce *melborP*.

Q04.34 Define the strings below:

(a) Define a string a as *coffee*, define a string b as *it's*, define a string c as *hot!* and string d as , (a comma).

(b) Combine the strings a, b, c and d to produce the string *coffee, it's hot* (notice the comma)

(c) Print out the statement *she said "coffee, it's hot"* using the variables a, b, c and d.

Q04.35 Create the string `path` with the value *C:\Users\Gabby\Documents*

Q04.36 Convert the string `Problem` to the list `['P','r','o','b','l','e','m']` without writing the list from scratch.

Q04.37 Use the string `over board` and slicing to produce the following words:

(a) `over`

(b) `board`

(c) `oar`

Q04.38 Use the string `rotten tomatoes` and slicing to produce the following words:

(a) `to`

(b) `no`

(c) `ten`

(d) `oat`

4.8. REVIEW QUESTIONS

Lists

Q04.40 Create a list that contains the numbers 1, 2.9×10^8, and the word *game*.

Q04.41 Create a list that contains the words *problem, solving, with, python*.

Q04.42 Create a list with one value, the number 6. Convert the list to a boolean with the `bool()` function.

Q04.43 Create an empty list. Convert the empty list to a boolean with the `bool()` function.

Q04.44 Create a list with the letters *C*, *D*, and *R*. Pull the letters *C* and *D* out of your list with indexing.

Q04.45 Create a list with the numbers 1 to 10 (counting by ones). Use slicing to pull out the number 5 from the list.

Q04.46 Create a list with the numbers 1 to 10 (counting by ones). Use slicing to pull out all of the numbers 5 or less.

Q04.47 Create a list with the numbers 1 to 10 (counting by ones). Use slicing to pull out all of the numbers 5 and greater.

Q04.48 Create a list with the numbers 1 to 10 (counting by ones). Use slicing to pull out all of the even numbers from the list.

Q04.49 Create a list with the numbers 1 to 10 (counting by ones). Use slicing to pull out every odd number from the list.

Q04.50 Create a list with the numbers 1 to 10 (counting by ones). Use slicing to return the list in reverse order (the returned list starts with 10 and ends with 1).

Q04.51 Create a Python list containing the values 1, 2, 5.6, and 9 in that order and store it in a variable called x.

Dictionaries

Q04.60 Create a dictionary called `capitals` that contains the states and state capitals. Include `Washington`, capital `Olympia` and `Oregon`, capital `Salem`.

Q04.61 Create a dictionary called `capitals` that contains the states and state capitals. Include `Washington`, capital `Olympia` and `Oregon`, capital `Salem`. In the line after the dictionary is created add the state `New York`, capital `Albany`.

Q04.62 Create a dictionary `numbers = {'one':1, 'two':2, 'three':3}`. Pull out the number '2' by calling the key 'two'.

Q04.63 Create a dictionary `colors = {'red':' #FF0000', 'green':'#008000', 'blue':'#0000FF'}`. Pull out all the keys and add them to a list called `colors_list` with the `.keys()` method.

Q04.64 Create a dictionary `colors = {'red':' #FF0000', 'green':'#008000', 'blue':'#0000FF'}`. Pull out all the values and add them to a list called `colors_hex` with the `.values()` method.

Q04.65 Create a dictionary `colors = {'red':' #FF0000', 'green':'#008000', 'blue':'#0000FF'}`. Pull out all the items from the dictionary and add them to a list called `color_items` with the `.items()` method.

Q04.66 Create a dictionary `groups = {'solo':1, 'duo':'2'}`. Add the key *trio* and the corresponding value 3.

Q04.67 Create a dictionary groups = {'solo':1, 'duo':'2'}. Then remove the key 'duo' and the value '2' so that only 'solo':1 remains.

Q04.68 Create a dictionary college = {'name': 'University of Oregon'}. Add the following two keys: *abbreviation, mascot* and the corresponding two values: *UofO, ducks*.

Tuples

Q04.70 Create a tuple with the numbers 8, 9, and 10.

Q04.71 Create a tuple that has a single entry, the number 10.

Q04.72 Create a list and a tuple that both contains the strings: *one, two* and *three*. Pull the word *two* out of both the list and the tuple.

Q04.73 Create a list and a tuple that both contains the strings: *one, two* and *three*. Try to substitute the number 2 for the word *two* in both the list and tuple using indexing (square brackets).

Q04.74 Code the following lines:

```
t1 = (9)
t2 = (9,)
t3 = ('9')
```

Use Python's type() function to find the object type of each variable.

Q04.75 Create a tuple that returns True when converted to a boolean. Use the bool() function to demonstrate your tuple converts to True.

Q04.76 Create a tuple that returns False when converted to a boolean. Use the bool() function to demonstrate your tuple converts to False.

Errors, Explanations, and Solutions

Q04.80 Run the following lines of code and explain the error in your own words. Then rewrite the lines of code to run error free:

```
n = 503
n[2]
```

Q04.81 Run the following lines of code and explain the error in your own words. Then rewrite the lines of code to run error free:

```
a = 321
b = 'go!'
c = a + b
```

Q04.82 Run the following lines of code and explain the error in your own words. Then rewrite the lines of code to run error free:

```
d = {one:1, two:2, three:3}
d[one]
```

Q04.83 Run the following lines of code and explain the error in your own words. Then rewrite the lines of code to run error free:

4.8. REVIEW QUESTIONS

```
f = false
not f
```

Q04.84 Run the following lines of code and explain the error in your own words. Then rewrite the lines of code to run error free:

```
comp = 0.1 - 4.3i
comp + 5
```

Q04.85 Run the following lines of code and explain the error in your own words. Then rewrite the lines of code to run error free:

```
empty = ''
bool(empty)
```

Q04.86 Run the following lines of code and explain the error in your own words. Then rewrite the lines of code to run error free:

```
lst = [1,3,5]
lst[3]
```

Q04.87 Run the following lines of code and explain the error in your own words. Then rewrite the lines of code to run error free:

```
dict = ['key': 8, 'pair': 9]
dict['key']
```

Q04.88 Run the following lines of code and explain the error in your own words. Then rewrite the lines of code to run error free:

```
s = ['Problem Solving']
s[8:]
```

Chapter 5

NumPy and Arrays

5.1 Introduction

By the end of this chapter you will be able to:

- Explain the difference between a Python list and a NumPy array
- Create NumPy arrays
- Modify NumPy arrays
- Index NumPy arrays
- Run mathematical operations on NumPy arrays
- Solve a system of linear equations using matrices

5.2 NumPy

NumPy is a Python package used for numerical computation. NumPy is one of the foundational packages for scientific computing with Python. NumPy's core data type is the array and NumPy functions operate on arrays.

5.3 Installing NumPy

Before NumPy's functions and methods can be used, NumPy must be installed. Depending on which distribution of Python you use, the installation method is slightly different.

Install NumPy on Anaconda

If you installed the Anaconda distribution of Python, NumPy comes pre-installed and no further installation steps are necessary.

If you use a version of Python from python.org or a version of Python that came with your operating system, the **Anaconda Prompt** and **conda** or **pip** can be used to install NumPy.

Install NumPy with the Anaconda Prompt

To install NumPy, open the **Anaconda Prompt** and type:

```
> conda install numpy
```

Type y for yes when prompted.

Install NumPy with pip

To install NumPy with **pip**, bring up a terminal window and type:

```
$ pip install numpy
```

This command installs NumPy in the current working Python environment.

Verify NumPy installation

To verify NumPy is installed, invoke NumPy's version using the Python REPL. Import NumPy and call the `.__version__` attribute common to most Python packages.

```
In [1]: import numpy as np
        np.__version__

Out[1]: '1.14.3'
```

A version number like '1.16.1' indicates a successful NumPy installation.

5.4 Python Lists and NumPy Arrays

NumPy is a Python package used for numerical calculations, working with arrays of homogeneous values, and scientific computing. This section introduces NumPy arrays then explains the difference between Python lists and NumPy arrays.

Python Lists

NumPy is used to construct homogeneous arrays and perform mathematical operations on arrays. A NumPy array is different from a Python list. The data types stored in a Python list can all be different.

```
python_list = [ 1, -0.038, 'gear', True]
```

The Python list above contains four different data types: 1 is an integer, -0.038 is a float, 'gear' is a string, and 'True' is a boolean.

The code below prints the data type of each value store in `python_list`.

```
In [1]: python_list = [1, -0.038, 'gear', True]
        for item in python_list:
            print(type(item))

<class 'int'>
<class 'float'>
<class 'str'>
<class 'bool'>
```

NumPy Arrays

The values stored in a NumPy array must all share the same data type. Consider the NumPy array below:

```
np.array([1.0, 3.1, 5e-04, 0.007])
```

All four values stored in the NumPy array above share the same data type: 1.0, 3.1, 5e-04, and 0.007 are all floats.

The code below prints the data type of each value stored in the NumPy array above.

```
In [2]: import numpy as np

        np_array = [1, -0.038, 'gear', True]
        for value in np.array([1.0, 3.1, 5e-04, 0.007]):
            print(type(value))

<class 'numpy.float64'>
<class 'numpy.float64'>
```

```
<class 'numpy.float64'>
<class 'numpy.float64'>
```

If the same four elements stored in the previous Python list are stored in a NumPy array, NumPy forces all of the four items in the list to conform to the same data type.

In the next code section, all four items are converted to type '<U32', which is a string data type in NumPy (the U refers Unicode strings; all strings in Python are Unicode by default).

```
In [3]: np.array([1, -0.038, 'gear', True])

Out[3]: array(['1', '-0.038', 'gear', 'True'], dtype='<U32')
```

NumPy arrays can also be two-dimensional, three-dimensional, or up to n-dimensional. In practice, computer resources limit array size. Remember that regardless of size, all elements in a NumPy array must be the same type.

NumPy arrays are useful because mathematical operations can be run on an entire array simultaneously. If numbers are stored in a regular Python list and the list is multiplied by a scalar, the list extends and repeats- instead of multiplying each number in the list by the scalar.

The code below demonstrates list repetition using the multiplication operator, *.

```
In [4]: lst = [1, 2, 3, 4]
        lst*2

Out[4]: [1, 2, 3, 4, 1, 2, 3, 4]
```

To multiply each element in a Python list by the number 2, a loop can be used:

```
In [5]: lst = [1, 2, 3, 4]
        for i, item in enumerate(lst):
            lst[i] = lst[i]*2
        lst

Out[5]: [2, 4, 6, 8]
```

The method above is relatively cumbersome and is also quite *computationally expensive*. An operation that is computationally expensive is an operation that takes a lot of processing time or storage resources like RAM and CPU bandwidth.

Another way of completing the same action as the loop above is to use a NumPy array.

Array Multiplication

An entire NumPy array can be multiplied by a scalar in one step. The scalar multiplication operation below produces an array with each element multiplied by the scalar 2.

5.5. ARRAY CREATION

```
In [6]: nparray= np.array([1,2,3,4])
        2*nparray

Out[6]: array([2, 4, 6, 8])
```

If we have a very long list of numbers, we can compare the amount of time it takes each of the two computation methods above, a list with a loop compared to array multiplication to complete the same operation. This comparison highlights an advantage of arrays compared to lists- speed.

Timing Arrays

Jupyter notebooks have a nice built-in method to time how long a line of code takes to execute. In a Jupyter notebook, when a line starts with %timeit followed by code, the kernel runs the line of code multiple times and outputs an average of the time spent to execute the line of code.

We can use %timit to compare a mathematical operation on a Python list using a for loop to the same mathematical operation on a NumPy array.

```
In [7]: lst = list(range(10000))
        %timeit for i, item in enumerate(lst): lst[i] = lst[i]*2

3.09 ms ś 927 ţs per loop (mean ś std. dev. of 7 runs, 1000 loops each)


In [8]: nparray= np.arange(0,10000,1)
        %timeit 2*nparray

7.21 ţs ś 105 ns per loop (mean ś std. dev. of 7 runs, 100000 loops each)
```

With 10,000 integers, the Python list and for loop takes an average of single milliseconds, while the NumPy array completes the same operation in tens of microseconds. This is a speed increase of over 100x by using the NumPy array (1 millisecond = 1000 microseconds).

For larger lists of numbers, the speed increase using NumPy is considerable.

5.5 Array Creation

NumPy arrays are created with the np.array() function. The arguments provided to np.array() needs to be a list or iterable. An example is below. Note how the list [1,2,3] is passed into the function with square brackets at either end.

```
In [1]: import numpy as np
        np.array([1,2,3])

Out[1]: array([1, 2, 3])
```

The data type can be passed into the `np.array()` function as a second optional keyword argument. Available data types include `'int64'`, `'float'`, `'complex'` and `'>U32'` (a string data type).

```
In [1]: import numpy as np
        np.array([1,2,3], dtype='float')

Out[1]: array([1., 2., 3.])
```

The data type used in a NumPy array can be determined using the `.dtype` attribute. For instance, an array of `floats` returns `float64`.

```
In [2]: import numpy as np
        my_array = np.array([1,2,3], dtype='float')
        my_array.dtype

Out[2]: dtype('float64')
```

In addition to `np.array()`, there are other functions you can use to create NumPy arrays.

Arrays of Regularly Spaced Numbers

There are multiple ways to create arrays of regularly spaced numbers with NumPy. The next section introduces five NumPy functions to create regular arrays.

np.arange()

NumPy's `np.arange()` function creates a NumPy array according the arguments `start, stop, step`.

```
my_array = np.arange(start, stop, step)
```

The `np.arange()` function is useful for creating an array of regularly spaced numbers where you know the step size.

Consider creating a NumPy array of even numbers between 0 and 10. Note that just like counting in Python, counting in NumPy starts at 0 and ends at n-1.

```
In [4]: np.arange(0,10+2,2)

Out[4]: array([ 0, 2, 4, 6, 8, 10])
```

np.linspace()

NumPy's `np.linspace()` function creates a NumPy array according the arguments `start, stop, number of elements`.

```
my_array = np.linspace(start, stop, number of elements)
```

5.5. ARRAY CREATION

The np.linspace() function is useful for creating an array of regularly spaced numbers where the spacing is not known, but the number of values is. Consider creating a NumPy array of 10 numbers between 0 and 2pi.

```
In [5]: np.linspace(0,2*np.pi,10)

Out[5]: array([0.        , 0.6981317 , 1.3962634 , 2.0943951 , 2.7925268 ,
               3.4906585 , 4.1887902 , 4.88692191, 5.58505361, 6.28318531])
```

np.logspace()

NumPy's np.logspace() function creates a NumPy array according the arguments start, stop,number of elements, but unlike np.linspace(), np.logspace() produces a logarithmically spaced array.

```
    my_array = np.logspace(start, stop, number of elements, base=<num>)
```

The np.logspace() function is useful for creating an array of logarithmically spaced numbers where the spacing interval is not known but the number of values is. Consider creating a NumPy array of 4 logarithmically spaced numbers between 10 and 100. The function call is np.logspace(1, 2, 4). The start is $10^1 = 10$ and the stop is $10^2 = 100$, and the number of elements is 4. Be careful about putting large numbers in for stop because the stop argument is the power of 10, not the stop value.

```
In [6]: np.logspace(1, 2, 4)

Out[6]: array([ 10.        , 21.5443469 , 46.41588834, 100.        ])
```

Large numbers passed to np.logspace() will produce errors. Remember to pass exponents to np.logspace(). The code below throws an error because 10^{1000} is bigger than the largest floating point number supported by a 64 bit computer.

```
In [4]: np.logspace(10,1000,4)

RuntimeWarning: overflow encountered in power
  return _nx.power(base, y)

Out[4]: array([1.e+10,   inf,    inf,   inf])
```

np.zeros()

NumPy's np.zeros() function creates a NumPy array containing all zeros of a specific size. np.zeros() is useful when the size of an array is known, but the values that will go into the array have not been created yet.

```
    my_array = np.zeros((rows,cols))
```

```
In [7]: np.zeros((5,5))
```

```
Out[7]: array([[0., 0., 0., 0., 0.],
               [0., 0., 0., 0., 0.],
               [0., 0., 0., 0., 0.],
               [0., 0., 0., 0., 0.],
               [0., 0., 0., 0., 0.]])
```

np.ones()

NumPy's np.ones() function creates a NumPy array containing all 1's of a specific size. Like np.zeros(), np.ones() is useful when the size of an array is known, but the values that will go into the array have not been created yet.

```
my_array = np.ones((rows,cols))
```

```
In [8]: np.ones((3,5))

Out[8]: array([[1., 1., 1., 1., 1.],
               [1., 1., 1., 1., 1.],
               [1., 1., 1., 1., 1.]])
```

In the next section, you'll learn how to create array of random numbers with NumPy.

Arrays of Random Numbers

NumPy has functions to create arrays of many different types of random numbers in the np.random module. A few of the common random number types are detailed below.

Array of Random Integers

Arrays of random integers can be created with NumPy's np.random.randint() function. The general syntax is:

```
np.random.randint(lower limit, upper limit, number of values)
```

The code below creates an array of 5 random integers, each random integer between 1 and 10:

```
In [5]: np.random.randint(0,10,5)

Out[5]: array([9, 8, 2, 5, 2])
```

Array dimensions can be provided as the third argument to the np.random.randint() function. The code below creates a 5 × 5 array of random numbers between 1 and 10:

```
In [6]: np.random.randint(0,10,[5,5])

Out[6]: array([[1, 6, 7, 8, 2],
               [2, 0, 6, 3, 2],
               [8, 8, 2, 3, 9],
               [8, 4, 7, 2, 0],
               [1, 3, 5, 9, 9]])
```

5.5. ARRAY CREATION

Array of Random Floats

Arrays of random floating point numbers can be created with NumPy's `np.random.rand()` function. The general syntax is:

```
np.random.rand(number of values)
```

To create an array of 5 random floats between 0 and 1:

```
In [13]: np.random.rand(5)
```

```
Out[13]: array([0.74876036, 0.5403639 , 0.87934604, 0.08373662, 0.18713551])
```

The upper and lower ranges of random floats can me modified with arithmetic.

To expand the range of random floats to between 0 and 10, multiply the result by 10

```
In [15]: np.random.rand(5)*10
```

```
Out[15]: array([4.07650792, 5.94007487, 3.83427467, 1.0336569 , 3.40368341])
```

To change the range to between 11 and 13, we multiply the range by 2 (range 0-3), then add 11 to the result.

```
In [16]: np.random.rand(5)*2+11
```

```
Out[16]: array([12.51534171, 12.27391119, 12.11401002, 11.55578106, 12.6999884 ])
```

Random Array Choice from a List

```
np.random.choice(list of choices, number of choices)
```

To choose three numbers at random from a list of [1,5,9,11] use:

```
In [12]: lst = [1,5,9,11]
         np.random.choice(lst,3)
```

```
Out[12]: array([11, 1, 11])
```

Random Array with a Normal Distribution

`np.random.randn()` returns an array of random numbers with a normal distribution, assuming a mean of 0 and variance of 1.

```
np.random.randn(number of values)
```

```
In [13]: np.random.randn(10)
```

```
Out[13]: array([-0.8587019 ,  0.51022209,  1.52989165, -0.62763827,  0.42359871,
                -0.12794222, -0.05960913,  0.1018347 , -0.13226924,  1.21221629])
```

To specify a mean `mu` and a standard deviation `sigma`, the function can be wrapped with:

```
In [14]: mu = 70
         sigma = 6.6

         sigma * np.random.randn(10) + mu
```

```
Out[14]: array([83.08982467, 63.75617079, 54.80340275, 65.64987114, 60.86298488,
                71.15108776, 72.68180092, 67.74486107, 62.88712717, 71.53153691])
```

Matplotlib's `plt.hist()` function can be used to quickly plot a normal distribution created with NumPy's `np.random.randn()` function.

```
In [15]: import matplotlib.pyplot as plt
         import numpy as np
         %matplotlib inline

         mu = 70
         sigma = 6.6

         sample = sigma * np.random.randn(1000) + mu
         plt.hist(sample)
         plt.show()
```

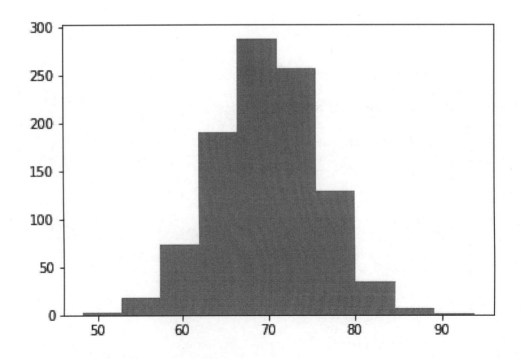

5.5. ARRAY CREATION

The next section introduces methods to create 2D NumPy arrays.

2-D Arrays

np.meshgrid()

NumPy's np.meshgrid() function takes in two positional arguments which are 1D NumPy arrays. The two input arrays do not have to contain the same number of elements. The outputs of the np.meshgrid() function are two 2D arrays. One of the 2D arrays has the same values in each row; the other 2D array has the same values in each column.

```
np.meshgrid(array1, array2)
```

```
In [16]: x = np.arange(0,6)
         y = np.arange(0,11,2)
         X, Y = np.meshgrid(x,y)
         print(X)
         print(Y)

[[0 1 2 3 4 5]
 [0 1 2 3 4 5]
 [0 1 2 3 4 5]
 [0 1 2 3 4 5]
 [0 1 2 3 4 5]
 [0 1 2 3 4 5]]
[[ 0  0  0  0  0  0]
 [ 2  2  2  2  2  2]
 [ 4  4  4  4  4  4]
 [ 6  6  6  6  6  6]
 [ 8  8  8  8  8  8]
 [10 10 10 10 10 10]]
```

Note how the first array X has the same numbers in each row, and the second array Y has the same numbers in each column.

np.mgrid[]

NumPy's np.mgrid[] function is similar to np.meshgrid(), but has a "MATLAB-like" syntax and behavior.

Use square brackets [ ] after the np.mgrid function name. Separate the two "lists" passed as input arguments with a comma and use the start:stop:step indexing method. The outputs of the np.mgrid[] function are two 2D arrays. The first 2D array has the same values in each row; the second 2D array has the same values in each column.

```
np.mgrid[start:stop:step, start:stop:step]
```

```
In [17]: X, Y = np.mgrid[0:5,0:11:2]
         print(X)
         print(Y)

[[0 0 0 0 0 0]
 [1 1 1 1 1 1]
 [2 2 2 2 2 2]
 [3 3 3 3 3 3]
 [4 4 4 4 4 4]]
[[ 0  2  4  6  8 10]
 [ 0  2  4  6  8 10]
 [ 0  2  4  6  8 10]
 [ 0  2  4  6  8 10]
 [ 0  2  4  6  8 10]]
```

Section Summary

Below is a list of NumPy functions and associated descriptions used in this section.

Function	Description
`np.array([list, of, numbers])`	Array from a list
`np.arange(start, stop, step)`	Array with know step
`np.linspace(start, stop, num)`	Array with known num
`np.logspace(start, stop, num)`	Logarithmically spaced array
`np.zeros((rows, cols))`	Array of zeros
`np.ones((rows, cols))`	Array of ones
`np.random.randint(start, stop, num)`	Random integers
`np.random.rand(num)`	Random float 0 to 1
`np.random.choice(list, num)`	Randome choice from a list
`np.random.randn(num)`	Random normal distribution
`np.meshgrid(array1, array2)`	Two 2D arrays from two 1D arrays
`np.mgrid[start:stop:step, start:stop:step]`	MATLAB meshgrid

5.6 Array Indexing

Elements in NumPy arrays can be accessed by *indexing*. Indexing is an operation that pulls out a select set of values from an array. The *index* of a value in an array is that value's *location* within the array. There is a difference between *the value* and *where the value is stored* in an array.

An array with 3 values is created in the code section below.

```
In [3]: import numpy as np

        a = np.array([2,4,6])
        print(a)
```

5.6. ARRAY INDEXING

```
[2 4 6]
```

The array above contains three values: 2, 4 and 6. Each of these values has a different index.

Remember counting in Python starts at 0 and ends at n-1.

The value 2 has an index of 0. We could also say 2 is in location 0 of the array. The value 4 has an index of 1 and the value 6 has an index of 2. The table below shows the index (or location) of each value in the array.

Index (or location)	Value
0	2
1	4
2	6

Individual values stored in an array can be accessed with indexing.

The general form to index a NumPy array is below:

```
<value> = <array>[index]
```

Where <value> is the value stored in the array, <array> is the array object name and [index] specifies the index or location of that value.

In the array above, the value 6 is stored at index 2.

```
In [4]: import numpy as np

        a = np.array([2,4,6])
        print(a)
        value = a[2]
        print(value)

[2 4 6]
6
```

Multi-dimensional Array Indexing

Multi-dimensional arrays can be indexed as well. A simple 2-D array is defined by a list of lists.

```
In [3]: import numpy as np

        a = np.array([[2,3,4],[6,7,8]])
        print(a)

[[2 3 4]
 [6 7 8]]
```

Values in a 2-D array can be accessed using the general notation below:

```
<value> = <array>[row,col]
```

Where `<value>` is the value pulled out of the 2-D array and `[row,col]` specifies the row and column index of the value. Remember Python counting starts at 0, so the first row is row zero and the first column is column zero.

We can access the value 8 in the array above by calling the row and column index [1,2]. This corresponds to the 2nd row (remember row 0 is the first row) and the 3rd column (column 0 is the first column).

```
In [2]: import numpy as np

        a = np.array([[2,3,4],[6,7,8]])
        print(a)
        value = a[1,2]
        print(value)

[[2 3 4]
 [6 7 8]]
8
```

Assigning Values with Indexing

Array indexing is used to *access* values in an array. And array indexing can also be used for *assigning* values of an array.

The general form used to assign a value to a particular index or location in an array is below:

```
<array>[index] = <value>
```

Where `<value>` is the new value going into the array and `[index]` is the location the new value will occupy.

The code below puts the value 10 into the second index or location of the array a.

```
In [5]: import numpy as np
        a = np.array([2,4,6])
        a[2] = 10
        print(a)

[ 2  4 10]
```

Values can also be assigned to a particular location in a 2-D arrays using the form:

```
<array>[row,col] = <value>
```

The code example below shows the value 20 assigned to the 2nd column and 3rd row of the array.

5.7. ARRAY SLICING

```
In [6]: import numpy as np

        a = np.array([[2,3,4],[6,7,8]])
        print(a)

        a[1,2]=20
        print(a)

[[2 3 4]
 [6 7 8]]
[[ 2  3  4]
 [ 6  7 20]]
```

5.7 Array Slicing

Multiple values stored within an array can be accessed simultaneously with array *slicing*. To pull out a section or slice of an array, the colon operator : is used when calling the index. The general form is:

<slice> = <array>[start:stop]

Where <slice> is the slice or section of the array object <array>. The index of the slice is specified in [start:stop]. Remember Python counting starts at 0 and ends at n-1. The index [0:2] pulls the first two values out of an array. The index [1:3] pulls the second and third values out of an array.

An example of slicing the first two elements out of an array is below.

```
In [1]: import numpy as np

        a = np.array([2, 4, 6])
        b = a[0:2]
        print(b)

[2 4]
```

On either sides of the colon, a blank stands for "default".

- [:2] corresponds to [start=default:stop=2]
- [1:] corresponds to [start=1:stop=default]

Therefore, the slicing operation [:2] pulls out the first through the third values in an array. The slicing operation [1:] pull out the second through the last values in an array.

The example below illustrates the default stop value is the last value in the array.

```
In [2]: import numpy as np

        a = np.array([2, 4, 6, 8])
        print(a)
        b = a[1:]
        print(b)

[2 4 6 8]
[4 6 8]
```

The next examples shows the default start value is the first value in the array.

```
In [3]: import numpy as np

        a = np.array([2, 4, 6, 8])
        print(a)
        b = a[:3]
        print(b)

[2 4 6 8]
[2 4 6]
```

The following indexing operations output the same array.

```
In [4]: import numpy as np

        a = np.array([2, 4, 6, 8])
        b = a[0:4]
        print(b)
        c = a[:4]
        print(c)
        d = a[0:]
        print(d)
        e = a[:]
        print(e)

[2 4 6 8]
[2 4 6 8]
[2 4 6 8]
[2 4 6 8]
```

Slicing 2D Arrays

2D NumPy arrays can be sliced with the general form:

5.8. ARRAY OPERATIONS

```
<slice> = <array>[start_row:end_row, start_col:end_col]
```

The code section below creates a two row by four column array and indexes out the first two rows and the first three columns.

```
In [5]: import numpy as np

        a = np.array([[2, 4, 6, 8], [10, 20, 30, 40]])
        print(a)
        b = a[0:2, 0:3]
        print(b)

[[ 2  4  6  8]
 [10 20 30 40]]
[[ 2  4  6]
 [10 20 30]]
```

The code section below slices out the first two rows and all columns from array a.

```
In [6]: import numpy as np

        a = np.array([[2, 4, 6, 8], [10, 20, 30, 40]])
        b = a[:2, :]   #[first two rows, all columns]
        print(b)

[[ 2  4  6  8]
 [10 20 30 40]]
```

Again, a blank represents defaults the first index or the last index. The colon operator all by itself also represents "all" (default start: default stop).

```
In [7]: import numpy as np

        a = np.array([[2, 4, 6, 8], [10, 20, 30, 40]])
        b = a[:,:]   #[all rows, all columns]
        print(b)

[[ 2  4  6  8]
 [10 20 30 40]]
```

5.8 Array Operations

Mathematical operations can be completed using NumPy arrays.

Scalar Addition

Scalars can be added and subtracted from arrays and arrays can be added and subtracted from each other:

```
In [1]: import numpy as np

        a = np.array([1, 2, 3])
        b = a + 2
        print(b)
```

[3 4 5]

```
In [2]: a = np.array([1, 2, 3])
        b = np.array([2, 4, 6])
        c = a + b
        print(c)
```

[3 6 9]

Scalar Multiplication

NumPy arrays can be multiplied and divided by scalar integers and floats:

```
In [3]: a = np.array([1,2,3])
        b = 3*a
        print(b)
```

[3 6 9]

```
In [4]: a = np.array([10,20,30])
        b = a/2
        print(b)
```

[5. 10. 15.]

Array Multiplication

NumPy array can be multiplied by each other using matrix multiplication. These matrix multiplication methods include element-wise multiplication, the dot product, and the cross product.

5.8. ARRAY OPERATIONS

Element-wise Multiplication

The standard multiplication sign in Python * produces element-wise multiplication on NumPy arrays.

```
In [5]: a = np.array([1, 2, 3])
        b = np.array([4, 5, 6])
        a * b

Out[5]: array([ 4, 10, 18])
```

Dot Product

```
In [6]: a = np.array([1, 2, 3])
        b = np.array([4, 5, 6])
        np.dot(a,b)

Out[6]: 32
```

Cross Product

```
In [7]: a = np.array([1, 2, 3])
        b = np.array([4, 5, 6])
        np.cross(a, b)

Out[7]: array([-3,  6, -3])
```

Exponents and Logarithms

np.exp()

NumPy's np.exp() function produces element-wise e^x exponentiation.

```
In [8]: a = np.array([1, 2, 3])
        np.exp(a)

Out[8]: array([ 2.71828183,  7.3890561 , 20.08553692])
```

Logarithms

NumPy has three logarithmic functions.

- np.log() - natural logarithm (log base e)
- np.log2() - logarithm base 2
- np.log10() - logarithm base 10

```
In [9]: np.log(np.e)

Out[9]: 1.0

In [10]: np.log2(16)

Out[10]: 4.0

In [11]: np.log10(1000)

Out[11]: 3.0
```

Trigonometry

NumPy also contains all of the standard trigonometry functions which operate on arrays.

- `np.sin()` - sin
- `np.cos()` - cosine
- `np.tan()` - tangent
- `np.asin()` - arc sine
- `np.acos()` - arc cosine
- `np.atan()` - arc tangent
- `np.hypot()` - given sides of a triangle, returns hypotenuse

```
In [12]: import numpy as np
         np.set_printoptions(4)

         a = np.array([0, np.pi/4, np.pi/3, np.pi/2])
         print(np.sin(a))
         print(np.cos(a))
         print(np.tan(a))
         print(f"Sides 3 and 4, hypotenuse {np.hypot(3,4)}")

[0.     0.7071 0.866  1.    ]
[1.0000e+00 7.0711e-01 5.0000e-01 6.1232e-17]
[0.0000e+00 1.0000e+00 1.7321e+00 1.6331e+16]
Sides 3 and 4, hypotenuse 5.0
```

NumPy contains functions to convert arrays of angles between degrees and radians.

- `deg2rad()` - convert from degrees to radians
- `rad2deg()` - convert from radians to degrees

```
In [13]: a = np.array([np.pi,2*np.pi])
         np.rad2deg(a)
```

5.9 Systems of Linear Equations

```
Out[13]: array([180., 360.])

In [14]: a = np.array([0,90, 180, 270])
         np.deg2rad(a)

Out[14]: array([0.     , 1.5708, 3.1416, 4.7124])
```

5.9 Systems of Linear Equations

Systems of linear equations can be solved with arrays and NumPy.

A system of linear equations is shown below:

$$8x + 3y - 2z = 9$$

$$-4x + 7y + 5z = 15$$

$$3x + 4y - 12z = 35$$

NumPy's `np.linalg.solve()` function can be used to solve this system of equations for the variables x, y and z.

The steps to solve the system of linear equations with `np.linalg.solve()` are below:

- Create NumPy array A as a 3 by 3 array of the coefficients
- Create a NumPy array b as the right-hand side of the equations
- Solve for the values of x, y and z using `np.linalg.solve(A, b)`.

The resulting array has three entries. One entry for each variable.

```
In [1]: import numpy as np

        A = np.array([[8, 3, -2], [-4, 7, 5], [3, 4, -12]])
        b = np.array([9, 15, 35])
        x = np.linalg.solve(A, b)
        x

Out[1]: array([-0.58226371, 3.22870478, -1.98599767])
```

We can plug the valusue of x, y and z back into one of the equations to check the answer.

x is the first entry of the array, y is the second entry of the array, and z is the third entry of the array.

x = x[0]

y = x[1]

z = x[2]

When these values are plugged into the equation from above:

$$8x + 3y - 2z = 9$$

The answer should be 9.0.

```
In [2]: 8*x[0] + 3*x[1] - 2*x[2]

Out[2]: 9.0
```

5.10 Summary

In this chapter, you learned how to work with NumPy arrays. NumPy is a Python package used for numerical calculations and arrays. An array is a data structure which only contains objects that share the same data type. Arrays are faster than lists in large-scale numerical calculations.

You learned how to create arrays in a variety of ways:

- Create an array from a Python list with `np.array()`
- Create an array of regularly spaced numbers with `np.arange()`, `np.linspace()`, and `np.logspace`
- Create an array of random numbers with `np.random.ranint()`, `np.random.rand()`, and `np.random.randn()`
- Create two 2D arrays from two 1D arrays with `np.meshgrid()` and `np.mgrid()`

You learned how to index and slice arrays. Slicing NumPy arrays share the same syntax used to slice Python lists and strings.

At the end of the chapter, you learned how to run mathematical operations on arrays. NumPy's mathematical functions operate on arrays like Python's math functions operate on integers and floats. NumPy has additional functions like `np.dot()` and `np.cross()` that cannot be applied to scalars. NumPy's `np.linalg.solve()` function can be used to solve systems of linear equations.

Key Terms and Concepts

NumPy	homogenous	iterable
array	homogenous data type	logarithmically spaced numbers
scalar	element-wise	normal distribution
computationally expensive	system of linear equations	meshgrid
slice	attribute	matrix multiplication methods
index	scientific computing	dot product
data type	Unicode	cross product

5.11 Review Questions

Array Creation

Q05.01 Create an array of the numbers 1, 5, 19, 30

Q05.02 Create an array of the numbers -3, 15, 0.001, 6.02e23

Q05.03 Create an array of integers between -10 and 10

Q05.04 Create an array of 10 equally spaced angles between 0 and 2π

Q05.05 Create an array of logarithmically spaced numbers between 1 and 1 million. Hint: remember to pass exponents to the `np.logspace()` function.

Q05.06 Create an array of 20 random integers between 1 and 10

Q05.07 Create an array of 30 random numbers with a normal distribution

Q05.08 Create an array of 30 random numbers with a normal distribution that has an mean μ of 78.5 and a standard deviation σ of 5.2

Q05.09 Create an array of 18 random floating point numbers between 0 and 1

Q05.10 Create an array of 18 random floating point numbers between -1 and 0

Q05.11 Create an array of 18 random floating point numbers between 0 and 10

Q05.12 Create a variable x that is an NumPy array which contains values 0, 0.1, 0.2, ..., 4.9, 5.0. Hard coding the values one will be time consuming, use a NumPy function to create the array instead.

Q05.13 Create a Python list containing the values 1, 2, 5.6, and 9 and store the Python list in a variable called x. Then create a NumPy array of the same values and store it in a variable called y.

Q05.14 Create an array called r of 200 evenly spaced numbers between and including 0 to 2π, then create an array y such that $y = 10sin(3r)$.

Q05.15 Create an array of 25 regularly spaced values beginning at 10 and ending with 18.

Q05.16 Create an array of regularly spaced numbers beginning at 10, ending with 18.4 using an increment of 0.6.

Array Manipulation

Q05.20 Create a NumPy array called A and store the values 5, 8, -8, 99, and 0 in array A in a single row, five columns. Reshape A to an array with one column and 5 rows.

Array Slicing

Q05.30 Create an array B that contains integers 0 to 24 (including 24) in one row. Then reshape B into a 5 row by 5 column array.

(a) Extract the 2nd row from B. Store it as a one column array called x.

(b) Store the number of elements in array x in a new variable called y.

(c) Extract the last column of B and store it in an array called z.

(d) Store a transposed version of B in an array called t.

Q05.31 Run the following code to create a NumPy array C

```
C = np.array(range(11)) + 5
```

(a) Extract the 4th value in array C into a variable called x.

(b) Extract the 2nd-to-last value in array C into a variable called y.

5.11. REVIEW QUESTIONS

(c) Extract the values from array C starting from the 3rd value up to and including the 7th value into a variable called z.

Q05.32 Run the following code to create a NumPy array D

```
D = np.array(range(18)) + 3
```

(a) Extract every other value from array D starting from the 2nd value through the 10th value. Store the result in a variable called x.

(b) Extract every other value from array D starting from the 10th value through the 2nd value. Store the result a variable called y.

(c) Create a variable z that contains all of the values in D in reverse order.

Q05.33 The 1D NumPy array F is defined below. But construct your code to work with any 1D NumPy array filled with numbers.

```
F = np.array([5, -4.7, 99, 50, 6, -1, 0, 50, -78, 27, 10])
```

(a) Select all the elements from F that are greater than 5 and store them in x.

(b) Select all of the elements from F that are between 5 and 30. Store them in y.

(c) Select all of the elements from F that are between 5 and 30 or that are equal to 50. Store them in z.

Hint: To perform the logical OR or AND operations, on boolean arrays of the same dimensions, NumPy functions are needed. The standard Python "or" and "and" will not work.

Hint: You can use either logical indexing or np.where() to get the appropriate values from A.

Q05.34 The 1D NumPy array B is defined below. But your code should work with any 1D NumPy array filled with numeric values.

```
G = np.array([5, -4.7, 99, 50, 6, -1, 0, 50, -78, 27, 10])
```

(a) Select all of the positive numbers in G and store them in x.

(b) Select all the numbers in G between 0 and 30 and store them in y.

(c) Select all of the numbers in G that are either less than −50 or greater than 50 and store them in z.

Q05.35 Define an integer c which is a random integer between 100 and 999 (including 100 and 999)

(a) pull the first digit out of c and assign it to the variable x

(b) pull the second digit out of c and assign it to the variable y

(c) pull the third digit out of c and assign it the the variable z.

Meshgrids

Q05.40 Create two 2D arrays from the two 1D arrays below using NumPy's `np.meshgrid()` function.

```
x = [0.0, 0.1, 0.2, 0.3, 0.4, 0.5]

y = [0, 2, 4, 6]
```

Q05.41 Create a meshgrid of the two arrays below:

```
x = [1, 2, 3, 4, 5, 6, 7, 8, 9, 10]

y = [1, 2, 3, 4, 5, 6, 7, 8, 9, 10]
```

Use element-wise multiplication to multiply each element in the first resulting 2D array with the corresponding element is the second array to build a multiplication table.

Array Operations

Q05.50 Create the two arrays below and perform each calculation.

```
a = [2 4 6]
b = [-1 0 1]
```

(a) $a + b$

(b) $1.5a - 2b$

(c) $0.5ab$

(d) $\frac{b^2}{a}$

Q05.51 Create an array of angles between (and including) 0 and 2π radians in increments of $\pi/2$ radians.

(a) Calculate the sine of each angle in the array

(b) Calculate the cosine of each angle in the array

(c) Convert each angle in the array to degrees

Q05.52 Create the two arrays F1, F2 below and then perform the following operations.

```
F1 = [-1, 0, 2]
F2 = [5, -2, 0]
```

(a) Calculate the dot product of F1 and F2

(b) Calculate cross product of F1 and F2

5.11. REVIEW QUESTIONS

(c) Calculate the element-wise product (element-wise multiplication of F1 and F2)

Q05.53 Compute all possible prices of flooring that can have lengths of 2, 4, 6, and 8 meters and widths of 1, 1.5, and 2 meters if the flooring costs $32.19 per square meter. Store the result in a 2D array. The lengths should increase from top to bottom and widths should increase from left to right.

Q05.54 Create an array H defined by the code below:

H = np.array([-5, 10, 12, 500, 20, 10, -46, 16])

(a) Create a boolean array x based on the variable H. x should be True everywhere H equals 10 and False everywhere else.

(b) Create a boolean array y based on the variable H. y should be True everywhere H is not equal to 10. y should be False everywhere else.

(c) Create a boolean array z based on the variable H. z should be True everywhere H is less than or equal to 20. z should be False everywhere else.

Q05.55 Create an array J using the code below:

```
J = np.array(range(7*5)).reshape((7, 5))
J[4, 3] = 500
```

(a) Store the row index of the number 500 in a variable called row_500.

(b) Store the column index of the number 500 in a variable called col_500.

Q05.56 Create an array K using the code below:

```
K = np.random.randint(100, 500, 7*7).reshape(7, 7)
K[2, 6] = 250
```

(a) Extract all of the values from K that are greater or equal to 250```` and store them in an array called x'''.

(b) Extract all of the values from K that are less than 250 and store them in an array called y.

(c) Programmatically determine which column and which row the number 250 is stored inside of K.

Linear Algebra

Q05.70 Use the system of linear equations below to calculate the values of x and y.

$$4x - 2y = -42$$

$$-6x + y = 31$$

Q05.71 Use the system of linear equations below to calculate the values of x, y and z.

$$\frac{x}{2} + 2y - z = 5$$

$$x + 3y - 4z = -1$$

$$-x - 3y + 2z = -5$$

Chapter 6

Plotting with Matplotlib

6.1 Introduction

By the end of this chapter you will be able to:

- Import Matplotlib into a Python script or Jupyter notebook
- Construct line plots with Matplotlib
- Use Matplotlib's object-oriented interface
- Construct bar charts and pie charts with Matplotlib
- Add error bars to bar charts and line plots
- Plot histograms
- Make box plots and violin plots
- Plot contours
- Create quiver plots and stream plots
- Construct 3D mesh grid plots

6.2 What is Matplotlib?

Matplotlib is a popular Python package used to build plots. Matplotlib started as a project in the early 2000's partly to use Python to visualize the electronic signals in the brain of epilepsy patients. Matplotlib's creator, John D. Hunter, was a neurobiologist. He was looking for a way to replicate MATLAB's plotting capability with Python. In addition to starting Matplotlib, Dr. Hunter was part of the founding group that created Numfocus. The Numfocus group oversees some major Python projects including Matplotlib, NumPy, Pandas, and Jupyter.

Why use Matplotlib?

Matplotlib is useful for creating static 2D plots, the kind of plots included in scientific publications and presentations. Almost any plot created in Microsoft Excel can be created with Matplotlib. Matplotlib can also be used to make 3D plots and animations.

6.3 Installing Matplotlib

Before Matplotlib's plotting functions can be used, Matplotlib needs to be installed. Depending on which distribution of Python is installed on your computer, the installation methods are slightly different.

Use the Anaconda distribution of Python

The simplest way to install Matplotlib is to download and install the Anaconda distribution of Python. The Anaconda distribution of Python comes with Matplotlib pre-installed and no further installation steps are necessary.

Below are additional methods to install Matplotlib if you are not using the Anaconda distribution of Python.

Install Matplotlib with the Anaconda Prompt

Matplotlib can be installed using with the **Anaconda Prompt**. If the **Anaconda Prompt** is available on your machine, it can usually be seen in the Windows Start Menu. To install Matplotlib, open the **Anaconda Prompt** and type:

```
> conda install matplotlib
```

Type y for yes when prompted.

Install Matplotlib with pip

Matplotlib can also be installed using the Python package manager, **pip**. To install Matplotlib with **pip**, open a terminal window and type:

```
$ pip install matplotlib
```

6.4. LINE PLOTS

This command installs Matplotlib in the current working Python environment.

Verify the installation

To verify that Matplotlib is installed, try to invoke Matplotlib's version at the Python REPL. Use the commands below that include calling the `.__version__` an attribute common to most Python packages.

```
>>> import matplotlib
>>> matplotlib.__version__
'3.1.1'
```

6.4 Line Plots

Line plots can be created in Python with Matplotlib's `pyplot` library.

To build a line plot, first import Matplotlib. It is a standard convention to import Matplotlib's `pyplot` library as `plt`. The `plt` alias will be familiar to other Python programmers.

If using a Jupyter notebook, include the line `%matplotlib inline` after the imports. `%matplotlib inline` is a Jupyter notebook magic command which causes Matplotlib plots to display directly inside Jupyter notebook output cells.

To build our first plot, we will also use NumPy, a numerical computing library for Python. NumPy is typically imported with the alias np.

```
In [1]: import matplotlib.pyplot as plt
        import numpy as np
        # if using a Jupyter notebook, include:
        %matplotlib inline
```

NumPy's `np.arange()` function creates an array of numbers with the parameters `np.arange(start,stop,step)`. NumPy's `np.sin()` and `np.pi` functions do what you expect, calculate the sine of an array and compute π. We use these functions to create two arrays of numbers x and y.

```
In [2]: x = np.arange(0, 4 * np.pi, 0.1)
        y = np.sin(x)
```

To create a line plot, pass an array or list of numbers as an *argument* to Matplotlib's `plt.plot()` function. The command `plt.show()` is needed at the end to show the plot. Make sure to include the double parenthesis () in `plt.show()`.

```
In [3]: plt.plot(x, y)
        plt.show()
```

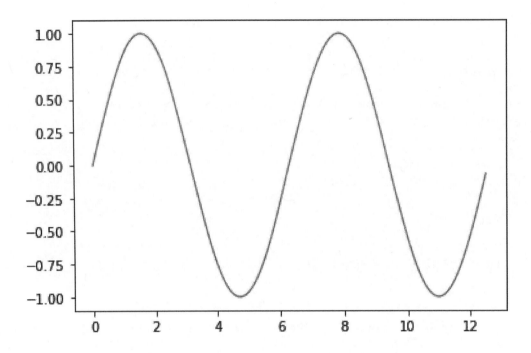

The result is a line plot that shows sin(x) from 0 to 4π.

Features of a Matplotlib plot

A variety of features on a Matplotlib plot can be specified. The following is a list of commonly defined features:

Line Color, Line Width, Line Style, Line Opacity and Marker Options

The color, width, and style of line in a Matplotlib plot can be specified. Line color, line width, and line style are included as extra keyword arguments in the `plt.plot()` function call.

```
plt.plot(<x-data>,<y-data>,
         linewideth=<float or int>,
         linestyle='<linestyle abbreviation>',
         color='<color abbreviation>',
         marker='<marker abbreviation>')
```

An example `plt.plot()` function call including line color, line width, and line style options is:

```
plt.plot(x, y,
         linewidth=2.0,
         linestyle='+',
         color='b',
         alpha=0.5,
         marker='o')
```

6.4. LINE PLOTS

Below is a list of linewidths (many other widths are also available).

`linewidth=<float or int>`	Line Width
0.5	0.5 pixels wide
1	1 pixel wide
1.5	1.5 pixels wide
2	2 pixels wide
3	3 pixels wide

Below is a list of line styles.

`linestyle='<style abbreviation>'`	Line Style
`'-'` or `'solid'`	solid line (default)
`'--'` or `'dashed'`	dashed line
`'-.'` or `'dashdot'`	dash-dot line
`':'` or `'dotted'`	dotted line
`'None'` or `' '` or `''`	no line

Below is a list of color abbreviations. Note `'b'` is used for blue and `'k'` is used for black.

`color ='<color abbreviation>'`	Color Name
`'b'`	blue
`'c'`	cyan
`'g'`	green
`'k'`	black
`'m'`	magenta
`'r'`	red
`'w'`	white
`'y'`	yellow

Colors can also be specified in hexadecimal form surrounded by quotation marks like `'#FF69B4'` or in RGBA (red, green, blue, opacity) color surrounded by parenthesis like (255,182,193,0.5).

`color ='<color abbreviation>'`	Color Format
`'#FF69B4'`	hexadecimal
(255,182,193,0.5)	RGBA

Below is a list of alpha (opacity) values (any alpha value between 0.0 and 1.0 is possible).

`alpha = <float or int>`	Opacity
0	transparent
0.5	half transparent
1.0	opaque

Below is a list of maker styles.

`marker='<marker abbreviation>'`	Marker Style
`'.'`	point
`','`	one pixel
`'o'`	circle
`'v'`	triangle_down
`'^'`	triangle_up
`'8'`	octagon
`'s'`	square
`'p'`	pentagon
`'*'`	star
`'h'`	hexagon 1
`'H'`	hexagon 2
`'+'`	plus
`'P'`	filled plus
`'x'`	x
`'X'`	filled x
`'D'`	diamond
`'d'`	thin diamond

In addition to `marker='<marker style>'`, the color of the marker edge, the color of the marker face and the size of the marker can be specified with:

```
plt.plot( ....
         markeredgecolor='<color abbreviation>',
         markerfacecolor='<color abbreviation>',
         markersize=<float or int>
         ....)
```

Title

The plot title will be shown above the plot. The `plt.title()` command accepts a string as an argument.

```
plt.title('My Plot Title')
```

x-axis label

The x-axis label is shown below the x-axis. The `plt.xlabel()` command accepts a string as an argument.

```
plt.xlabel('My x-axis label')
```

y-axis label

The y-axis label is shown to the left of the y-axis. The `plt.ylabel()` command also accepts a string as an argument.

6.4. LINE PLOTS

```
plt.ylabel('My y-axis label')
```

Legend

You can use the `plt.legend()` command to insert a legend on a plot. The legend appears within the plot area, in the upper right corner by default. The `plt.legend()` command accepts a list of strings and optionally accepts a `loc=` argument to specify the legend location.

```
plt.legend(['entry1','entry2'], loc = 0)
```

The following are the legend location codes. These numbers need to be placed after `loc=` in the `plt.legend()` call.

Legend Location	loc = <number>
'best'	0
'upper right'	1
'upper left'	2
'lower left'	3
'lower right'	4
'right'	5
'center left'	6
'center right'	7
'lower center'	8
'upper center'	9
'center'	10

Grid

A grid can be added to a Matplotlib plot using the `plt.grid()` command. By default, the grid is turned off. To turn on the grid use:

```
plt.grid(True)
```

The only valid options are `plt.grid(True)` and `plt.grid(False)`. Note that `True` and `False` are capitalized and are not enclosed in quotes.

Tick Labels

Tick labels can be specified on a Matplotlib plot using `plt.xticks()` and `plt.yticks()`. To add tick labels use:

```
plt.xticks([locations list],[labels list])
plt.yticks([locations list],[labels list])
```

The [locations list] can be a Python list or NumPy array of tick locations. The [labels list] is a Python list or NumPy array of strings.

Build a plot in five steps

The steps below show a logical progression to build a plot with Matplotlib:

1. Imports
2. Define data
3. Plot data including options
4. Add plot details
5. Show the plot

Details of each step is explained below.

1. Imports

Import `matplot.pyplot as plt`, as well as any other modules needed to work with the data such as NumPy or Pandas. If using a Jupyter notebook, include the line `%matplotlib inline` in the import section.

2. Define data

The plot needs to contain data. Data is defined after the imports. Typically, data for plots is contained in Python lists, NumPy arrays or Pandas dataframes.

3. Plot data including options

Use `plt.plot()` to plot the data you defined. Note the `plt.plot()` line needs to be called before any other plot details are specified. Otherwise, the details have no plot to apply to.

Besides data, the `plt.plot()` function can include keyword arguments such as:

- `linewideth= <float or int>`
- `linestyle='<linestyle abbreviation>'`
- `color='<color abbreviation>'`
- `alpha= <float or int>`
- `marker='<marker abbreviation>'`
- `markeredgecolor='<color abbreviation>'`
- `markerfacecolor='<color abbreviation>'`
- `markersize=<float or int>`

4. Add plot details

After the `plt.plot()` line, add details such as a title, axis labels, legend, grid, and tick labels. Plot details to add include:

- `plt.title('<title string>')`
- `plt.xlabel('<x-axis label string>')`
- `plt.ylabel('<y-axis label string>')`

6.4. LINE PLOTS

- plt.legend(['list','of','strings'])
- ptl.grid(<True or False>)
- plt.xticks([locations list or array], [labels list])
- plt.yticks([locations list or array], [labels list])

5. Show the plot

Use the plt.show() command to show the plot. plt.show() causes the plot to display in a Jupyter notebook or pop out in a new window if the plot is constructed in a separate *.py* file. Note that plt.show() needs to be called after plt.plot() and any plot details such as plt.title().

The next code section utilizes the 5 steps to build a plot. The resulting plot is shown after the code.

```
In [4]:  # 1. Imports
         import numpy as np
         import matplotlib.pyplot as plt
         # if using a Jupyter notebook, include:
         %matplotlib inline

         # 2. Define data
         x = np.arange(0, 4 * np.pi, 0.2)
         y = np.sin(x)

         # 3. Plot data including options
         plt.plot(x, y,
             linewidth=0.5,
             linestyle='--',
             color='r',
             marker='o',
             markersize=10,
             markerfacecolor=(1, 0, 0, 0.1))

         # 4. Add plot details
         plt.title('Plot of sin(x) vs x from 0 to 4 pi')
         plt.xlabel('x (0 to 4 pi)')
         plt.ylabel('sin(x)')
         plt.legend(['sin(x)']) # list containing one string
         plt.xticks(
             np.arange(0, 4*np.pi + np.pi/2, np.pi/2),
             ['0','pi/2','pi','3pi/2','2pi','5pi/2','3pi','7pi/2','4pi'])
         plt.grid(True)

         # 5. Show the plot
         plt.show()
```

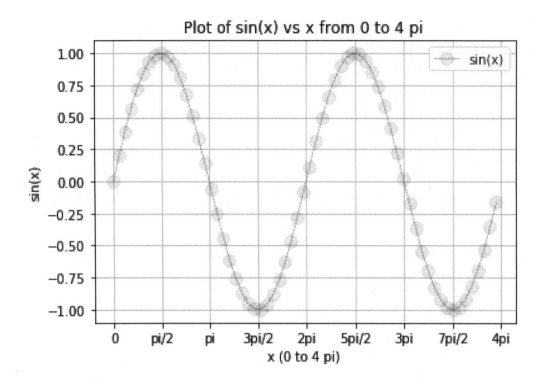

6.5 Saving plots

Matplotlib plots can be saved as image files using the `plt.savefig()` function.

The `plt.savefig()` function needs to be called right above the `plt.show()` line. All the features of the plot must be specified before the plot is saved as an image file. If the figure is saved after the `plt.show()` command; the figure will not be saved until the plot window is closed. Calling `plt.savefig()` after calling `plt.show()` can be problematic when building plots in a Jupyter notebook with `%matplotlib inline` enabled.

A standard `savefig()` command is:

```
plt.savefig('plot.png', dpi=300, bbox_inches='tight')
```

Where `'plot.png'` is the name of the saved image file. Matplotlib infers the image file format (*.png*, *.jpg*, etc) based on the extension specified in the filename.

The keyword argument `dpi=` specifies how many dots per inch (image resolution) are in the saved image. `dpi=72` is fine for web images. `dpi=300` is better for an image designed to go in a written report or *.pdf* document.

The keyword argument `bbox_inches='tight'` is optional. If the axis labels in the plot are cut off in the saved image, set `bbox_inches='tight'`.

The following code section constructs a line plot and saves the plot to the image file ***plot.png***.

6.5. SAVING PLOTS

```
In [1]: import matplotlib.pyplot as plt
        # if using a Jupyter notebook, include:
        %matplotlib inline

        x = [0, 2, 4, 6]
        y = [1, 3, 4, 8]

        plt.plot(x,y)

        plt.xlabel('x values')
        plt.ylabel('y values')
        plt.title('plotted x and y values')
        plt.legend(['line 1'])

        # save the figure
        plt.savefig('plot.png', dpi=300, bbox_inches='tight')

        plt.show()
```

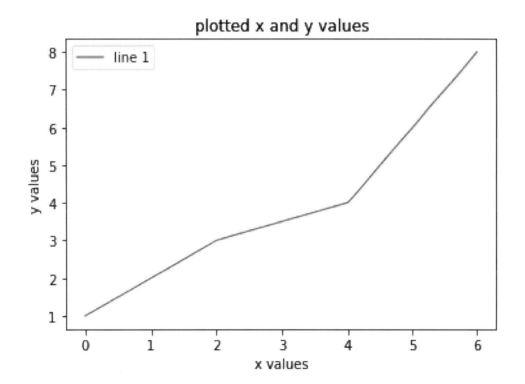

6.6 Multi Line Plots

Multi-line plots are created using Matplotlib's `pyplot` library. This section builds upon the work in the previous section where a plot with one line was created. This section also introduces Matplotlib's *object-oriented* approach to building plots. The object-oriented approach to building plots is used in the rest of this chapter.

The Matplotlib's object-oriented interface

An object-oriented plotting interface is an interface where components of the plot (like the axis, title, lines, markers, tick labels, etc.) are treated as programmatic *objects* that have *attributes* and *methods* associated with them.

To create a new *object* is called *instantiation*. Once an object is created, or *instantiated*, the properties of that object can be modified, and methods can be called on that object.

The basic anatomy of a Matplotlib plot includes a couple of layers, each of these layers is a Python *object*:

- Figure object: The bottom layer. Think of the figure object as the figure window which contains the minimize, maximize, and close buttons. A figure window can include one plot or multiple plots.
- Plot objects: A plot builds on the figure layer. If there are multiple plots, each plot is called a subplot.
- Axis objects: An axis is added to a plot layer. Axis can be thought of as sets of x and y axis that lines and bars are drawn on. An Axis contains daughter attributes like axis labels, tick labels, and line thickness.
- Data objects: data points, lines, shapes are plotted on an axis.

Matplotlib's `plt.subplot()` function is used to build figure objects. The `plt.subplot()` function creates both a figure *object* and axis *objects*. We say the `plt.subplot()` function *instantiates* a figure *object* and *instantiates* an axis object. For now, we'll leave the `subplot()` arguments blank. By default, the `subplot()` function creates a single figure object and a single axis object. By convention we'll call the figure object `fig` and the axis object `ax`. Note these two outputs of the `plt.subplots()` function are separated by a comma.

```
fig, ax = plt.subplots()
```

We instantiated a figure object and axis object, now both of these objects need attributes. We add attributes to the axis object to build a plot. NumPy arrays or Python lists `x`, `y`, and `z` can be added to axis object `ax`.

```
ax.plot(x,y)
ax.plot(x,z)
```

We add a plot attribute (a line) to our axis object `ax` using the object-oriented structure `<object>.<attribute>`. In this case, `ax` is the object and `plot` is the attribute.

The next code section demonstrates how to build a multi-line plot with Matplotlib's object-oriented interface.

6.6. MULTI LINE PLOTS

```
In [1]: import numpy as np
        import matplotlib.pyplot as plt
        # if using a Jupyter notebook, inlcude:
        %matplotlib inline

        x = np.arange(0,4*np.pi,0.1)
        y = np.sin(x)
        z = np.cos(x)

        fig, ax = plt.subplots()

        ax.plot(x,y)
        ax.plot(x,z)

        plt.show()
```

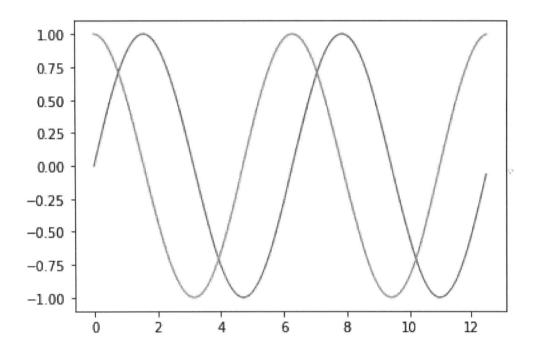

The ax object has many *methods* and *attributes*. In Python a method is sort of like a function, but methods typically modify the object they are associated with, while functions modify their input arguments.

Two methods we can run on the ax object include ax.set_title() and ax.legend(). A couple daughter objects include ax.xaxis and ax.yaxis. These daughter objects in turn have methods such as ax.xaxis.set_label_text() and ax.yaxis.set_label_text().

The code section below demonstrates using objects, attributes, and methods to build a multi-line plot.

```
In [2]: import numpy as np
        import matplotlib.pyplot as plt
        # if using a Jupyter notebook, include:
        %matplotlib inline

        x = np.arange(0,4*np.pi,0.1)
        y = np.sin(x)
        z = np.cos(x)

        fig, ax = plt.subplots()

        ax.plot(x,y)
        ax.plot(x,z)

        ax.set_title('Two Trig Functions')
        ax.legend(['sin','cos'])
        ax.xaxis.set_label_text('Angle $\Theta$')
        ax.yaxis.set_label_text('Sine and Cosine')

        plt.show()
```

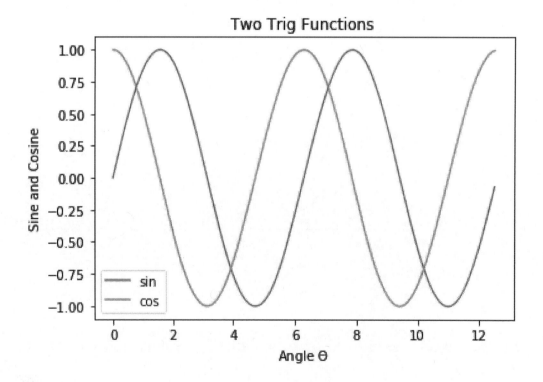

The table below shows common commands to build plots using Matplotlib's object-oriented interface.

Object-oriented command	Description	Corresponding plt. command
`fig, ax = plt.subplots()`	create a figure and axis object	-
`ax.plot(x,y)`	create a line plot	`plt.plot(x,y)`
`ax.set_title('My Title')`	plot title	`plt.title('My Title')`
`ax.set_xlabel('x label')`	x-axis label	`plt.xlabel('x label')`
`ax.set_ylabel('x label')`	y-axis label	`plt.ylabel('x label')`
`ax.legend(['line1','line2'])`	legend	`plt.legend(['line1','line2'])`
`ax.set_xlim([0, 5])`	x-axis limits	`plt.xlim([0, 5])`
`ax.set_ylim([-1, 1])`	y-axis limits	`plt.ylim([-1, 1])`
`ax.axis([-x, +x, -y, +y])`	both axis limits	-
`ax.grid(True)`	grid in both directions	`plt.grid(True)`
`ax.xaxis.grid(True)`	vertical grid lines	-
`ax.yaxis.grid(True)`	horizontal grid lines	-
`ax.xaxis.set_xticks([loc])`	x-axis tick locations	`plt.xticks([loc],[label])`
`ax.xaxis.set_xticklabels([labels])`	x-axis tick labels	`plt.xticks([loc],[label])`
`ax.yaxis.set_yticks([loc])`	y-axis tick locations	`plt.yticks([loc],[label])`
`ax.yaxis.set_yticklabels([labels])`	y-axis tick labels	`plt.yticks([loc],[label])`
`ax.xaxis.set_ticks([])`	remove x tick labels	`plt.xticks([],[])`
`ax.yaxis.set_ticks[]`	remove y tick labels	`plt.yticks([],[])`
`ax.set_aspect('equal')`	equal axis scales	-
`fig.tight_layout()`	adjust padding	`plt.tight_layout()`
`plt.show()`	show the plot	`plt.show()`

6.7 Bar Charts and Pie Charts

Bar charts and pie charts can be created with Matplotlib's `pyplot` library.

Bar Charts

To construct a bar plot using Matplotlib, first import Matplotlib's `pyplot` library. The alias `plt` is commonly used to substitute `matplotlib.pyplot`. If using a Jupiter notebook, include the line `%matplotlib inline`. In the next example, NumPy is used. So NumPy must be included in the imports as well as Matplotlib.

```
In [1]: import numpy as np
        import matplotlib.pyplot as plt
        # if using a Jupyter notebook, include:
        %matplotlib inline
```

We need some data to add to our bar chart. In this case, the data is from a set of *coefficient of thermal expansion* lab measurements. The coefficient of thermal expansion (CTE) is a material property that describes how much a material will change in length as a result of a change in temperature. Different materials have different CTE's and we can use the lab data to determine which material will expand the most if all three materials are heated up to the same temperature (assuming all three materials start at the same temperature).

First, we need to input the lab measurement data as NumPy arrays:

```
In [2]: # Data
        aluminum = np.array([
            6.4e-5, 3.01e-5, 2.36e-5, 3.0e-5, 7.0e-5, 4.5e-5, 3.8e-5, 4.2e-5, 2.62e-5,
            3.6e-5
        ])
        copper = np.array([
            4.5e-5, 1.97e-5, 1.6e-5, 1.97e-5, 4.0e-5, 2.4e-5, 1.9e-5, 2.41e-5, 1.85e-5,
            3.3e-5
        ])
        steel = np.array([
            3.3e-5, 1.2e-5, 0.9e-5, 1.2e-5, 1.3e-5, 1.6e-5, 1.4e-5, 1.58e-5, 1.32e-5,
            2.1e-5
        ])
```

Next, calculate the average or *mean* of each data set using NumPy's np.mean() function.

```
In [3]: # Calculate the average
        aluminum_mean = np.mean(aluminum)
        copper_mean = np.mean(copper)
        steel_mean = np.mean(steel)
```

Then build a list of materials and CTE's. Note the list of materials is a list of strings, the list of x-positions x_pos is an array of numbers [0,1,2], and the list CTEs is a list of three numbers from the np.mean() calculation above. Python's len() function returns the length of a list, array, dictionary or tuple.

```
In [4]: # Create arrays for the plot
        materials = ['Aluminum', 'Copper', 'Steel']
        x_pos = np.arange(len(materials))
        CTEs = [aluminum_mean, copper_mean, steel_mean]
```

After the materials, x_pos, and CTEs (the labels below the bars) are defined, the bar chart is created using the ax.bar() method.

Mathplotlib's ax.bar() method requires two positional arguments, a list of bar positions and a list of bar heights. In this bar chart, x_pos is the list of bar positions and CTEs is the list of bar heights.

The list of materials is passed to the ax.set_xticklabels() method.

```
In [5]: # Build the plot
        fig, ax = plt.subplots()

        ax.bar(x_pos, CTEs, align='center', alpha=0.5)
        ax.set_ylabel('Coefficient of Thermal Expansion ($\degree C^{-1}$)')
        ax.set_xticks(x_pos)
        ax.set_xticklabels(materials)
        ax.set_title('Coefficent of Thermal Expansion (CTE) of Three Metals')
```

6.7. BAR CHARTS AND PIE CHARTS

```
    ax.yaxis.grid(True)

# Save the figure and show
plt.tight_layout()
plt.savefig('bar_plot.png')
plt.show()
```

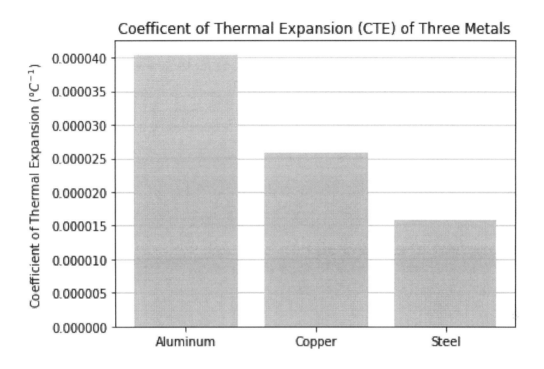

Pie Charts

Pie charts can be constructed with Matplotlib's `ax.pie()` method. The one required *positional argument* supplied to the `ax.pie()` method is a list of pie piece sizes. Optional *keyword arguments* include a list of pie piece labels (`label=`) and if the percentages will be auto-calculated and in what format (`autopct=`).

For our first pie chart, the data we will plot describes the number of students who choose different engineering majors at colleges in the US each year.

The following table lists the approximate numbers of engineering graduates in different engineering disciplines:

Discipline	Number of graduates
Civil Engineering	15,000 graduates
Electrical Engineering	50,000 graduates

Discipline	Number of graduates
Mechanical Engineering	45,000 graduates
Chemical Engineering	10,000 graduates

We will plot this data on a pie chart with Matplotlib's ax.pie() method. The pie piece labels are defined as a list of strings, and the pie piece sizes are defined as a list of integers. The line ax.axis('equal') is needed to ensure the pie chart is a circle. If you leave out ax.axis('equal'), the pie chart may look like an oval instead of a circle.

The code section below builds a pie chart with four pie pieces, each pie piece labeled with a relative size auto-calculated to the nearest 10th of a percent.

In [6]:
```
import numpy as np
import matplotlib.pyplot as plt
# if using a Jupyter notebook, include:
%matplotlib inline

# Pie chart, where the slices will be ordered and plotted counter-clockwise:
labels = ['Civil', 'Electrical', 'Mechanical', 'Chemical']
sizes = [15, 50, 45, 10]

fig, ax = plt.subplots()
ax.pie(sizes, labels=labels, autopct='%1.1f%%')
ax.axis('equal')  # Equal aspect ratio ensures the pie chart is circular.
ax.set_title('Engineering Diciplines')

plt.show()
```

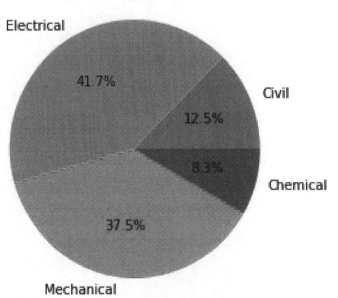

6.7. BAR CHARTS AND PIE CHARTS

Pie pieces can be highlighted by "exploding" them out. Exploded pie pieces are applied to a Matplotlib pie chart by supplying the `explode=` keyword argument to the `ax.pie()` method. `shadow=True` and `startangle=` are two additional keyword arguments that can be passed to the `ax.pie()` method to control the angle and rotation of the pieces on a pie chart.

The code section below creates a pie chart with the pie pieces separated and the "Chemical" piece exploded out.

```
In [7]: import numpy as np
        import matplotlib.pyplot as plt
        # if using a Jupyter notebook, include:
        %matplotlib inline

        # Pie chart, where the slices will be ordered and plotted counter-clockwise
        labels = ['Civil', 'Electrical', 'Mechanical', 'Chemical']
        sizes = [15, 30, 45, 10]

        # Explode out the 'Chemical' pie piece by offsetting it a greater amount
        explode = (0.1, 0.1, 0.1, 0.4)
        fig, ax = plt.subplots()
        ax.pie(sizes,
               explode=explode,
               labels=labels,
               autopct='%1.1f%%',
               shadow=True,
               startangle=90)
        ax.axis('equal')  # Equal aspect ratio ensures the pie chart is circular.
        ax.set_title('Engineering Diciplines')

        plt.show()
```

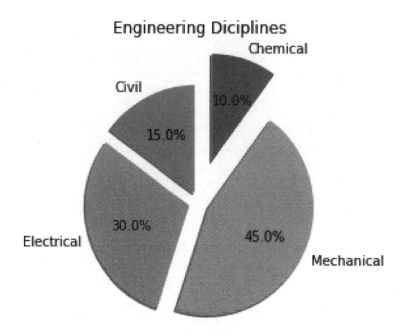

6.8 Error Bars

Matplotlib line plots and bar charts can include error bars. Error bars are useful to problem solvers because error bars show the confidence or precision in a set of measurements or calculated values. Bar charts without error bars give the illusion that a measured or calculated value is known to high precision or high confidence.

Error bars in bar plots

To construct a bar plot with error bars, first import Matplotlib. If using a Jupyter notebook, include the line %matplotlib inline

```
In [1]: import numpy as np
        import matplotlib.pyplot as plt
        # include if using a Jupyter notebook
        %matplotlib inline
```

We'll apply error bars to the Coefficient of Thermal Expansion data used in a previous section. First the data is stored in three NumPy arrays. Then the mean or average of each array is calculated. The mean of each array will be the height of the bars in the bar plot. Next, the standard deviation of each array is calculated. The standard deviation will be the height of the error bars. Finally, a couple lists are created that correspond to the bar labels (labels), bar positions (x_pos), bar heights (CTEs), and the error bar heights (error).

6.8. ERROR BARS

```
In [2]: # Data
        aluminum = np.array([6.4e-5 , 3.01e-5 , 2.36e-5, 3.0e-5, 7.0e-5, 4.5e-5, 3.8e-5,
                             4.2e-5, 2.62e-5, 3.6e-5])
        copper = np.array([4.5e-5 , 1.97e-5 , 1.6e-5, 1.97e-5, 4.0e-5, 2.4e-5, 1.9e-5,
                           2.41e-5 , 1.85e-5, 3.3e-5 ])
        steel = np.array([3.3e-5 , 1.2e-5 , 0.9e-5, 1.2e-5, 1.3e-5, 1.6e-5, 1.4e-5,
                          1.58e-5, 1.32e-5 , 2.1e-5])

        # Calculate the average
        aluminum_mean = np.mean(aluminum)
        copper_mean = np.mean(copper)
        steel_mean = np.mean(steel)

        # Calculate the standard deviation
        aluminum_std = np.std(aluminum)
        copper_std = np.std(copper)
        steel_std = np.std(steel)

        # Define labels, positions, bar heights and error bar heights
        labels = ['Aluminum', 'Copper', 'Steel']
        x_pos = np.arange(len(labels))
        CTEs = [aluminum_mean, copper_mean, steel_mean]
        error = [aluminum_std, copper_std, steel_std]


In [3]: # Build the plot
        fig, ax = plt.subplots()
        ax.bar(x_pos, CTEs,
               yerr=error,
               align='center',
               alpha=0.5,
               ecolor='black',
               capsize=10)
        ax.set_ylabel('Coefficient of Thermal Expansion ($\degree C^{-1}$)')
        ax.set_xticks(x_pos)
        ax.set_xticklabels(labels)
        ax.set_title('Coeffcient of Thermal Expansion (CTE) of Three Metals')
        ax.yaxis.grid(True)

        # Save the figure and show
        plt.tight_layout()
        plt.savefig('bar_plot_with_error_bars.png')
        plt.show()
```

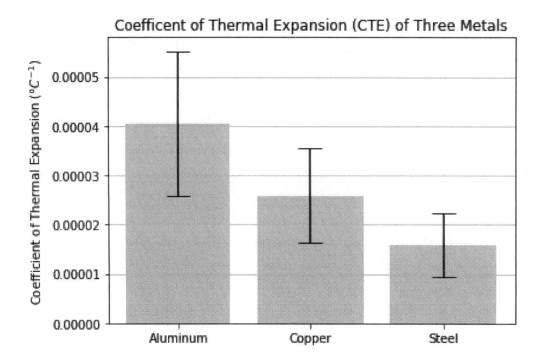

The resulting plot contains three error bars. We can see the standard deviation of the aluminum data is greater than the standard deviation of the steel by looking at the error by lengths.

Error bars in line plots

Error bars can also be added to line plots created with Matplotlib. The `ax.errorbar()` method is used to create a line plot with error bars. The two positional arguments supplied to `ax.errorbar()` are the lists or arrays of x, y data points. The two keyword arguments `xerr=` and `yerr=` define the error bar lengths in the x and y directions.

The general format of Matplotlib's `ax.errorbar()` method is below:

```
ax.errorbar(x, y,
            xerr=<error bar width>
            yerr=<error bar height>
            fmt=<format>)
```

The following code section builds a line plot with horizontal and vertical error bars included on each point in the plot. The error bar widths and heights are created using NumPy's `random_sample` function.

```
In [4]: import numpy as np
        import matplotlib.pyplot as plt
        # if using a Jupyter notebook, include:
        %matplotlib inline
```

6.8. ERROR BARS

```python
x = np.linspace(0,5.5,10)
y = 10*np.exp(-x)
xerr = np.random.random_sample(10)
yerr = np.random.random_sample(10)

fig, ax = plt.subplots()

ax.errorbar(x, y,
            xerr=xerr,
            yerr=yerr,
            fmt='-o')

ax.set_xlabel('x-axis')
ax.set_ylabel('y-axis')
ax.set_title('Line plot with error bars')

plt.show()
```

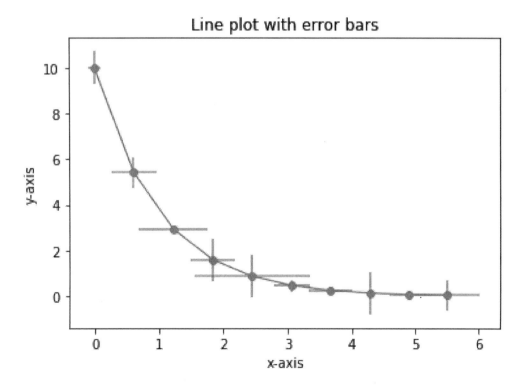

6.9 Histograms

Histograms are a useful type of statistics plot for problem solvers. A histogram is a type of bar plot that shows the frequency or number of values compared to a set of value ranges. Matplotlib's `ax.hist()` function creates histogram plots.

In this example, we'll use NumPy's `np.random.normal()` function to create an array of random numbers with a normal distribution. The three arguments passed to NumPy's `np.random.normal()` function are `mu` (mean), `sigma` (standard deviation) and `size=` (length of the array).

Matplotlib's `ax.hist()` method is used to build the histogram. The first argument passed to `ax.hist()` corresponds to the list or array of values to plot. The second argument corresponds to the number of bins, or number of bars on the histogram. The general format of Matplotlib's `ax.hist()` method is below.

```
ax.hist(data, num_bins)
```

In this example, we'll specify 20 bins (20 bars).

The line `plt.style.use('fivethirtyeight')` is included to style the plot to look like plots on fivethirtyeight.com. Matplotlib styles are addressed in a subsequent section of this chapter.

The code section below builds a histogram that contains 20 bins.

```
In [1]: import numpy as np
        import matplotlib.pyplot as plt
        # if using a Jupyter notebook, include:
        %matplotlib inline
        plt.style.use('fivethirtyeight')

        mu = 80
        sigma = 7
        x = np.random.normal(mu, sigma, size=200)

        fig, ax = plt.subplots()

        ax.hist(x, 20)
        ax.set_title('Historgram')
        ax.set_xlabel('bin range')
        ax.set_ylabel('frequency')

        fig.tight_layout()
        plt.show()
```

6.10. BOX PLOTS AND VIOLIN PLOTS

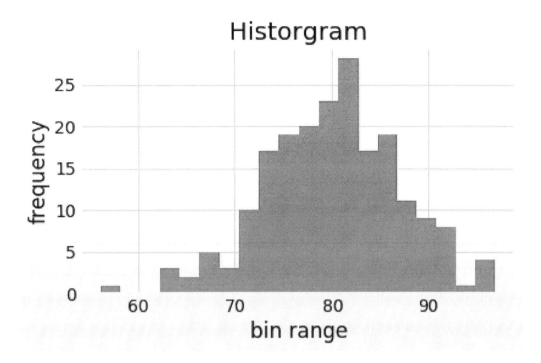

The resulting histogram has 20 bars and shows a roughly normal distribution.

6.10 Box Plots and Violin Plots

In addition to histograms, a couple other useful statistical plots are box plots and violin plots.

Box Plots

To create a box plot with Matplotlib, the `ax.boxplot()` method is used. The general syntax is:

```
ax.boxplot(data)
```

The `data` passed to the `ax.boxplot()` method can be a Python list or NumPy array. To create multiple box plots side by side, pass in a list of lists or a 2D NumPy array.

The code section below creates a box plot with four elements.

```
In [1]: import numpy as np
        import matplotlib.pyplot as plt
        # if using a Jupyter notebook, include:
        %matplotlib inline

        # generate some random data
```

```python
data1 = np.random.normal(0, 6, 100)
data2 = np.random.normal(0, 7, 100)
data3 = np.random.normal(0, 8, 100)
data4 = np.random.normal(0, 9, 100)
data = list([data1, data2, data3, data4])

fig, ax = plt.subplots()

# build a box plot
ax.boxplot(data)

# title and axis labels
ax.set_title('box plot')
ax.set_xlabel('x-axis')
ax.set_ylabel('y-axis')
xticklabels=['category 1', 'category 2', 'category 3', 'category 4']
ax.set_xticklabels(xticklabels)

# add horizontal grid lines
ax.yaxis.grid(True)

# show the plot
plt.show()
```

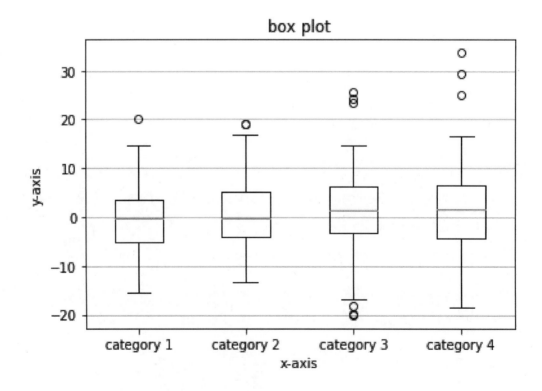

Violin Plots

Violin plots are another type of statistical plot. A violin plot is similar to a box plot, but a violin plot shows some additional information. The sides of the "violins" in a violin plot corresponds to a kernel density estimation (kind of like a histogram) flipped vertically.

To create a violin plot with Matplotlib, use the `ax.violinplot()` method. The general syntax is:

```
ax.violinplot(data)
```

A couple of extra keyword arguments that can be included are `showmeans=` and `showmedians=`.

```
ax.violinplot(data, showmeans=True, showmedians=False)
```

The following code section builds a violin plot with 4 "violins" using randomly generated data.

```
In [2]: import numpy as np
        import matplotlib.pyplot as plt
        # if using a Jupyter notebook, include:
        %matplotlib inline

        # generate some random data
        data1 = np.random.normal(0, 6, 100)
        data2 = np.random.normal(0, 7, 100)
        data3 = np.random.normal(0, 8, 100)
        data4 = np.random.normal(0, 9, 100)
        data = list([data1, data2, data3, data4])

        fig, ax = plt.subplots()

        # build a violin plot
        ax.violinplot(data, showmeans=False, showmedians=True)

        # add title and axis labels
        ax.set_title('violin plot')
        ax.set_xlabel('x-axis')
        ax.set_ylabel('y-axis')

        # add x-tick labels
        xticklabels = ['category 1', 'category 2', 'category 3', 'category 4']
        ax.set_xticks([1,2,3,4])
        ax.set_xticklabels(xticklabels)

        # add horizontal grid lines
        ax.yaxis.grid(True)

        # show the plot
        plt.show()
```

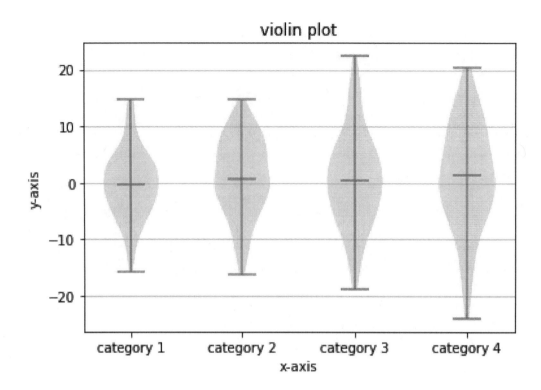

6.11 Scatter Plots

Scatter plots of (x,y) point pairs are created with Matplotlib's `ax.scatter()` method.

The required positional arguments supplied to `ax.scatter()` are two lists or arrays. The first positional argument specifies the x-value of each point on the scatter plot. The second positional argument specifies the y-value of each point on the scatter plot.

The general syntax of the `ax.scatter()` method is shown below.

```
ax.scatter(x-points, y-points)
```

The next code section shows how to build a scatter plot with Matplotlib.

First, 150 random (but semi-focused) x and y-values are created using NumPy's `np.random.randn()` function. The x and y-values are plotted on a scatter plot using Matplotlib's `ax.scatter()` method. Note the number of x-values is the same as the number of y-values. The size of the two lists or two arrays passed to `ax.scatter()` must be equal.

```
In [1]: import numpy as np
        import matplotlib.pyplot as plt
        # if uising a Jupyter notebook, include:
        %matplotlib inline
```

6.11. SCATTER PLOTS

```
# random but semi-focused data
x1 = 1.5 * np.random.randn(150) + 10
y1 = 1.5 * np.random.randn(150) + 10
x2 = 1.5 * np.random.randn(150) + 4
y2 = 1.5 * np.random.randn(150) + 4
x = np.append(x1,x2)
y = np.append(y1,y2)

fig, ax = plt.subplots()
ax.scatter(x,y)

plt.show()
```

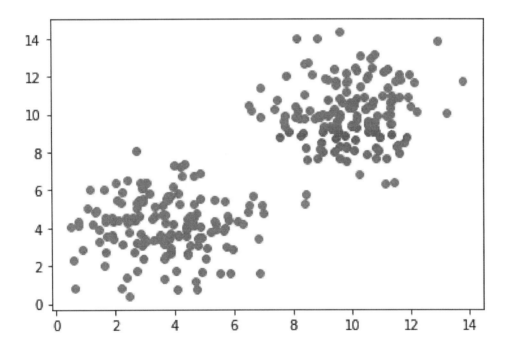

Matplotlib scatter plots can be customized by supplying additional keyword arguments to the ax.scatter() method. Note the keyword arguments used in ax.scatter() are a little different from the keyword arguments used in other Matplotlib plot types.

scatter plot feature	ax.scatter() keyword	Example
marker size	s=	ax.scatter(x, y, s=10)
marker color	c=	ax.scatter(x, y, c=(122, 80, 4))
marker opacity	alpha=	ax.scatter(x, y, alpha=0.2)

Each of these keyword arguments can be assigned an individual value which applies to the whole scatter plot. The `ax.scatter()` keyword arguments can also be assigned to lists or arrays. Supplying a list or array controls the properties of each marker in the scatter plot.

The code section below creates a scatter plot with randomly selected colors and areas.

```
In [2]: import numpy as np
        import matplotlib.pyplot as plt
        # if uising a Jupyter notebook, include:
        %matplotlib inline

        x1 = 1.5 * np.random.randn(150) + 10
        y1 = 1.5 * np.random.randn(150) + 10
        x2 = 1.5 * np.random.randn(150) + 4
        y2 = 1.5 * np.random.randn(150) + 4
        x = np.append(x1,x2)
        y = np.append(y1,y2)
        colors = np.random.rand(150*2)
        area = np.pi * (8 * np.random.rand(150*2))**2

        fig, ax = plt.subplots()

        ax.scatter(x, y, s=area, c=colors, alpha=0.6)
        ax.set_title('Scatter plot of x-y pairs semi-focused in two regions')
        ax.set_xlabel('x value')
        ax.set_ylabel('y value')

        plt.show()
```

6.12. PLOT ANNOTATIONS

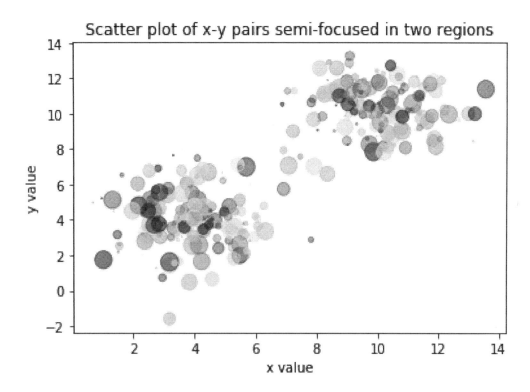

6.12 Plot annotations

Sometimes it is useful for problem solvers to annotate plots. Text can be included on a plot to indicate a point of interest or highlight a specific feature of a plot.

The code section below builds a simple line plot and applies three annotations (three arrows with text) on the plot. Matplotlib's `ax.annotate()` method creates the annotations. Multiple keyword arguments can be passed to `ax.annotate()` method to specify the annotation location and style the annotation.

```
ax.annotate('text', xy= , xycoodrs= , xytext= , arrowprops= )
```

The keyword argument to pay attention to in the next code section is `xycoords=`. Each of the three annotations in the next figure has a different `xycoords=` keyword argument. The annotation can be located relative to the plot data, located relative to the axis, or located relative to the figure window.

In the first annotation, `xycoords='data'`. This means the annotation is placed relative to the data. Since `xy=(0, 0)`, the annotation arrow points to the data point 0,0.

In the second annotation, `xycoords='axes fraction'`. This means the second annotation is placed relative to the axis. Since `xy=(0, 0.5)`, the annotation arrow points all the way to the left edge of the x-axis and half way up the y-axis.

In the third annotation, `xycoords='figure pixels'`. This means the third annotation is placed relative to the figure window. Since xy=(20, 75), the third annotation arrow points 20 pixels to the right and 75 pixels up from the bottom left corner of the figure window.

The chart below summarizes Matplotlib's `ax.annotate()` keyword arguments.

ax.annotate() keyword	description
xy = (0,0)	annotation location
xycoords = 'data'	annotation location relative to data
xycoords = 'axis fraction'	annotation location relative to axis
xycoords = 'figure pixels'	annotation location relative to figure window
bbox = <dict>	define bounding box properties with a dictionary
arrowprops = <dict>	define arrow properties with a dictionary
horizontalalignment='left'	horizontal alignment of annotation
verticalalignment='top'	vertical alignment of annotation

The next code section builds a figure with three annotation arrows.

```
In [1]: import numpy as np
        import matplotlib.pyplot as plt
        # if using a Jupyter notebook, include:
        %matplotlib inline

        x = np.arange(-5, 5, 0.01)
        y = x**2

        fig, ax = plt.subplots()

        # Plot a line
        ax.plot(x, y)

        # first annotation relative to the data
        ax.annotate('function minium \n relative to data',
                 xy=(0, 0),
                 xycoords='data',
                 xytext=(2, 3),
                 arrowprops=
                     dict(facecolor='black', shrink=0.05),
                 horizontalalignment='left',
                 verticalalignment='top')

        # second annotation relative to the axis limits
        bbox_props = dict(boxstyle="round,pad=0.5", fc="w", ec="k", lw=2)

        ax.annotate('half of range \n relative to axis limits',
                 xy=(0, 0.5),
                 xycoords='axes fraction',
                 xytext=(0.2, 0.5),
                 bbox=bbox_props,
```

6.12. PLOT ANNOTATIONS

```
                arrowprops=
                    dict(facecolor='black', shrink=0.05),
                horizontalalignment='left',
                verticalalignment='center')

# third annotation relative to the figure window
bbox_props = dict(boxstyle="larrow,pad=0.5", fc="w", ec="k", lw=2)

ax.annotate('outside the plot \n relative to figure window',
            xy=(20, 75),
            xycoords='figure pixels',
            horizontalalignment='left',
            verticalalignment='top',
            bbox=bbox_props)

ax.set_xlim(-5,5)
ax.set_ylim(-1,10)
ax.set_title('Parabolic Function with Text Notation')

plt.show()
```

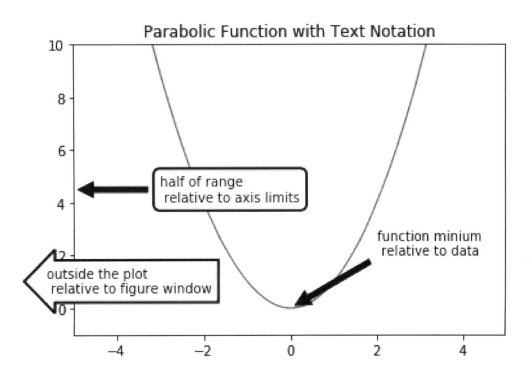

6.13 Subplots

Sometimes it is useful for problem solvers to include a couple plots in the same figure window. This can be accomplished using Matplotlib *subplots*. Matplotlib's `plt.subplot()` function can include two positional arguments for the number of rows of subplots in the figure and the number of columns of subplots in the figure. The general format is:

```
fig, <ax objects> = plt.subplots(rows, cols)
```

Where `rows` and `cols` are integers that control the subplot layout. The `<ax objects>` needs to have dimensions that correspond to `rows` and `cols`.

If a 2 row by 2 column array of plots is created, the `<ax object>` must to be arrayed as shown below:

```
fig, ( (ax1,ax2), (ax3,ax4) ) = plt.subplots(2,2)
```

If a 2 row by 3 column array of plots is created, the `<ax objects>` must be arrayed to correspond to these dimensions:

```
fig, ( (ax1,ax2,a3), (ax4,ax5,ax6) ) = plt.subplots(2, 3)
```

Subplots are useful if you want to show the same data on different scales. The plot of an exponential function looks different on a linear scale compared to a logarithmic scale. Matplotlib contains three plotting methods which scale the x and y-axis linearly or logarithmically. The table below summarizes Matplotlib's axis scaling methods.

Matplotlib method	axis scaling
`ax.plot()`	linear x, linear y
`ax.semilogy()`	linear x, logarithmic y
`ax.semilogx()`	logarithmic x, linear y
`ax.loglog()`	logarithmic x, logarithmic y

The code section below builds a 2 row by 2 column array of subplots in one figure. The axes of each subplot is scaled in a different way.

```
In [1]: import matplotlib.pyplot as plt
        import numpy as np
        # if using a Jupyter notebook, include:
        %matplotlib inline

        # Data for plotting
        t = np.arange(0.01, 20.0, 0.01)

        # Create a figure with 2 rows and 2 cols of subplots
        fig, ((ax1, ax2), (ax3, ax4)) = plt.subplots(2, 2)

        # linear x and y axis
        ax1.plot(t, np.exp(-t / 5.0))
        ax1.set_title('linear x and y')
```

6.13. SUBPLOTS

```
    ax1.grid()

    # log y axis
    ax2.semilogy(t, np.exp(-t / 5.0))
    ax2.set_title('semilogy')
    ax2.grid()

    # log x axis
    ax3.semilogx(t, np.exp(-t / 5.0))
    ax3.set_title('semilogx')
    ax3.grid()

    # log x and y axis
    ax4.loglog(t, 20 * np.exp(-t / 5.0), basex=2)
    ax4.set_title('loglog base 2 on x')
    ax4.grid()

    fig.tight_layout()
    plt.show()
```

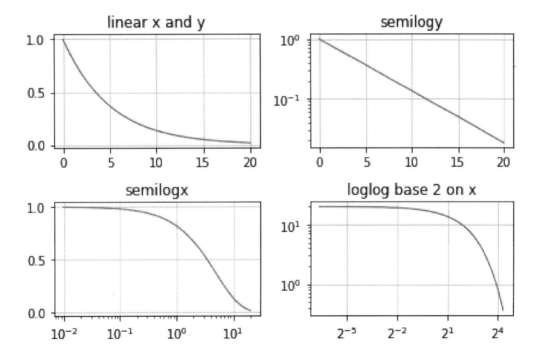

6.14 Plot Styles

Colors, font sizes, line thickness, and many other plot attributes all have default values in Matplotlib. In addition to the default style for these plot attributes, additional styles are available.

To use the default style, either don't specify a style or use the line `plt.style.use('default')`. If you want to apply a different style to a plot use the line:

```
plt.style.use('style')
```

The `'style'` is supplied to the method as a string, surrounded by quotes.

The code below builds a plot with `'fivethirtyeight'` style, a style similar to the plots on fivethirtyeight.com.

```
In [1]: import numpy as np
        import matplotlib.pyplot as plt
        # if using a Jupyter notebook, include:
        %matplotlib inline

        x = np.linspace(0, 10)
        fig, ax = plt.subplots()

        plt.style.use('fivethirtyeight')

        for n in range(-20,30,10):
            ax.plot(x, np.cos(x) + np.random.randn(50) + n)

        ax.set_title("'fivethirtyeight' style")

        plt.show()
```

6.14. PLOT STYLES

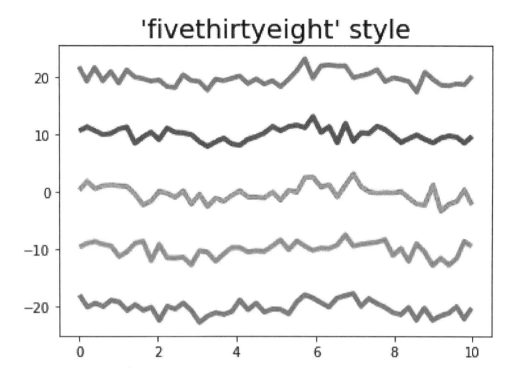

There are many different styles available. You can list the available Matplotlib styles with the command:

```
In [2]: for style in plt.style.available:
            print(style)
```

```
bmh
classic
dark_background
fast
fivethirtyeight
ggplot
grayscale
seaborn-bright
seaborn-colorblind
seaborn-dark-palette
seaborn-dark
seaborn-darkgrid
seaborn-deep
seaborn-muted
seaborn-notebook
seaborn-paper
seaborn-pastel
```

```
seaborn-poster
seaborn-talk
seaborn-ticks
seaborn-white
seaborn-whitegrid
seaborn
Solarize_Light2
tableau-colorblind10
_classic_test
```

The code section below displays a couple of Matplotlib's available plot styles including `'default'`, `'seaborn'` and Matplotlib's older `'classic'` style.

```
In [3]: def pl(ax,st):
            x = np.linspace(0, 10)
            for n in range(-20,30,10):
                ax.plot(x, np.cos(x) + np.random.randn(50) + n)

        def his(ax):
            x = np.random.randn(50)
            ax.hist(x)

        def lb(ax,s):
            ax.text(0.2,0.5,s, fontsize=14)
            ax.xaxis.set_ticklabels([])
            ax.yaxis.set_ticklabels([])

        def make_fig(st):
            with plt.style.context(st):
                fig,[ax1,ax2,ax3] = plt.subplots(1,3,figsize=(9,1.5))
                lb(ax1,st)
                his(ax2)
                pl(ax3,st)

        s = ['default','fivethirtyeight','seaborn', 'Solarize_Light2','classic']

        for st in s:
            make_fig(st)

        plt.show()
```

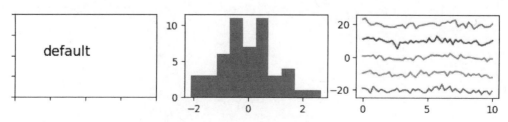

6.14. PLOT STYLES

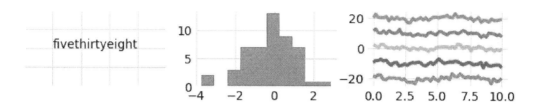

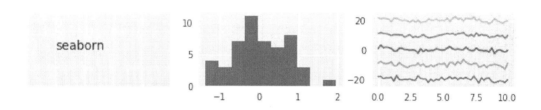

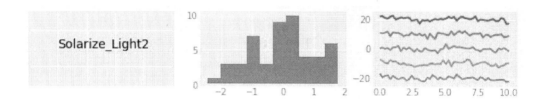

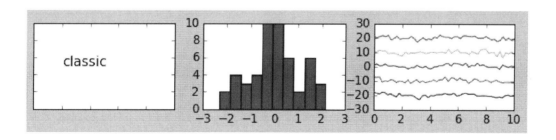

6.15 Contour Plots

Contour plots can be created with Matplotlib. In Civil Engineering a contour plot could show the topology of a building sight. In Mechanical Engineering a contour plot could show the stress gradient across part surface.

Matplotlib's `plt.contourf()` method

Building contour plots with Matplotlib entails using the `ax.contour()` method. The basic `ax.contour()` method call is below.

```
ax.contour(X, Y, Z)
```

Where X and Y are 2D arrays of the x and y points, and Z is a 2D array of points that determines the "height" of the contour, which is represented by color in a 2D plot.

The code section below includes NumPy's `np.meshgrid()` function which produces two 2D arrays from two 1D arrays.

```
In [1]: import numpy as np
        import matplotlib.pyplot as plt
        # if using a Jupyter notebook, include:
        %matplotlib inline

        x = np.arange(-3.0, 3.0, 0.1)
        y = np.arange(-3.0, 3.0, 0.1)
        X, Y = np.meshgrid(x, y)

        Z = np.sin(X)*np.cos(Y)

        fig, ax = plt.subplots(figsize=(6,6))

        ax.contour(X,Y,Z)

        plt.show()
```

6.15. CONTOUR PLOTS

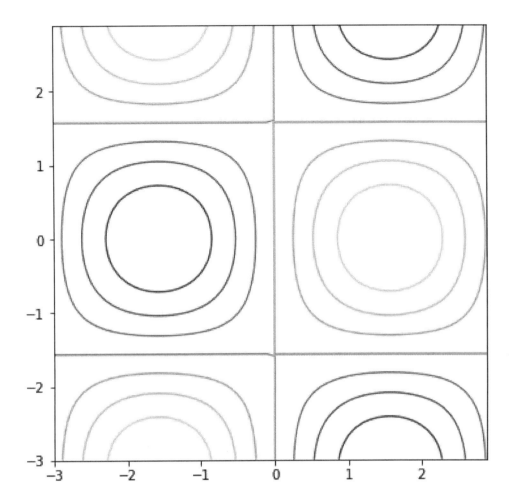

Matplotlib's `plt.contourf()` method

Matplotlib's `ax.contourf()` method is similar to `ax.contour()` except that `ax.contourf()` produces contour plots that are "filled". Instead of lines in a `ax.contour()` plot, shaded areas are produced by a `ax.contourf()` plot. The general method call for `ax.contourf()` is similar to `ax.contour()`.

```
ax.contourf(X, Y, Z)
```

Where X and Y are 2D arrays of the x and y points, and Z is a 2D array of points that determines the color of the areas on the 2D plot.

The next code section builds a shaded contour plotting using Matplotlib's `ax.contourf()` method.

```
In [2]: import numpy as np
        import matplotlib.pyplot as plt
```

```
# if using a Jupyter notebook, include:
%matplotlib inline

x = np.arange(-3.0, 3.0, 0.1)
y = np.arange(-3.0, 3.0, 0.1)

X, Y = np.meshgrid(x, y)

Z = np.sin(X)*np.cos(Y)

fig, ax = plt.subplots(figsize=(6,6))

ax.contourf(X,Y,Z)

plt.show()
```

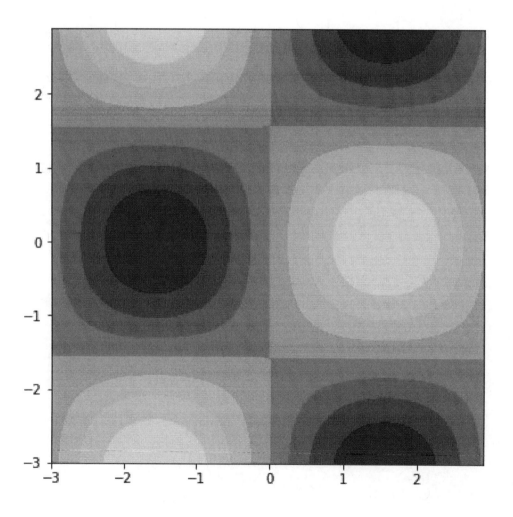

6.15. CONTOUR PLOTS

Color bars on contour plots

Because colors represent a third dimension (like "hight") on a 2D plot, it is useful to have a scale to what each color means. A color scale is typically represented besides a plot.

Color bars are added to Matplotlib contour plots using the `fig.colorbar()` method. Since the color bar is not part of the contour plot, the color bar needs to be applied to the figure object, often called `fig`. A contour plot needs to be passed into the `fig.colorbar()` method. Therefore, when you add a color bar to a figure, a plot object needs to be available. A plot object is the output of the `ax.contourf()` method.

Previously, the output of the `ax.contourf()` method was not assigned to a variable. But to include a color bar on a contour plot, the plot object needs to be saved to a variable, so that the plot object can be passed to the `fig.colorbar()` method.

```python
cf = ax.contourf(X,Y,Z)
fig.colorbar(cf, ax=ax)
```

Where `cf` is the plot object created by `ax.contourf(X, Y, Z)`. The axis object that contains the contour plot, `ax` is passed to the `fig.colorbar()` method along with the `cf` plot object.

The code section below creates a filled contour plot with a color bar placed beside the plot.

```python
In [3]: import numpy as np
        import matplotlib.pyplot as plt
        # if using a Jupyter notebook, include:
        %matplotlib inline

        x = np.arange(-3.0, 3.0, 0.1)
        y = np.arange(-3.0, 3.0, 0.1)

        X, Y = np.meshgrid(x, y)

        Z = np.sin(X)*np.cos(Y)

        fig, ax = plt.subplots(figsize=(6,6))

        ax.set_aspect('equal')
        cf = ax.contourf(X,Y,Z)
        fig.colorbar(cf, ax=ax)

        plt.show()
```

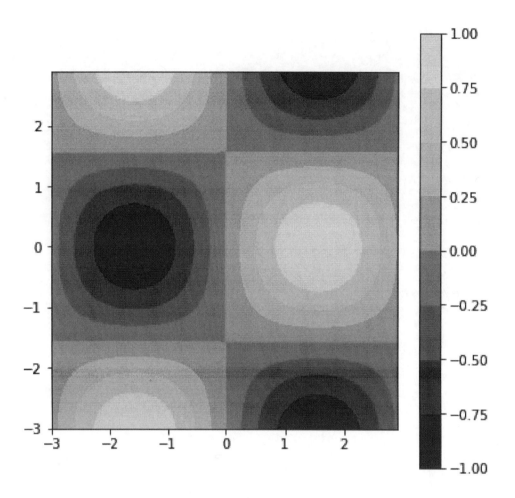

Color maps on contour plots

The default color scheme of Matplotlib contour and filled contour plots can be modified. A general way to modify the color scheme is to call Matplotlib's plt.get_cmap() function that outputs a color map object. There are many different colormaps available to apply to contour plots. A complete list is available in the Matplotlib documentation (https://matplotlib.org). The colormap object is then passed to the ax.contourf() or ax.contour() method as a keyword argument.

```
mycmap = plt.get_cmap('gist_earth')
ax.contourf(X, Y, Z, cmap=mycmap)
```

The code section below produces two filled contour plots, contour plot has a different color map.

```
In [4]: import matplotlib.pyplot as plt
        import numpy as np
        # if using a Jupyter notebook, include:
```

6.15. CONTOUR PLOTS

```
%matplotlib inline

x = np.arange(-3.0, 3.0, 0.1)
y = np.arange(-3.0, 3.0, 0.1)

X, Y = np.meshgrid(x, y)

Z = np.sin(X)*np.cos(Y)

fig, (ax1, ax2) = plt.subplots(1, 2, figsize=(12,6))

mycmap1 = plt.get_cmap('gist_earth')
ax1.set_aspect('equal')
ax1.set_title('Colormap: gist_earth')
cf1 = ax1.contourf(X,Y,Z, cmap=mycmap1)

fig.colorbar(cf1, ax=ax1)

mycmap2 = plt.get_cmap('gnuplot2')
ax2.set_aspect('equal')
ax2.set_title('Colormap: gnuplot2')
cf2 = ax2.contourf(X,Y,Z, cmap=mycmap2)

fig.colorbar(cf2, ax=ax2)

plt.show()
```

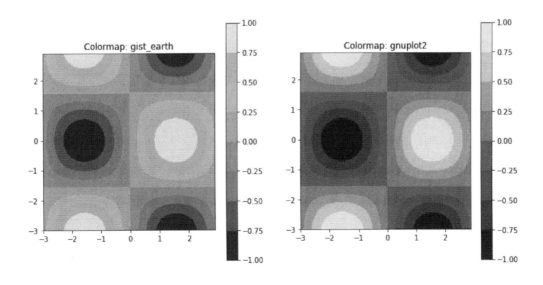

6.16 Quiver and Stream Plots

In this section, you will learn how to build quiver and stream plots using Matplotlib.

Quiver Plots

A quiver plot is a type of 2D plot that shows vector lines as arrows. Quiver plots are useful in Electrical Engineering to visualize electrical potential and useful in Mechanical Engineering to show stress gradients.

Quiver plot with one arrow

First, we'll build a simple quiver plot that contains one arrow to demonstrate how Matplotlib's `ax.quiver()` method works. The `ax.quiver()` method takes four positional arguments:

```
ax.quiver(x_pos, y_pos, x_direct, y_direct)
```

Where `x_pos` and `y_pos` are the arrow starting positions and `x_direct`, `y_direct` are the arrow directions.

Our first plot contains one quiver arrow at the starting point `x_pos = 0`, `y_pos = 0`. The quiver arrow's direction is pointing up and to the right `x_direct = 1`, `y_direct = 1`.

The following code section builds a quiver plot that contains one arrow.

```
In [1]: import numpy as np
        import matplotlib.pyplot as plt
        # if using a Jupyter notebook, include:
        %matplotlib inline

        fig, ax = plt.subplots()

        x_pos = 0
        y_pos = 0
        x_direct = 1
        y_direct = 1

        ax.quiver(x_pos, y_pos, x_direct, y_direct)
        ax.set_title('Quiver plot with one arrow')

        plt.show()
```

6.16. QUIVER AND STREAM PLOTS

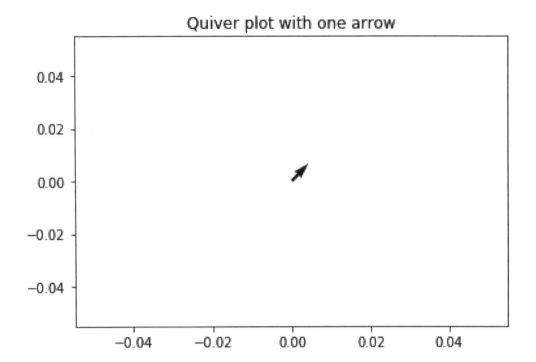

The quiver plot contains one arrow. The arrow starts at point 0, 0 and ends at point 1, 1.

Quiver plot with two arrows

Now let's add a second arrow to the quiver plot by passing in two starting points and two arrow directions.

We'll keep our original arrow starting position at the origin 0,0 and pointing up and to the right (in the 1,1 direction). We'll define a second arrow with a starting position of -0.5,0.5 which points straight down (in the 0,-1 direction).

An additional keyword argument to add the the `ax.quiver()` method is `scale=5`. Including `scale=5` scales the arrow lengths so the arrows look longer and show up better on the quiver plot.

To see the start and end of both arrows, we'll set the axis limits between -1.5 and 1.5 using the `ax.axis()` method and pass in a list of axis limits in the form [xmin, xmax, ymin, ymax].

We can see two arrows. One arrow points to the upper right and the other arrow points straight down.

```
In [2]: fig, ax = plt.subplots()

        x_pos = [0, 0]
        y_pos = [0, 0]
        x_direct = [1, 0]
```

```
        y_direct = [1, -1]

    ax.quiver(x_pos,y_pos,x_direct,y_direct,
              scale=5)
    ax.axis([-1.5, 1.5, -1.5, 1.5])

    plt.show()
```

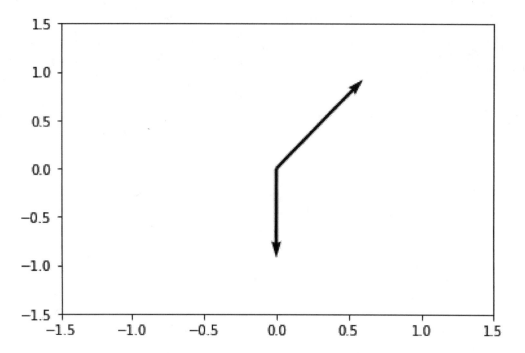

We see a plot with two arrows. Both arrows start at the origin. One arrow points to the upper right, the other arrow points straight down.

Quiver plot using a meshgrid

A quiver plot with two arrows is a good start, but it is tedious and repetitive to add quiver plot arrows one by one. To create a complete 2D surface of arrows, we'll utilize NumPy's `meshgrid()` function.

First, we need to build a set of arrays that denote the x and y starting positions of each quiver arrow on the plot. The quiver arrow starting position arrays will be called X and Y.

We can use the x, y arrow starting *positions* to define the x and y components of each quiver arrow *direction*. We will call the quiver arrow direction arrays u and v. For this plot, we will define the quiver arrow direction based upon the quiver arrow starting point using the equations below.

$$x_{direction} = \cos(x_{starting\ point})$$

6.16. QUIVER AND STREAM PLOTS

$$y_{direction} = sin(y_{starting\ point})$$

The code section below builds the X and Y position arrays using NumPy's np.meshgrid() function.

```
In [3]: import numpy as np
        import matplotlib.pyplot as plt
        # if using a Jupyter notebook, include:
        %matplotlib inline

        x = np.arange(0,2.2,0.2)
        y = np.arange(0,2.2,0.2)

        X, Y = np.meshgrid(x, y)
        u = np.cos(X)*Y
        v = np.sin(y)*Y
```

Next, we can build the quiver plot using Matplotlib's ax.quiver() method. Recall the ax.quiver() method accepts four positional arguments:

```
ax.quiver(x_pos, y_pos, x_direct, y_direct)
```

In this quiver plot, x_pos and y_pos are 2D arrays which contain the starting positions of the arrows and x_direct, y_direct are 2D arrays which contain the arrow directions.

The commands ax.xaxis.set_ticks([]) and ax.yaxis.set_ticks([]) removes the tick marks from the axis and ax.set_aspect('equal') sets the aspect ratio of the plot to 1:1.

```
In [4]: fig, ax = plt.subplots(figsize=(7,7))
        ax.quiver(X,Y,u,v)

        ax.xaxis.set_ticks([])
        ax.yaxis.set_ticks([])
        ax.axis([-0.2, 2.3, -0.2, 2.3])
        ax.set_aspect('equal')

        plt.show()
```

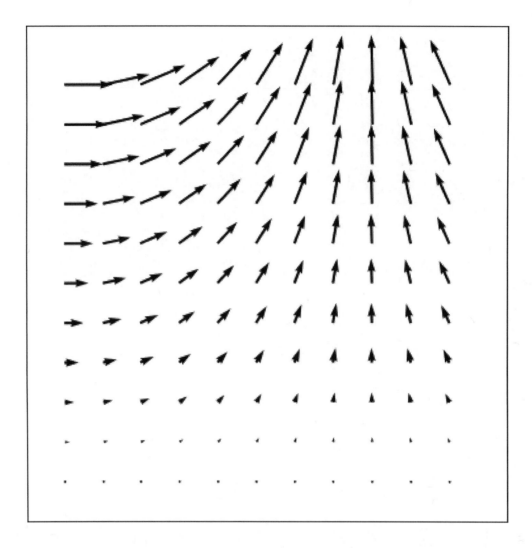

Now let's build another quiver plot where the $\hat{i}$ and $\hat{j}$ components (the direction) of the force arrows, $\vec{F}$ are dependent on the arrow starting point x, y according to the function:

$$\vec{F} = \frac{x}{5}\hat{i} - \frac{y}{5}\hat{j}$$

Again, we will use NumPy's `np.meshgrid()` function to build the arrow starting position arrays, then apply our function $\vec{F}$ to the X and Y arrow starting point arrays.

```
In [5]: x = np.arange(-1,1,0.1)
        y = np.arange(-1,1,0.1)

        X, Y = np.meshgrid(x, y)
```

6.16. QUIVER AND STREAM PLOTS

```
u = np.cos(X)*Y
v = np.sin(Y)*Y

X,Y = np.meshgrid(x,y)

u = X/5
v = -Y/5

fig, ax = plt.subplots(figsize=(9,9))

ax.quiver(X,Y,u,v)

ax.xaxis.set_ticks([])
ax.yaxis.set_ticks([])
ax.set_aspect('equal')

plt.show()
```

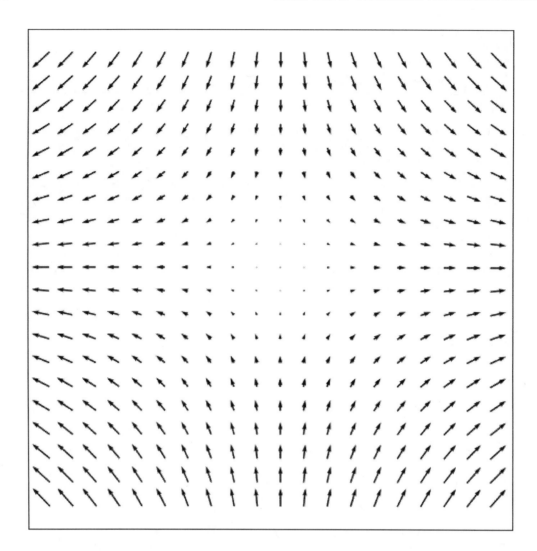

Quiver plot containing a gradient

Next let's build a quiver plot that shows a gradient function. The gradient function has the form:

$$z = xe^{-x^2-y^2}$$

We can use NumPy's `np.gradient()` function to apply the gradient function to every arrow's x, y starting position.

```
In [6]: import numpy as np
        import matplotlib.pyplot as plt
        # if using a Jupyter notebook, include:
```

6.16. QUIVER AND STREAM PLOTS

```
%matplotlib inline

x = np.arange(-2,2.2,0.2)
y = np.arange(-2,2.2,0.2)

X, Y = np.meshgrid(x, y)
z = X*np.exp(-X**2 -Y**2)
dx, dy = np.gradient(z)

fig, ax = plt.subplots(figsize=(9,9))

ax.quiver(X,Y,dx,dy)

ax.xaxis.set_ticks([])
ax.yaxis.set_ticks([])
ax.set_aspect('equal')

plt.show()
```

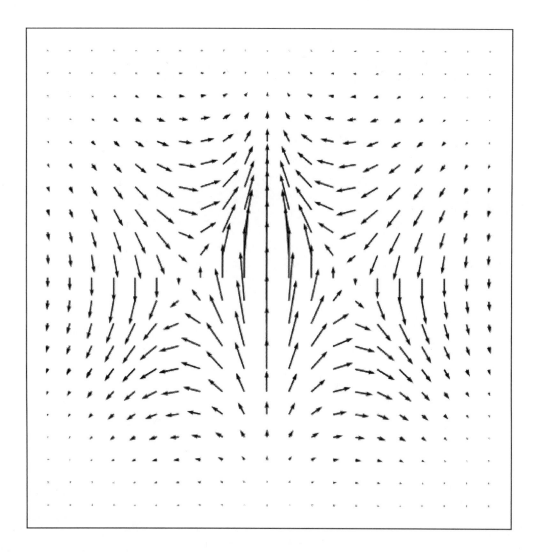

Quiver plot with four vortices

Now let's build a quiver plot that contains four vortices. The function $\vec{F}$ which describes the 2D field that has four vortices is shown below.

$$\vec{F} = sin(x)cos(y)\,\hat{i} - cos(x)sin(y)\,\hat{j}$$

The code section below builds a quiver plot with four vortices.

```
In [7]: import numpy as np
        import matplotlib.pyplot as plt
        # if using a Jupyter notebook, include:
```

6.16. QUIVER AND STREAM PLOTS

```
%matplotlib inline

x = np.arange(0,2*np.pi+2*np.pi/20,2*np.pi/20)
y = np.arange(0,2*np.pi+2*np.pi/20,2*np.pi/20)

X,Y = np.meshgrid(x,y)

u = np.sin(X)*np.cos(Y)
v = -np.cos(X)*np.sin(Y)

fig, ax = plt.subplots(figsize=(9,9))

ax.quiver(X,Y,u,v)

ax.xaxis.set_ticks([])
ax.yaxis.set_ticks([])
ax.axis([0,2*np.pi,0,2*np.pi])
ax.set_aspect('equal')

plt.show()
```

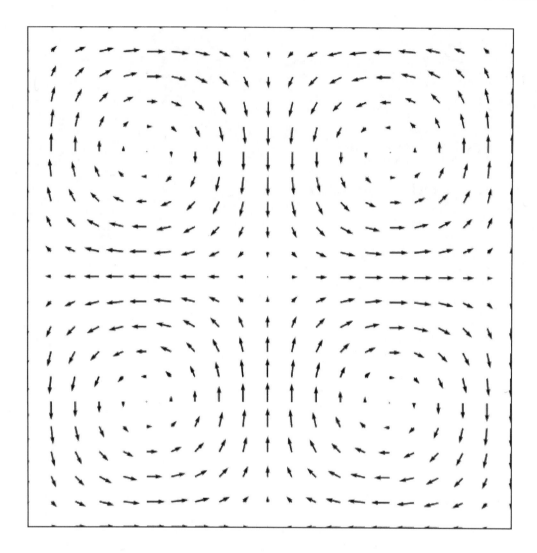

Quiver plots with color

Finally, let's add some color to our quiver plots. The `ax.quiver()` method has an optional fifth positional argument that specifies the quiver arrow color. The quiver arrow color argument needs to have the same dimensions as the position and direction arrays.

```
ax.quiver(x_pos, y_pos, x_direct, y_direct, color)
```

Using Matplotlib subplots, we can build a figure which contains three quiver plots. Each quiver plot will be in color.

The code section below builds a figure with three subplots. Each subplot is a colored quiver plot.

```
In [8]: import numpy as np
```

6.16. QUIVER AND STREAM PLOTS

```python
import matplotlib.pyplot as plt
%matplotlib inline

fig, (ax1,ax2,ax3) = plt.subplots(1,3)

# first subplot
x = np.arange(0,2.2,0.2)
y = np.arange(0,2.2,0.2)
X, Y = np.meshgrid(x, y)
u = np.cos(X)*Y
v = np.sin(y)*Y
n = -2
color = np.sqrt(((v-n)/2)**2 + ((u-n)/2)**2)

ax1.quiver(X,Y,u,v,color, alpha=0.8)

ax1.xaxis.set_ticks([])
ax1.yaxis.set_ticks([])
ax1.axis([-0.2, 2.3, -0.2, 2.3])
ax1.set_aspect('equal')
ax1.set_title('meshgrid function')

# second subplot
x = np.arange(-2,2.2,0.2)
y = np.arange(-2,2.2,0.2)
X, Y = np.meshgrid(x, y)
z = X*np.exp(-X**2 -Y**2)
dx, dy = np.gradient(z)
n = -2
color = np.sqrt(((dx-n)/2)**2 + ((dy-n)/2)**2)

ax2.quiver(X,Y,dx,dy,color)

ax2.xaxis.set_ticks([])
ax2.yaxis.set_ticks([])
ax2.set_aspect('equal')
ax2.set_title('gradient')

# third subplot
x = np.arange(0,2*np.pi+2*np.pi/20,2*np.pi/20)
y = np.arange(0,2*np.pi+2*np.pi/20,2*np.pi/20)
X,Y = np.meshgrid(x,y)
u = np.sin(X)*np.cos(Y)
v = -np.cos(X)*np.sin(Y)
n = -1
color = np.sqrt(((dx-n)/2)**2 + ((dy-n)/2)**2)

ax3.quiver(X,Y,u,v,color)
```

```
        ax3.xaxis.set_ticks([])
        ax3.yaxis.set_ticks([])
        ax3.axis([0,2*np.pi,0,2*np.pi])
        ax3.set_aspect('equal')
        ax3.set_title('four vortices')

        # save and show the figure
        plt.tight_layout()
        fig.savefig('3_quiver_plots.png', dpi=300, bbox_inches='tight')

        plt.show()
```

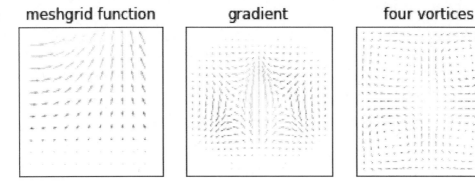

Stream Plots

A stream plot is a type of 2D plot used to show fluid flow and 2D field gradiants.

The basic method to build a stream plot in Matplotlib is:

```
    ax.streamplot(x_grid,y_grid,x_vec,y_vec, density=spacing)
```

Where x_grid and y_grid are arrays of x, y points. The arrays x_vec and y_vec denote the stream velocity at each point on the grid. The keyword argument density=spacing specifies how close the streamlines are drawn together.

A simple stream plot

Let's start with a stream plot that contains stream lines on a 10 x 10 grid. All the stream lines on the plot are parallel and point to the right.

The following code section builds a stream plot that contains horizontal parallel lines pointing to the right.

```
In [9]: import numpy as np
        import matplotlib.pyplot as plt
```

6.16. QUIVER AND STREAM PLOTS

```
# if using a Jupyter notebook, include:
%matplotlib inline

x = np.arange(0,10)
y = np.arange(0,10)

X, Y = np.meshgrid(x,y)
u = np.ones((10,10)) # x-component to the right
v = np.zeros((10,10)) # y-component zero

fig, ax = plt.subplots()

ax.streamplot(X,Y,u,v, density = 0.5)
ax.set_title('Stream Plot of Parallel Lines')
plt.show()
```

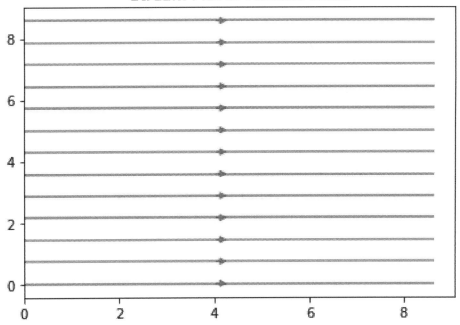

The plot contains parallel streamlines all pointing to the right.

Stream plot of a field

We can build a stream plot which shows field lines based on a defined 2D vector field.

```
In [10]: import numpy as np
         import matplotlib.pyplot as plt
```

```python
# if using a Jupyter notebook, include:
%matplotlib inline

x = np.arange(0,2.2,0.1)
y = np.arange(0,2.2,0.1)

X, Y = np.meshgrid(x, y)
u = np.cos(X)*Y
v = np.sin(y)*Y

fig, ax = plt.subplots()

ax.streamplot(X,Y,u,v, density = 1)
ax.axis([0.5,2.1,0,2])
ax.xaxis.set_ticks([])
ax.yaxis.set_ticks([])
ax.set_title('Stream Plot of Field Lines')

plt.show()
```

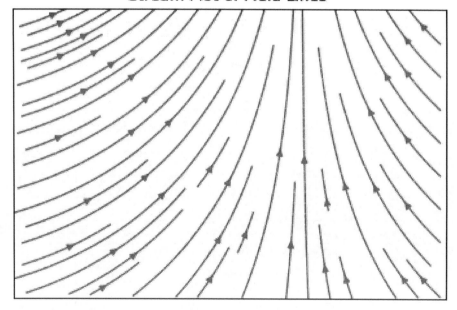

Stream plot of two point charges

Finally, we will build a stream plot to demonstrate the electric field due to two point charges. The electric field at any point on a 2D surface depends on the position and distance relative to the two

6.16. QUIVER AND STREAM PLOTS

point charges.

```
In [11]: import numpy as np
         import matplotlib.pyplot as plt
         # if using a Jupyter notebook, include:
         %matplotlib inline

         x = np.arange(-4,4,0.2)
         y = np.arange(-4,4,0.2)

         X,Y = np.meshgrid(x,y)
         Ex = (X + 1)/((X+1)**2 + Y**2) - (X - 1)/((X-1)**2 + Y**2)
         Ey = Y/((X+1)**2 + Y**2) - Y/((X-1)**2 + Y**2)

         fig, ax = plt.subplots(figsize=(6,6))

         ax.streamplot(X,Y,Ex,Ey)

         ax.set_aspect('equal')
         ax.plot(-1,0,'-or')
         ax.plot(1,0,'-ob')
         ax.set_title('Stream Plot of Two Point Charges')

         plt.show()
```

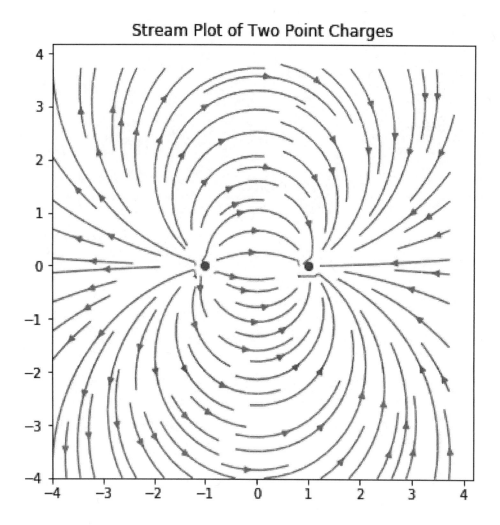

6.17 3D Surface Plots

3D surface plots can be created with Matplotlib.

The axes3d submodule included in Matplotlib's `mpl_toolkits.mplot3d` toolkit provides the methods necessary to create 3D surface plots with Python.

Surface Plots

Surface plots are created with Matplotlib's `ax.plot_surface()` method. By default, surface plots are a single color. The general format of Matplotlib's `ax.plot_surface()` method is below.

```
ax.plot_surface(X, Y, Z)
```

6.17. 3D SURFACE PLOTS

Where X and Y are 2D array of x and y points and Z is a 2D array of heights.

An example of a 3D surface plot is in the next code section. Note how the keyword argument `projection='3d'` is included in the `fig.add_subplot()` method.

```
In [1]: from mpl_toolkits.mplot3d import axes3d
        import matplotlib.pyplot as plt
        import numpy as np
        #if using a Jupyter notebook, include:
        %matplotlib inline

        x = np.arange(-5,5,0.1)
        y = np.arange(-5,5,0.1)
        X,Y = np.meshgrid(x,y)
        Z = X*np.exp(-X**2 - Y**2)

        fig = plt.figure(figsize=(6,6))
        ax = fig.add_subplot(111, projection='3d')

        # Plot a 3D surface
        ax.plot_surface(X, Y, Z)

        plt.show()
```

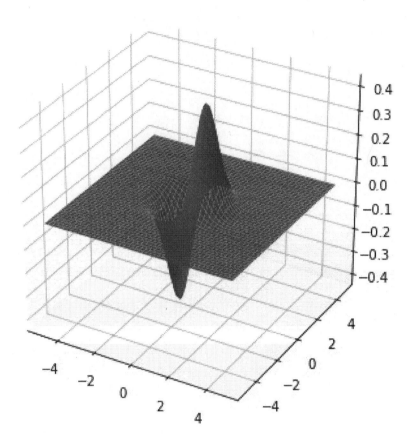

Wire Frame Plots

Wire frame plots are similar to surface plots, but on a wire frame plot the entire 3d surface is not shown. Instead, the surface is approximated with "wires" laid over the 3D surface. Wire frame 3D surface plots can be constructed using Matplotlib's ax.plot_wireframe() method. The general method is below.

```
ax.plot_wireframe(X, Y, Z, rstride=10, cstride=10)
```

Where X and Y are 2D array of x and y points and Z is a 2D array of heights. The keyword arguments rstride= and cstride= determine the row step size and the column step size. These keyword arguments control how close together the "wires" in the wire frame plot are drawn.

The next code section draws two wire frame plots side by side.

```
In [2]: import numpy as np
        import matplotlib.pyplot as plt
```

6.17. 3D SURFACE PLOTS

```
from mpl_toolkits.mplot3d import axes3d
# if using a Jupyter notebook, include:
%matplotlib inline

fig = plt.figure(figsize=(12,6))
ax1 = fig.add_subplot(121, projection='3d')
ax2 = fig.add_subplot(122, projection='3d')

x = np.arange(-5,5,0.1)
y = np.arange(-5,5,0.1)
X,Y = np.meshgrid(x,y)
Z = X*np.exp(-X**2 - Y**2)

# Plot a basic wireframe
ax1.plot_wireframe(X, Y, Z, rstride=10, cstride=10)
ax1.set_title('row step size 10, column step size 10')

ax2.plot_wireframe(X, Y, Z, rstride=20, cstride=20)
ax2.set_title('row step size 20, column step size 20')

plt.show()
```

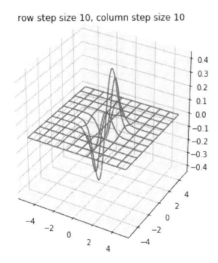
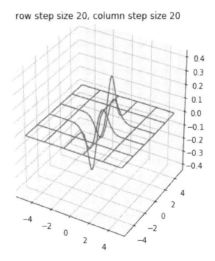

Gradient Surface Plots

Gradient surface plots combine a 3D surface plot with a 2D contour plot. In a gradient surface plot, the 3D surface is colored like a 2D contour plot. High parts of the surface contain a different color than low parts of the surface. The general method call is below. Note the cmap= keyword argument.

```
surf = ax.plot_surface(X, Y, Z,
```

```
                    cmap=<color map>,
                    linewidth=0,
                    antialiased=False)
```

The keyword argument cmap=<color map> assigns the colors to the surface. There is a wide array of color map options in Matplotlib. Options include 'coolwarm', 'gist_earth', and 'ocean'. Find all of Matplotlib's colormaps in the Matplotlib documentation at matplotlib.org/tutorials/colors/colormaps. A color bar can be added along side the plot by calling the fig.colorbar() method and passing in the surface plot object.

The next code section builds a gradient surface plot using the 'gist_earth' color map.

```
In [3]: import numpy as np
        import matplotlib.pyplot as plt
        from mpl_toolkits.mplot3d import axes3d
        # if using a Jupyter notebook, include:
        %matplotlib inline

        fig = plt.figure(figsize=(10,6))
        ax1 = fig.add_subplot(111, projection='3d')

        x = np.arange(-5,5,0.1)
        y = np.arange(-5,5,0.1)
        X,Y = np.meshgrid(x,y)
        Z = X*np.exp(-X**2 - Y**2)

        mycmap = plt.get_cmap('gist_earth')
        ax1.set_title('gist_earth color map')
        surf1 = ax1.plot_surface(X, Y, Z, cmap=mycmap)
        fig.colorbar(surf1, ax=ax1, shrink=0.5, aspect=5)

        plt.show()
```

6.17. 3D SURFACE PLOTS

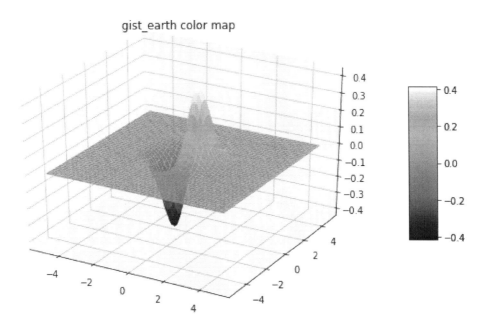

3D Surface Plots with 2D Contour Plot Projections

3D Surface plots created with Matplotlib can be projected onto 2D surfaces. Below is a code section that creates a 3D surface plot. The projections of the 3D surface are visualized on 2D contour plots.

```
In [4]: from mpl_toolkits.mplot3d import axes3d
        import matplotlib.pyplot as plt
        from matplotlib import cm

        x = np.arange(-5,5,0.1)
        y = np.arange(-5,5,0.1)
        X,Y = np.meshgrid(x,y)
        Z = X*np.exp(-X**2 - Y**2)

        fig = plt.figure(figsize=(12,6))
        ax = fig.add_subplot(111, projection='3d')

        surf = ax.plot_surface(X, Y, Z, rstride=8, cstride=8, alpha=0.8, cmap=cm.ocean)
        cset = ax.contourf(X, Y, Z, zdir='z', offset=np.min(Z), cmap=cm.ocean)
        cset = ax.contourf(X, Y, Z, zdir='x', offset=-5, cmap=cm.ocean)
        cset = ax.contourf(X, Y, Z, zdir='y', offset=5, cmap=cm.ocean)

        fig.colorbar(surf, ax=ax, shrink=0.5, aspect=5)
```

```
    ax.set_xlabel('X')
    ax.set_xlim(-5, 5)
    ax.set_ylabel('Y')
    ax.set_ylim(-5, 5)
    ax.set_zlabel('Z')
    ax.set_zlim(np.min(Z), np.max(Z))
    ax.set_title('3D surface with 2D contour plot projections')

plt.show()
```

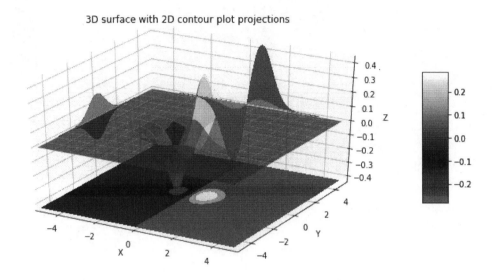

6.18 Summary

In this chapter, you learned how to create plots using Python and Matplotlib. You learned what Matplotlib is and why problem solvers should learn how to use Matplotlib. Matplotlib installation was shown at the start of the chapter. Then, you learned how to build line plots and save plots as image files. You learned how to customize plots by including axis label, titles, and legends on your plots. You also learned how to add annotations to plots.

The types of plots detailed in this chapter are shown in the table below.

Chart Type	Matplotlib method
line plot	ax.plot(x,y)
multi-line plot	ax.plot(x,y) ax.plot(x,z)
bar graph	ax.bar(x_pos, heights)
pie chart	ax.pie(sizes, labels=[labels])
bar graphs with error bars	ax.bar(x_pos, heights, yerr=[error])
line plot with error bars	ax.errorbar(x, y, xerr= , yerr=)
histogram	ax.hist(data, n_bins)
box plot	ax.boxplot([data list])
violin plot	ax.violinplot([data list])
scatter plot	ax.scatter(x_points, y_points)
plot annotations	ax.annotate('text',xy=loc,xy_coords=)
subplots	fig, (ax1,ax2,ax3) = plt.subplots(1,3)
plot styles	plt.style.use('style')
2D contour plot	ax.contour(X, Y, Z)
2D filled contour plot	ax.contourf(X, Y, Z)
color bars	fig.colorbar(cf, ax=ax)
color maps	mycmap = plt.get_cmap('map')
quiver plot	ax.quiver(x_pos, y_pos, x_dir, y_dir)
stream plot	ax.streamplot(x,y,x_d,y_d, density=)
3D surface plot	ax.plot_surface(X, Y, Z)
3D wireframe plot	ax.plot_wireframe(X,Y,Z)

Key Terms and Concepts

plot	object-oriented programming	reference frame
dpi	method	contour plot
invoke	image resolution	quiver plot
library	error bars	stream plot
parameters	box plot	gradient
RGBA	violin plot	field
object	histogram	wire frame plot
attribute	annotation	projection

Additional Resources

Matplotlib official documentation: `https://matplotlib.org/contents.html`

Matplotlib summary notebook on Kaggle: `https://www.kaggle.com/grroverpr/matplotlib-plotting-guide/notebook`

Python Plotting With Matplotlib (Guide) on Real Python: `https://realpython.com/python-matplotlib-guide/#why-can-matplotlib-be-confusing`

Python For Data Science: Matplotlib Cheat Sheet from DataCamp: `https://s3.amazonaws.com/assets.datacamp.com/blog_assets/Python_Matplotlib_Cheat_Sheet.pdf`

6.19 Review Questions

Line plots

Q06.01 Create a plot of the function $y = \cos(x)$ from $x = -2\pi$ to 2π

Q06.02 Create a plot of the function $y = \frac{1}{2}e^x$ from $x = 0$ to 5

Q06.03 Create a plot of the function $y = \sqrt{2x}$ from $x = 1$ to 10

Q06.04 Create a plot of the function $y = mx + b$, where $m = -1$ and $b = -4$. Limit the plot to values of $x = -5$ to 5.

Q06.05 Create a plot of the function $y = ax^2 + bx + c$, where $a = 1/2$, $b = -1/3$ and $c = 4$. Limit the plot to values of $x = -10$ to 10.

Q06.06 Create a plot of the function $y = x^3 + 3$ from $x = -3$ to 3.

Q06.07 Create a plot of the function $y = 2x^3 - 9x^2 + 7x + 6$ from $x = -3$ to 4.

Q06.08 Plot the data set below with a line plot. Use Matplotlib's default index system, or create a set of x values from $x = 0$ to 4.

$$y = [-1, 2, -3, 1, 0]$$

Q06.09 Plot the following three functions on the same set of axis. Use a different color line for each function.

$$x = \cos(t)$$

$$y = \cos(t/2)$$

$$z = \frac{1}{2}\cos(t)$$

Set values of $t = -4\pi$ to 4π

Q06.10 Plot the following three functions on the same set of axis. Specify a thick red line for the *cos* function, a thin blue line for the *sin* function, and a dashed green line for the *atan* function (the arc tangent function).

6.19. REVIEW QUESTIONS

$$x = cos(r/10)$$

$$y = sin(r/4)$$

$$z = atan(r)$$

Set values of $r = -1/2$ to $1/2$

Bar Charts and Pie Charts

Q06.30 According to the University of Waterloo, world energy consumption in 2006 from the five top energy resources were:

$$Natural\ Gas = 24\%$$

$$Hydro = 6\%$$

$$Nuclear = 6\%$$

$$Oil = 36\%$$

$$Coal = 28\%$$

Build a pie chart of the distribution of world energy consumption based on the data above.

Q06.31 According to the 2017 Python Developer's Survey, the computer operating system used by Python Developers breaks down as follows:

$$Windows = 49\%$$

$$Linux = 19\%$$

$$MacOS = 15\%$$

$$Other = 17\%$$

Build a pie chart of the computer operating system used by Python Developers in 2017.

Q06.32 According to the 2017 Python Developer's Survey, the commercial cloud providers used by Python Developers breaks down as follows:

$$Amazon\ Web\ Services = 67\%$$

$$Google\ Cloud = 29\%$$

$$Heroku = 26\%$$

$$Digital\ Ocean = 23\%$$

$$Microsoft\ Azure = 16\%$$

$$Other = 13\%$$

Build a pie chart of the commercial cloud providers used by Python Developers in 2017.

Q06.33 Re-create the pie chart in Q06.32 that shows which commercial cloud providers are used by Python Developers. Explode out the pie pieces on the chart and add a shadow to each piece.

Q06.34 Re-create the pie chart in Q06.31 that shows which operating system Python developers use. Explode out the Windows (49%) pie piece to highlight it.

Q06.35 A list of grades in a college engineering course and the corresponding number of students who earned each grade is shown below:

```
grades = ['A','B','C','D','F']

number_of_students = [3, 5, 8, 1, 2]
```

Build a bar plot of the grade distribution from the college engineering class.

Q06.36 The proof strength of four different grades of bolts is shown below:

Bolt Type	Proof Strength (psi)
Grade 2	33,000 psi
Grade 5	74,000 psi
Grade 8	120,000 psi
Grade A325	85,000 psi

Build a bar chart of the proof strength of the four types of bolts. Label the bars by bolt type and include a title and y-axis label with units.

Q06.37 According to the 2017 Python Developer's Survey, the IDE (Integrated Development Environment) used by *Scientific* Python Developers breaks down as follows:

$$PyCharm\ Professional = 12\%$$

$$PyCharm\ CE = 17\%$$

$$Sublime\ Text = 9\%$$

$$Vim = 8\%$$

$$IDLE = 7\%$$

$$Atom = 7\%$$

$$VS\ Code = 6\%$$

$$Notepad\ ++ = 6\%$$

$$Eclipse = 3\%$$

$$Emacs = 3\%$$

Build a bar chart of the IDE's used by Python Developers in 2017.

Q06.38 Create a plot of the function $y = x^3 + 3$ from $x = -3$ to $x = 3$.

Q06.39 The tensile strength of 4 steel heat treatments is shown in the table below:

Heat Treatment	Tensile Strength (MPa)
Annealed	390 MPa
Normalized	452 MPa
Oil Quench	734 MPa
Oil Quench and Temper	422 MPa

Build a bar plot of tensile strength vs. heat treatment using the steel heat treatment data above. Label the bars with the type of heat treatment and include a y-axis label with units and a title.

Histograms, Box Plots, and Violin Plots

Q06.50 Plot the histogram of a normal distribution of 100 random numbers. Use NumPy's `np.random.normal()` function to create the array of numbers. Set a mean $\mu = 20$ and a standard deviation $\sigma = 7$.

Q06.51 NumPy's `np.random.randint()` function creates an array of random numbers. NumPy's `np.random.randn()` function creates an array of normally-distributed random numbers. Use both of these functions to create a set of 200 random numbers. Plot both sets of numbers as histograms with Matplotlib's `ax.hist()` method. After you construct both histograms, explain how the two NumPy functions `np.random.randint()` and `np.random.randn()` compare.

Q06.52 Create a box plot with three elements (three "boxes"). Use NumPy's `np.random.randn()` function to create three arrays of 50 elements. Plot each array as a separate element on the box plot.

Q06.53 Create a violin plot with five elements (five "violins"). Use NumPy's `np.random.randn()` function to create five arrays of 50 elements. Plot each array as a separate element on the violin plot.

Q06.54 Use Matplotlib's `plt.subplots()` command to create a figure with three subplots. In the first subplot, build a historgram. In the second subplot build a box plot. In the third subplot build a violin plot. Plot the same set of 100 normally-distributed random numbers (using NumPy's `np.random.randn()` function) in each subplot. Include a title above each subplot that shows the plot type: Histogram, Box Plot, and Violin Plot.

Scatter Plots

Q06.60 Create a scatter plot with the following lists of x points and y points.

```
x = [1,2,3,4,5]
y = [8,12,4,2,6]
```

Q06.61 Create a scatter plot with the following arrays of x pints and y points generated with NumPy's `np.random.randint()` function.

```
x = np.random.randint(20)
y = np.random.randint(20)
```

Q06.62 Use the code below to create two arrays of semi-focused random points.

```
x1 = 1.5 * np.random.randn(150) + 10
y1 = 1.5 * np.random.randn(150) + 10
x2 = 1.5 * np.random.randn(150) + 4
y2 = 1.5 * np.random.randn(150) + 4
x = np.append(x1,x2)
y = np.append(y1,y2)
```

Plot the arrays x and y on a scatter plot. Set the color of the marker's on the scatter plot red. Set the marker opacity to 0.5.

Subplots

Q06.70 Create a figure that has four subplots all in one row. In each of the subplots plot the function:

$$y = e^x$$

Use the same values of x and y in each subplot. Set the values of x with NumPy's `arange()` function with the line `x = np.arange(0.01, 20.0, 0.01)` In the first subplot, use Matplotlibs's `ax.plot()` method. In the second subplot use Matplotlib's `ax.semilogy()` method. In the thrid subplot use

Matplotlib's `ax.semilogx()` method. In the four subplot use Matplotlib's `ax.loglog()` method. Label each subplot with a title that shows the plot type.

Q06.70 Use the data in Q06.31 to create a figure with two subplots. In the first subplot, build a bar chart of the data in Q06.31. In the second subplot, build a pie chart of he data in Q06.31.

Chapter 7

Functions and Modules

7.1 Introduction

In computer programming, functions are a way to bundle multiple lines of code together to run as one block of code. Many functions accept input, called arguments, and produce output. Python has many built-in functions such as `type()`, `len()` and `pow()`. In this chapter you will learn how to create user-defined functions in Python.

By the end of this chapter you will be able to:

- Call functions in Python
- Import functions into Python scripts
- Create user-defined functions
- Create functions with default arguments
- Utilize functions with positional and keyword arguments
- Write reusable code for other problem solvers to use

7.2 Why Functions?

Functions are an essential part of most programming languages. Functions are reusable pieces of code that can be called using a function's name. Functions can be called anywhere in a Python program, including calling functions within other functions.

Functions provide a couple of benefits:

- Functions allow the same piece of code to run multiple times
- Functions break long programs up into smaller components
- Functions can be shared and used by other programmers

Every function has a *function name*. The function name is used when the function is *called* in a program. Calling a function means running a function.

Functions can receive input from the program. The input provided to a function is called *input arguments* or just *arguments*. Arguments are the code passed to a function as input.

Functions can produce output. We say a function *returns* output to the program. The output of a function can be assigned to a variable for use in a program.

Below is an example calling Python's `pow()` a function:

```
In [1]: out = pow(3,2)
```

In the function call above, the function name is `pow`. `pow` is the power function. The `pow` function raises a number to a power. The input arguments are the numbers 3 and 2. The function output is assigned to the variable `out`. In this example, the function returns the value 9 (3 raised to the 2 power, $3^2 = 9$).

7.3 First Function

Defining Functions in Python

Function definitions in Python typically contain at least two lines. The first line defines the function name and arguments. The last line typically defines the function output. In between is the code that runs when the function is called.

```
def function_name(arguments):
    <code>
    return output
```

The first line of code above contains a couple of parts:

```
def
```

The keyword `def` needs to be the start of the line that declares the function. `def` stands for *definition* and indicates to the Python interpreter that a function definition will follow.

7.3. FIRST FUNCTION

```
function_name
```

Each function needs a name. The function name must start with a letter (or underscore) and is typically all lowercase (in Python, names that start with Uppercase are usually used to define *classes*). Function names can only contain letters, numbers and the underscore character. Just about any name will do, but it is best to avoid using any Python keywords such as `def`, `class`, `if`, `else`, `for`. A complete list of reserved Python keywords is in the Appendix.

```
(argument):
```

Function names are followed by a set of parenthesis ( ). Many functions have code, called *arguments* in between the parenthesis. The name used for the function argument(s) should be used in the body of the function. After the function name, parenthesis, and arguments comes a : colon. In Python, a colon is required to end the first line of all functions.

A colon : is required at the end of the first line of every function. If the : is not present the code will not run.

```
<code>
```

The body of the function contains the code that will run when the function is called. Any variables declared by the function arguments can be used in the body of the function. Any variables used in the body of the function are *local variables*. Local variables cannot be called or accessed by other scripts, or used outside the function body.

```
return
```

The `return` keyword is often the last line of a function. `return` indicates that whatever expression that follows is the output of the function. The `return` keyword is not a function or a method, and parenthesis are not used after `return`, just a space.

```
output
```

Whatever expression is included after `return` will be *returned* by the function. The output expression after `return` can be a single variable, value or be a complex expression that includes multiple variables.

Your First User-defined Function

When you write your own functions, called *user-defined functions*, consider these criteria:

- What will you name the function?
- What, if any, input arguments will the function accept?
- What will the function do? What is the purpose of the code that runs when the function is called?
- What, if any, output will the function return?

Let's write a simple function which adds two to any number. We will call our function `plustwo`. Our function has one input argument, a number. The function will return that number plus 2.

Let's apply this description to our four criteria:

- Function name: `plustwo`

- Input arguments: a number
- What does the function do: add 2 to any number
- Output: a number (2 + the input number)

Our plustwo() function will operate as shown below:

```
plustwo(3)
5
```

The code section below defines our plustwo() function.

```
In [1]: def plustwo(n):
            out = n + 2
            return out
```

The code section above includes the keyword def, a space and then the function name plustwo. The input argument, n, is enclosed in parenthesis ( ) after the function name. After the set of parenthesis is a colon :. The body of the function includes the code out = n + 2. The last line of the function includes the keyword return followed by a space and the variable out. Note variable n is a *local variable* and can only be used inside the function definition.

Let's run our plustwo() function and see the output.

```
In [2]: plustwo(3)

Out[2]: 5
```

The output of the plustwo() function can be assigned to variable.

```
In [3]: ans = plustwo(10)
        ans

Out[3]: 12
```

7.4 Functions with Multiple Arguments

Functions can be written to accept multiple input arguments. When multiple arguments are specified, the arguments are listed within the parenthesis after the function name and separated by a comma:

```
def function_name(argument1, argument2):
    <code>
    return output
```

A function that calculates the area of a triangle given the base and height of the triangle would accept two arguments base and height. The formula for the area A of a triangle given base b and height h is below.

7.4. FUNCTIONS WITH MULTIPLE ARGUMENTS

$$A = \frac{1}{2} b \times h$$

Let's name our function triarea and accept base and height as input arguments. The triarea function will return a number, the area of a triangle.

```
In [1]: def triarea(base, height):
            area = 0.5 * base * height
            return area
```

We can test our triarea() function with a couple of sets of input arguments.

```
In [2]: triarea(10,5)
```

```
Out[2]: 25.0
```

```
In [3]: A = triarea(1,4)
        A
```

```
Out[3]: 2.0
```

Note if only one input argument is supplied to the triarea() function, an error is returned:

```
In [ ]: triarea(2)
```

```
---------------------------------------------------------------------
TypeError                                 Traceback (most recent call last)
<ipython-input-4-ddd55ccdd949> in <module>()
----> 1 triarea(2)

TypeError: triarea() missing 1 required positional argument: 'height'
```

The variables base and height are local variables. If base or height is called outside the function definition, an error is returned.

```
In [ ]: triarea(base, height)
```

```
---------------------------------------------------------------------
NameError                                 Traceback (most recent call last)
<ipython-input-4-1dd955b62482> in <module>()
----> 1 triarea(base, height)

NameError: name 'base' is not defined
```

7.5 Functions with Default Arguments

Functions can be specified with *default arguments*. If values for these arguments are not supplied when the function is called, the default values are used. The general format to define a function with default arguments is below:

```
def function_name(argument1=default_value, argument2=default_value):
    <code>
    return output
```

An example a function with default arguments might be a function that calculates the distance an object falls based on time. The general formula for fall distance *d* based on fall time *t* can be modeled as:

$$d = \frac{1}{2}gt^2$$

Where g is the acceleration due to gravity. On earth the value of $g = 9.81 m/s^2$. But on the moon, $g = 1.625 m/s^2$. Our `falldist()` function will include the default value for earth's gravity and give programmers the option of specifying a different value for g if they choose.

```
In [1]: def falldist(t, g=9.81):
            d = 0.5 * g * t**2
            return d
```

On earth, the distance a ball that falls for three seconds is calculated by `falldist(3)`. In the function call `falldist(3)`, no value is specified for g, so the default value `9.81` is used.

```
In [2]: falldist(3)
```

```
Out[2]: 44.145
```

On earth, the ball falls 44.145 meters in 3 seconds.

However, on the moon gravity is much weaker than on earth. The acceleration of falling objects on the moon is $g = 1.625 m/s^2$. To calculate how far a ball falls on the moon in three seconds, two arguments need to be supplied to the `falldist()` function: 3 and 1.625. If a second argument is provided to the `falldist()` function, in this case 1.625, it overrides the default value assigned in the first line of the function.

```
In [3]: falldist(3, 1.625)
```

```
Out[3]: 7.3125
```

On the moon, the ball falls 7.3125 meters in 3 seconds.

7.6 Calling Functions from Other Files

User-defined functions can be called from other files. A function can be called and run in a different file than the file where the function is defined.

If a new file called *myfunctions.py* is created and contains two function definitions, `plustwo()` and `falldist()`, the functions `plustwo()` and `falldist()` can be used by a separate script as long as the file and function names are imported in the separate script first. It is essential that the file which contains the function definitions ends in the *.py* extension. Without a *.py* extension, the file where the functions are defined can not be imported.

Inside the file *myfuctions.py*, two functions are defined using the code below.

```
# myfunctions.py

def plustwo(n):
    out = n + 2
    return out


def falldist(t,g=9.81):
    d = 0.5 * g * t**2
    return d
```

This file, *myfunctions.py* can be imported into another script (another *.py* file), or Jupyter Notebook.

Remember the file that contains the function definitions and the file calling the functions must be in the same directory.

To use the functions written in one file inside another file include the import line, `from filename import function_name`. Note that although the file name must contain a *.py* extension, .py is not used as part of the filename during import.

The general syntax to import and call a function from a separate file is below:

```
from function_file import function_name

function_name(arguments)
```

An example using this syntax with the *myfunctions.py* file and the function `plustwo()` is below:

```
In [1]: from myfunctions import plustwo

        plustwo(3)

Out[1]: 5
```

Multiple functions can be imported from the same file by separating the imported functions with commas. The general syntax to import and call multiple functions from the same file is below:

```
from function_file import function_name1, function_name2
```

```
function_name1(arguments)
function_name2(arguments)
```

An example using this syntax with the *myfunctions.py* file and the functions plustwo() and falldist() is below:

```
In [2]: from myfunctions import falldist, plustwo

        out1 = falldist(3)
        out2 = plustwo(3)

        print(out1, out2)

44.145 5
```

Another way to import and use the functions from *myfunctions.py* into another script or Jupyter notebook is to import the entire *myfunctions.py* file with import myfunctions, then call the functions with the syntax below.

```
import function_file

function_file.function_name()
```

An example using this syntax with the *myfunctions.py* file is below.

```
In [3]: import myfunctions

        myfunctions.plustwo(3)

Out[3]: 5

In [4]: import myfunctions

        myfunctions.falldist(3)

Out[4]: 44.145
```

7.7 Docstrings in Functions

It is good programming practice to document your code. Reusable chunks of code are particularly relevant to document as other programmers may use the code, and you may use the code again at a different time.

Python has a couple of different ways for programmers to add documentation. One way is to use simple comments. Comments are lines of code that do not get run by the Python interpreter. Comments are meant to be viewed by humans. In Python, comment lines start with the pound symbol #. Any line that starts with a # symbol will not be run by the Python Interpreter.

7.7. DOCSTRINGS IN FUNCTIONS

Another way to document code is to use *docstrings*. Docstrings are comments which are surrounded with triple quotation marks and usually contain multiple lines of explanation. A function containing a docstring takes the form:

```
def function_name(arguments):
    """
    Docstring text



    """
    <code>

    return output
```

Doc strings are what you see when the `help()` function is called. As an example, running the `help()` function on the built-in function `sum` brings up:

```
In [1]: help(sum)

Help on built-in function sum in module builtins:

sum(iterable, start=0, /)
    Return the sum of a 'start' value (default: 0) plus an iterable of numbers

    When the iterable is empty, return the start value.
    This function is intended specifically for use with numeric values and may
    reject non-numeric types.
```

We can produce the same type of output when a user types types `help()` by adding docstrings to a function.

Let's create a new function that converts grams (g) to kilograms (kg). 1000 grams is equal to 1 kilogram. Let's call our function g2kg. Remember the **parenthesis**, **colon**, and **return** statement.

```
In [2]: def g2kg(g):
            kg = g/1000

            return kg
```

Now let's try and use our function. How many kilograms is 1300 grams? We expect the output to be 1.3 kilograms.

```
In [3]: g2kg(1300)

Out[3]: 1.3
```

If we call `help()` on our g2kg() function, nothing is returned. `help(g2kg)` does not return any output because our new g2kg() function does not contain a docstring yet.

```
In [4]: help(g2kg)

Help on function g2kg in module __main__:

g2kg(g)
```

If we insert a docstring into the function definition, `help(g2kg)` will return whatever text we included in the docstring.

The standard components of docstrings included in function definitions are:

- a summary of the function
- the function inputs
- the function outputs
- an example of the function running including the result

The docstring is included right below the `def` line and is enclosed in triple quotes `"""` `"""`. The triple quotes are typically included on their own lines. The syntax to add a docstring in a function definition is below.

```
def function_name(arguments):
    """

    <docstring text>

    """

    <code>

    return output
```

Let's include a docstring with our g2kg() function definition.

```
In [5]: def g2kg(g):
            """

            Function g2kg converts between g and kg

            input: number of grams, int or float
            output: number of kilograms, float

            Example:

                >>> g2kg(1300)

                1.3

            """
```

```
        kg = g/1000

    return kg
```

Now let's ask for `help()` on our `g2kg()` function and see the docstring we wrote in the `g2kg()` function definition printed back to us.

```
In [6]: help(g2kg)

Help on function g2kg in module __main__:

g2kg(g)
    Function g2kg converts between g and kg

    input: number of grams, int or float
    output: number of kilograms, float

    Example:

        >>> g2kg(1300)

        1.3
```

7.8 Positional and Keyword Arguments

Python functions can contain two types of arguments: *positional arguments* and *keyword arguments*. Positional arguments must be included in the correct order. Keyword arguments are included with a keyword and equals sign.

Positional Arguments

An *argument* is a variable, value or object passed to a function or method as input. *Positional arguments* are arguments that need to be included in the proper position or order.

The first positional argument always needs to be listed first when the function is called. The second positional argument needs to be listed second and the third positional argument listed third, etc.

An example of positional arguments can be seen in Python's `complex()` function. This function returns a complex number with a real term and an imaginary term. The order that numbers are passed to the `complex()` function determines which number is the real term and which number is the imaginary term.

If the complex number 3 + 5j is created, the two positional arguments are the numbers 3 and 5. As positional arguments, 3 must be listed first, and 5 must be listed second.

```
In [1]: complex(3, 5)
```

```
Out[1]: (3+5j)
```

On the other hand, if the complex number 5 + 3j needs to be created, the 5 needs to be listed first and the 3 listed second. Writing the same arguments in a different order produces a different result.

```
In [2]: complex(5, 3)
```

```
Out[2]: (5+3j)
```

Positional Arguments Specified by an Iterable

Positional arguments can also be passed to functions using an iterable object. Examples of iterable objects in Python include lists and tuples. The general syntax to use is:

```
function(*iterable)
```

Where `function` is the name of the function and `iterable` is the name of the iterable preceded by the ampersand * character.

An example of using a list to pass positional arguments to the `complex()` function is below. Note the ampersand * character is included before the `term_list` argument.

```
In [3]: term_list = [3, 5]
        complex(*term_list)
```

```
Out[3]: (3+5j)
```

Keyword Arguments

A *keyword argument* is an argument passed to a function or method which is preceded by a *keyword* and an equals sign. The general form is:

```
function(keyword=value)
```

Where `function` is the function name, `keyword` is the keyword argument and value is the value or object passed as that keyword.

Python's complex function can also accept two keyword arguments. The two keyword arguments are `real=` and `imag=`. To create the complex number 3 + 5j the 3 and 5 can be passed to the function as the values assigned to the keyword arguments `real=` and `imag=`.

```
In [4]: complex(real=3, imag=5)
```

```
Out[4]: (3+5j)
```

Keyword arguments are passed to functions after any required positional arguments. But the order of one keyword argument compared to another keyword argument does not matter. Note how both sections of code below produce the same output.

```
In [5]: complex(real=3, imag=5)
```

7.8. POSITIONAL AND KEYWORD ARGUMENTS

```
Out[5]: (3+5j)

In [6]: complex(imag=5, real=3)

Out[6]: (3+5j)
```

Keyword Arguments Specified by a Dictionary

Keyword arguments can also be passed to functions using a Python dictionary. The dictionary must contain the keywords as keys and the values as values. The general form is:

```
keyword_dict = {'keyword1': value1, 'keyword2': value2}
function(**keyword_dict)
```

Where function is the name of the function and keyword_dict is the name of the dictionary containing keywords and values preceded by the double ampersand ** character. Note that the keywords assigned as keys in a dictionary must be surrounded by quotes ' '. An example of using a dictionary to pass keyword arguments to the complex() function is below:

```
In [7]: keyword_dict = {'real': 3, 'imag': 5}
        complex(**keyword_dict)

Out[7]: (3+5j)
```

7.9 Summary

This chapter introduced user-defined functions. Functions are useful because functions are reusable pieces of code. All functions have names. Some functions take input arguments and produce output. Functions in Python are defined with the keyword `def`. You learned how to create functions with default arguments. You also learned the difference between positional arguments and keyword arguments. Positional arguments must be included in the proper order. Keyword arguments must include the keyword name and an equals sign. You learned how to call functions which are contained in a different file than the file that calls the function. One section of the chapter reviewed how docstrings work in Python functions and the results of calling Python's `help()` on a function that contains a docstring. At the end of the chapter you learned how to pass lists and dictionaries to Python functions.

Key Terms and Concepts

function	keyword	syntax
function definition	output	comments
arguments	docstring	documentation
default arguments	return	iterable
positional arguments	.py-file	
keyword arguments	import	

Python Commands

Command	Description
`def`	define a function
`return`	define the expression or value a function outputs
`import`	import a module or .py file
`from`	import a function or class from a module or .py file
`as`	name an alias for a function, method or class
`""" """`	define a docstring

7.10 Review Questions

User-defined functions

Q07.01 Write a function called `ft_to_in()` which converts feet to inches. Note the conversion factor is 1 foot = 12 inches. Convert 6 feet into inches using your function.

Q07.02 Write a function called `m_to_ft()` which converts meters to feet. Note the conversion factor is 1 meter = 3.28084 feet. Convert 5,000 meters into feet using your function.

7.10. REVIEW QUESTIONS

Q07.03 Use the functions in questions Q07.01 and Q07.02 to convert 2 meters into inches.

Q07.04 Write a function that calculates the area of a circle based on a circle's radius. The formula for the area of a circle is $A = \pi r^2$ where A is area and r is radius. Use your function to calculate the area of circle with a radius of 5.

Q07.05 Write a function that converts degrees Celsius (C) to degrees Fahrenheit (F). The formula to convert between the two temperature scales is $F = \frac{9}{5}C + 32$. Convert 100 degrees C to degrees F using your function.

Q07.06 Write a function that converts Kelvin temperature (K) to degrees Celsius (C). The formula to convert between the two temperature scales is $C = K - 273.15$.

Q07.07 Use the functions in questions Q07.05 and Q07.06 to convert to convert the temperature at Standard Temperature and Pressure (STP) of 273.15K into degrees F.

Q07.08 Use the functions in questions Q07.05 and Q07.06 to convert to convert the temperature at absolute zero, 0K into degrees Celsius and degrees Fahrenheit.

Q07.09 Write a function called `hp_to_kw()` which converts horse power (hp) into kilowatts (kW). Note the conversion factor is $1hp = 0.7457kW$. Convert the horsepower of the average horse, $14.9hp$, into kilowatts (kW).

Q07.10 Write a function called `fun_logic()` that accepts three boolean variables as its input (a, b, and c). The output of `fun_logic()` will be a single boolean variable that is only True when either a is True, or a, b, and c are all False.

Q07.11 Write a function called `pn()` that takes in a single number and outputs a string. If the input number is negative, output the string `'negative'`. If the input number is positive, output `'positive'`. Otherwise, output `'neither'`. Test your function with a negative number, a positive number and 0.

Functions with multiple arguments

Q07.20 Write a function called `cyl_v()` that calculates the volume V of a cylinder based on cylinder height h and cylinder radius r. The formula for the volume of a cylinder is below:

$$V = \pi r^2 h$$

Use your function `cyl_v()` to calculate the volume of a cylinder with height = 2.7 and radius = 0.73.

Q07.21 The universal gas law states that the pressure P, and temperature T of a volume V of gas with number of particles n is related by the equation below, where R is the universal gas constant.

$$PV = nRT$$

Write a function called `gas_v()` to calculate the volume V of a gas based on pressure P, temperature T, number of particles n and universal gas constant R. Use your function to find the volume of gas with the following parameters:

$$T = 273.15$$

$$n = 6.02 \times 10^{23}$$

$$R = 8.314$$

$$P = 101,325$$

Q07.22 Most professional bakers weight their ingredients, while many home bakers use measurements like cups and tablespoons to measure out ingredients. Create a function that takes two arguments: ingredient and cups. The function will output the number of grams of the specified ingredient. For example, a skeleton outline of your function might look like:

```
def bake_conv(ingredient, cups)
    <code>
    return grams
```

Your function needs to accept the following ingredients: 'flour' and 'sugar'. The conversion factor for flour is 1 cup flour = 128 grams flour. The conversion factor for sugar is 1 cup sugar = 200 grams sugar. Use your function to convert a recipe that calls for 3 cups of flour and a quarter cup of sugar.

Q07.23 The gravitational force between two celestial bodies (planets, moons, stars etc) is calculated according to:

$$F_g = \frac{GMm}{r^2}$$

where F_g is the gravitational force, M is the mass of one of the celestial bodies, m is the mass of the other the celestial body, r is the distance between the two celestial bodies and G is the universal gravitational constant. $G = 6.667408 \times 10^{-11} m^3 kg^{-1} s^{-2}$.

(a) Write a function called grav_force() that accepts the mass of two celestial bodies and outputs the gravitational force produced.

Celestial Body	Mass	Distance from sun
Sun	$1.989 \times 10^{30} kg$	0
Earth	$5.98 \times 10^{24} kg$	$149.6 \times 10^9 m$
Mars	$6.42 \times 10^{23} kg$	$228 \times 10^9 m$

(b) Use your function grav_force() and the table above to calculate the gravitational force between the earth and the sun.

(c) Use your function grav_force() and the table above to calculate the gravitational force between the mars and the sun.

Q07.24 Write a function called add3() that takes in 3 numbers and returns their sum. Only a single output variable (the sum of the three numbers) should be returned.

Test your function by writing code beneath the function definition that calls the function with input you create.

7.10. REVIEW QUESTIONS

Q07.25 Write a function called asq() that takes in two variables, A and B. Have asq() output 3 values: the sum, the difference and the quotient of A and B as defined below:

sum = A + B

difference = A - B

quotient = A/B

Your function should accept two input arguments and output three values.

Functions with default arguments

Q07.30 (a) Rewrite the function in problem Q07.20 called gas_v() with the default values $n = 6.02 \times 10^{23}$, $R = 8.314$ and $P = 101,325$.

(a) Use your modified function gas_v() to calculate the volume of a gas at $T = 500K$ using the default arguments.

(b) Use your modified function gas_v() to calculate the volume of a gas at $T = 500K$, under half the pressure $p = 101,325/2$.

Q07.31 In engineering mechanics, the tensile stress σ applied to a solid cylinder is equal to the tensile force on the cylinder F divided by the cylinder's cross sectional area A according to the formula below:

$$\sigma = \frac{F}{A}$$

The standard diameter d of a cylinder pulled in tension in a tensile test using the ASTM D8 standard is $d = 0.506$ inches.

$$A = \pi(d/2)^2$$

Use the formula for stress σ and area A above to write a function called stress() that calculates stress σ based on force F and diameter d. Use $d = 0.506$ as the default diameter, but allow the user to specify a different diameter if they want.

Use your stress() function to calculate the tensile stress σ in a cylinder with the default diameter and a tensile force $F = 12,000$.

Q07.32 One way to calculate how much an investment will be worth is to use the Future Value formula:

$$FV = I_0(1+r)^n$$

Where FV is the future value, I_0 is the initial investment, r is the yearly rate of return, and n is the number of years you plan to invest.

(a) Write a function called future_value() which accepts an initial investment I_0 and a number of years n and calculates the future value FV. Include $r = 0.05$ as the default yearly rate of return.

(b) Use your `future_value()` function to calculate the future value of an initial investment of 2000 dollars over 30 years with the default yearly rate of return

(c) Use your `future_value()` function to calculate the future value of the same initial investment of 2000 dollars over 30 years, but a rate of return of 8% (0.08).

(d) Use your `future_value()` function to determine when 2000 dollars is invested over 30 years, how much more do you make if the rate of return is 10% (0.10) instead of 5% (0.05).

Q07.33 Write a function called `s()` that takes in 3 variables, a, b, and c. Have your function `s()` output the sum of a, b and c. If no value is passed in for c, set c to the default value of 100.

Nested Functions

Q07.36 In mechanical engineering, there are a couple different units of *stress*. Units of stress include: Pascals (*Pa*), Mega Pascals (*MPa*), pounds per square inch (*psi*) and kilopounds per square inch (*ksi*).

(a) Write a function called `pa_to_mpa` to convert between Pascals (*Pa*) and Mega Pascals (*MPa*). The conversion factor is $1 MPa = 10^6 Pa$

(b) Write a function called `mpa_to_ksi` to convert between Mega Pascals (*MPa*) and kilopounds per square inch (*ksi*). The conversion factor is $1 ksi = 6.89476 MPa$

(c) Write a function called `ksi_to_psi` to convert between kilopounds per square inch (*ksi*) and pounds per square inch (*psi*). The conversion factor is $1000 psi = 1 ksi$

(d) Combine the three functions `pa_to_mpa`, `mpa_to_ksi`, `ksi_to_psi` into a single function `pa_to_psi`. Do this by calling the other functions as part of the `pa_to_psi` function, not by rewriting the same code you wrote in parts (a), (b), and (c).

(e) Convert 2,500 *Pa* into *psi* using your `pa_to_psi` function.

Functions in other files

Q07.40 Create a separate *.py* file called *greetings.py*. Inside of *greetings.py* include the code:

```
def hi():
    print("Hi!")
```

Import your newly created *greatings.py* file and run the function `hi()`.

Q07.41 Create a separate *.py* file called *greetings.py*. Inside of *greetings.py* include the code:

```
def hello(name):
    print("Hello " + name)
```

Import your newly created *greatings.py* file and run the function `hello()` with your name as an input argument.

Q07.42 Create a separate file *.py* file called *areas.py*. Inside of *areas.py* include the code:

7.10. REVIEW QUESTIONS

```
def triangle(base,height):
    area = 0.5*base*height
    print("Triangle Area: ", area)


def rectangle(length, width):
    area = length* width
    print("Rectangle Area: ", area)
```

Import your newly created *areas.py* file and run the functions `triangle()` and `rectangle()` with the same two input arguments: 2 and 3.

Errors, Explanations, and Solutions

For the sections of code below, run the lines of code. Then explain the error in your own words. Below your error explanation, rewrite and run an improved section of code that fixes the error.

Q07.80 Run the code below and explain the error. Rewrite the code and run it error free.

```
def add_me(num)
    return num + 2

add_me(1)
```

Q07.81 Run the code below and explain the error. Rewrite the code and run it error free.

```
def add_you[num]:
    return num + 2

add_you(2)
```

Q07.82 Run the code below and explain the error. Rewrite the code and run it error free.

```
def my_func():
    print('yup')

my_func('yup')
```

Q07.83 Run the code below and explain the error. Rewrite the code and run it error free.

```
def nothing():

nothing()
```

Q07.84 Run the code below and explain the error. Rewrite the code and run it error free.

```
def plus(2+2):
    return 4

nothing()
```

Q07.85 Run the code below and explain the error. Rewrite the code and run it error free.

```
def first_a(a):
    return a[0]

first_a(1)
```

Chapter 8

If Else Try Except

8.1 Introduction

In computer programming, selection structures run sections of code based on logical conditions. In this chapter you will learn about the selections structures if, else, and else if. The end of the chapter introduces another selection structure, the try / except block.

By the end of this chapter you will be able to:

- Utilize Python's input() function
- Use if, else if, and else selection structures
- Explain the difference between syntax errors and exception errors
- Use try-except statements
- Construct flowcharts to describe the flow of a Python program

8.2 User Input

To begin this chapter, Python's `input()` function is discussed.

Python can be used to ask users for input. The input entered by a user can be saved to a variable and used in subsequent parts of the program. The syntax of Python's `input()` function is below:

```
var = input('message')
```

Where `var` is the variable that stores the user's input and `'message'` is the message the user sees at the prompt. A string enclosed in quotes, like `'message'`, needs to be passed as an input argument to the `input()` function. Let's ask a user for their age:

```
In [1]: age = input('how old are you? ')

how old are you? 9
```

Since the user's input is assigned to a variable, further operations can be run on it. Now, let's print the user's age back to them. This can be accomplished with an f-string. Note the `f' '` inserted before the string. A set of curly braces `{ }` surrounds the variable's name and the variable's value is printed back to the user.

```
In [2]: age = input('how old are you? ')
        print(f'you are {age} years old')

how old are you? 9
you are 9 years old
```

Let's try another example. We will we ask the user for the base and height of a triangle and print out the area of the triangle.

But, there is a problem with the approach below. The code block does not run because a common error is present.

```
In [3]: b = input('base of triangle: ')
        h = input('height of triangle: ')
        A = (1/2)*b*h
        print(f'The area of the triangle is: {A}')

base of triangle: 5
height of triangle: 2
```

```
TypeError                                 Traceback (most recent call last)
```

8.3. SELECTION STATEMENTS

```
        <ipython-input-3-c9cb8f02e604> in <module>
          1 b = input('base of triangle: ')
          2 h = input('height of triangle: ')
    ----> 3 A = (1/2)*b*h
          4 print(f'The area of the triangle is: {A}')


        TypeError: can't multiply sequence by non-int of type 'float'
```

The previous section of code returns an error because of the *data type* of the variables b and h. We can investigate b and h's data type with Python's type() function.

```
In [4]: b = input('base of triangle: ')
        h = input('height of triangle: ')
        print(f'b and h are of type: {type(b)}, {type(h)}')

base of triangle: 5
height of triangle: 2
b and h are of type: <class 'str'>, <class 'str'>
```

Notice both b and h are strings, even though the numbers 5 and 2 were entered as input. The output of the input() function is always a string, even if the user enters a number.

To complete the area calculation, b and h first need to be converted to floats using Python's float() function, then the mathematical operation will run without error:

```
In [5]: b = input('base of triangle: ')
        h = input('height of triangle: ')
        A = (1/2)*float(b)*float(h)
        print(f'The area of the triangle is: {A}')

base of triangle: 5
height of triangle: 2
The area of the triangle is: 5.0
```

Now that you are familiar with Python's input() function, let's utilize a user's input to decide which lines of code will run. The concept of an selection statement is introduced the next section.

8.3 Selection Statements

Selection statements are used in programming to select particular blocks of code to run based on a logical condition. The primary selection statements in Python are:

- if

- else
- elif
- try
- except

So far in this text, all of the Python code has either been strictly linear or linear and include functions. A strictly linear program is a program that runs top to bottom. Every line of code in a linear program is executed. In a linear program with functions, the program still runs head to base, but the program takes side excursions to execute functions on the way down.

If this next couple chapters, you learn to write programs non-linearly. Non-linear programs do not run every line of code top to bottom. In non-linear programs, sections of code may not run based on selection statements like *if* and *try*. Non-linear programs can include loops. Inside loops are sections of code that run multiple times. Loops are defined by repetition structures like *for loops* and *while loops*.

To start our discussion of non-linear programs, we will begin with *if statements*.

8.4 If statements

The *if-statement* is one of the basic selection structures in Python. The syntax for a section of code that contains an if-statement is below:

```
if <logical_condition>:
    <code to run>
```

The keyword `if` begins the statement. Following `if`, a logical condition must to be included. A logical condition is an variable or expression that can be evaluated as `True` or `False`. An example of a logical condition is a<5. The logical condition a<5 returns `True` if a is less than 5. Otherwise, if a is 5 or greater a<5 returns `False`. Following the logical condition, a colon : is required. After the if-statement, a section of code to run when the condition is `True` is included. The section of `<code to run>` must be indented and every line in this section of code must be indented the same number of spaces. By convention, four space indentation is used in Python. Most Python code editors, including Jupyter notebooks, indent code after if-statements automatically four spaces.

The section of code below demonstrates an if-statement in Python:

```
In [1]: a = 2
        if a<5:
            print('less than five')

less than five
```

In the first line of code in the example above, the variable a is assigned the value 2. The second line of code is the if-statement. The if-statement starts with the keyword `if` and is followed by the logical condition a<5 and a colon :. The logical condition a<5 will return either `True` or `False` depending on the value of a. Since a=2, the logical condition a<5 evaluates as `True`. The line print('less than five') is indented after the if-statement. The line of code including the

8.4. IF STATEMENTS

`print()` statement will run if the if-statement is True. Since the if-statement *is* True, the indented line `print('less than five')` runs.

As a result of running these three lines of code, the user sees the text `less than five`.

Multiple if statements

If-statements can be chained together one after another to create a programmatic flow. For example, the following code block utilizes three different if-statements, each if-statement is followed by an indented code block.

```
In [2]: a = 2
        if a<0:
            print('is negative')
        if a == 0:
            print('is zero')
        if a>0:
            print('is positive')

is positive
```

Note how each if-statement is followed by a logical condition and a colon :. Also, note how the code below each if-statement is indented. If the code is left-justified (not indented), all three code lines run, and the output is different.

The code block below will not run unless at least one line of code is indented after the if-statement. Python's pass keyword is a line of code that does nothing when executed. pass is added under the if-statments so the code runs error-free.

```
In [3]: a = 2
        if a<0:
            pass
        print('a is negative')
        if a == 0:
            pass
        print('a is zero')
        if a>0:
            pass
        print('a is positive')

a is negative
a is zero
a is positive
```

8.5 If Else Statements

In Python, if-statements can include *else* clauses. An else clause is a section of code that runs if the if-statement is `False`. If the if-statement is `True`, the code section under the else clause does not run.

The general form of an if-statement with an else statement is below:

```
if <logical_condition>:
    <code block 1>
else:
    <code block 2>
```

The keyword `else` needs to be on its own line and be at the same indentation level as the `if` keyword that the `else` corresponds to. The keyword `else` needs to be followed by a colon :. Any code that is included as part of the else statement must be indented the same amount.

A sample if/else code section is below:

```
In [1]: a = 5
        if a>10:
            print('a is greater than 10')
        else:
            print('a is less than 10')

a is less than 10
```

Since a=5 assigns a value to a that is less than 10, a>10 is `False` and the code under the `if` statement does not run. Therefore, the code under the `else` statement does run, and "a is less than 10" is printed.

If the value of a is modified so that a is greater than 10, a>10 returns `True`, and the code under the if statement *will* run, and the code under the `else` keyword *will not*.

```
In [2]: a = 20
        if a>10:
            print('a is greater than 10')
        else:
            print('a is less than 10')

a is greater than 10
```

elif

The *else if* statement can be added to an if statement to run different sections of code depending on which one of many conditions are `True`. The basic syntax of an else if section of code is:

8.6. TRY-EXCEPT STATEMENTS

```
if <logical_condition>:
    <code block 1>
elif <logical_condition>:
    <code block 2>
else:
    <code block 3>
```

The keyword `elif` must be followed by a logical condition that evaluates as `True` or `False` followed by a colon `:`. The `<code block>` runs if the `elif` condition is `True` and is skipped if the `elif` condition is `False`.

An example section of code using `if`, `elif` and `else` is below:

```
In [3]: color = 'green'
        if color == 'red':
            print('The color is red')
        elif color == 'green':
            print('The color is green')
        else:
            print('The color is not red or green')

The color is green
```

If we modify the code and set `color = 'orange'`, the code under the `if` does not run, and the code under the `elif` does not run either. Only the code under the `else` is executed.

```
In [4]: color = 'orange'
        if color == 'red':
            print('The color is red')
        elif color == 'green':
            print('The color is green')
        else:
            print('The color is not red or green')

The color is not red or green
```

8.6 Try-Except Statements

Try-except statements are another selection structure in Python. Like `if`, `elif` and `else` statements, a try-except statements select a particular block of code to run based on a condition. Unlike `if`, `elif` and `else` clauses, try-except blocks are not based on *logical conditions*. Try-except blocks are based upon whether a line or section of code returns an error.

Therefore, before we learn how to use try-except statements, we need to understand two types of errors in Python: syntax errors and exception errors.

Syntax Errors

A *syntax error* is a type of error in Python that occur when the syntax in a line of code is not valid Python code. Syntax errors include quotes that are not closed and variable names that do not start with a letter.

The line of code below contains a syntax error. The string `"problem solving` is missing a quotation mark ".

```
In [1]: string = "problem solving
```

```
  File "<ipython-input-1-4c037f6284bc>", line 1
    string = "problem solving
                             ^
SyntaxError: EOL while scanning string literal
```

When you encounter syntax errors in Python, the Python interpreter displays `SyntaxError` and often a cryptic message.

Even if a line of code does not run when a program is executed, syntax errors in Python are not allowed. For instance, a line of code indented after the if-statement `if 'a' == 'b':` will not be executed. But if the indented line of code contains a syntax error, the Python interpreter still flags the error as a syntax error and does not complete the program.

```
In [2]: if 'a' == 'b':
            string = 10problems
```

```
  File "<ipython-input-2-532ae1edb2a2>", line 2
    string = 10problems
                 ^
SyntaxError: invalid syntax
```

Exception Errors

Syntax errors are lines of code that are not valid Python. Another type of error in Python is an *exception error*. Exception errors result when a *valid* line of Python code *cannot run*. Lines of code with exception errors contain *valid* Python code, but the line of code still cannot be executed.

For example, the statement `f = open('file.txt','r')` is valid Python code. But if the file *file.txt* does not exist, Python throws an exception error because `f = open('file.txt','r')` cannot be executed.

```
In [3]: f = open('file.txt','r')
```

8.6. TRY-EXCEPT STATEMENTS

```
-------------------------------------------------------------------
FileNotFoundError                        Traceback (most recent call last)
<ipython-input-3-cc3c27f5a0c3> in <module>
----> 1 f = open('file.txt','r')


FileNotFoundError: [Errno 2] No such file or directory: 'file.txt'
```

Another valid line of Python code is print(a[0]), but if a is defined as an integer, a can not be indexed and an exception error is shown.

```
In [4]: a = 1
        print(a[5])
```

```
-------------------------------------------------------------------
TypeError                                Traceback (most recent call last)
<ipython-input-4-0e1fa8aeb4c3> in <module>
      1 a = 1
----> 2 print(a[5])


TypeError: 'int' object is not subscriptable
```

Try except statements can be used to try to run sections of Python code that *may* return an exception error. The general syntax of a try except statement is below:

```
try:
    <code to try>
except:
    <code to run instead>
```

For instance, if the file *file.txt* does not exist, a line of code that tries to open *file.txt* can be included in a try statement.

```
In [5]: try:
            f=open('file.txt','r')
        except:
            print('file does not exist')

file does not exist
```

Similarly, we can wrap the code `a = 5` and `print(a[0])` in a try block and attempt to run it. If the line `a = 5` and `print(a[0])` throws an exception error, the code below `except` runs.

```
In [6]: try:
            a = 5
            print(a[0])
        except:
            print('variable a is not a list')
```

variable a is not a list

When the Python code in a try block does run and does not throw an exception error, the code in the `except` block does not run.

```
In [7]: try:
            a = 'Solution'
            print(a[0])
        except:
            print('variable a is not a list')
```

S

8.7 Flowcharts

Flowcharts graphically represent the flow of a program. There are four basic shapes used in a flow chart. Each shape has a specific use:

- oval: start / end
- parallelogram: input / output
- rectangle: calculations
- diamond: selection structures

Arrows connect the basic shapes in a flowchart. The shapes and arrows of a flowchart describe the flow of a program from start to end. Flowcharts typically flow from the top to the bottom or flow from the left to the right.

Below is the description of a simple program:

> The program starts. Then the program prints out "Output!". Finally, the program ends.

A flowchart that describes this simple program is shown.

The Python code that corresponds to this flowchart is:

```
# start
print("Output!")
# end
```

8.7. FLOWCHARTS

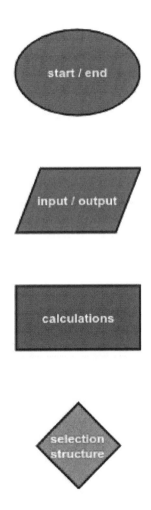

Figure 8.1. Four basic flow chart shapes: oval, parallelogram, rectangle and diamond

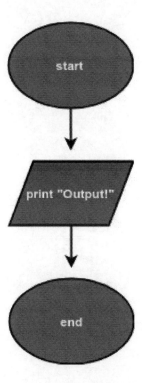

Figure 8.2. Flow chart of a simple print program

8.7. FLOWCHARTS

A description of a program that includes a calculation is below:

> The program starts. Next, the program asks a user for a number. Two is added to the number. Next, the resulting sum is printed. Finally, the program ends.

A flowchart that describes this program is is shown.

The Python code that corresponds to this flow chart is:

```
# start
num = input("Enter a number: ")
num = float(num)
num_plus_2 = num + 2
print(num_plus_2)
# end
```

The description of another program is below:

> The program starts. Next the program asks a user for a number. If the number is greater than zero, the program prints "Greater than 0", then the program ends.

A flow chart that describes this program is shown.

The Python code that corresponds to this flow chart is:

```
# start
num = input("Enter a number: ")
num = float(num)
if num > 0:
    print("Greater than 0")
# end
```

The description of a more complex program is below:

> The program starts. Next, the program asks a user for a number. If the number is greater than zero, the program prints "Greater than 0". If the number is less than zero, the program prints "Less than 0". Then the program prints "Done" and the program ends.

A flowchart that describes this program is below:

The Python code that corresponds to this flow chart is:

```
# start
num = input('Enter a number: ')
num = float(num)
if num > 0:
    print('num greater than zero')
if num < 0:
    print('num less than zero')
print('Done')
# end
```

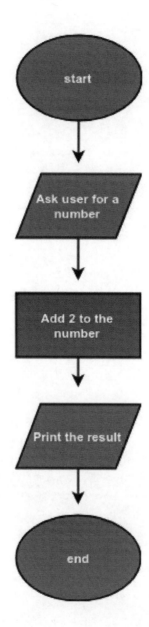

Figure 8.3. Flowchart of a program that includes input, output and a calculation

8.7. FLOWCHARTS

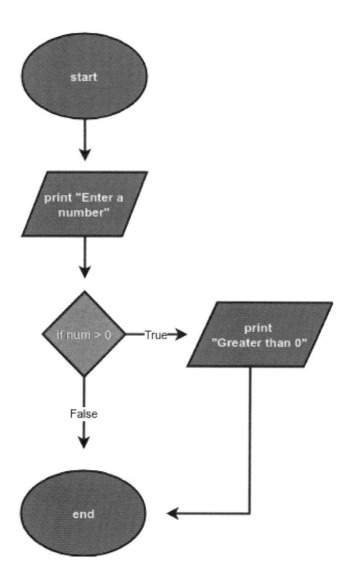

Figure 8.4. Flow chart of a program that contains user input and a selection structure

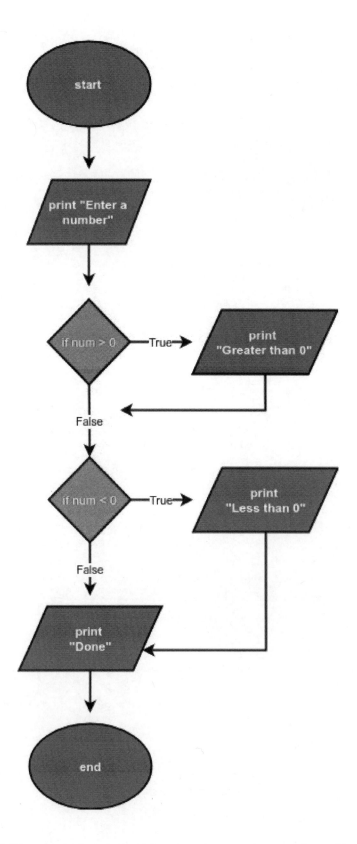

Figure 8.5. Flowchart of a program that contains user input and two if-statements

8.8 Summary

Selection structures in Python include `if`, `elif`, `else`, `try` and `except`. These selection structures allow certain blocks of code to run or not run based on logical conditions. Logical conditions are expressions or variables that can be evaluated as `True` or `False`. You learned to indent code segments after `if`, `elif`, and `else` statements. Standard indentation in Python is four spaces.

The difference between syntax errors and exception errors was demonstrated in this chapter. `try`/`except` blocks only check for exception errors.

At the end of the chapter, you learned how to use flowcharts to describe the flow of a program with four basic shapes and arrows.

Key Terms and Concepts

selection structures	pass	valid code
if	else	exception error
logical condition	else if	try
True	elif	except
False	exceptions	flow chart
programmatic flow	syntax	
indentation	syntax error	

8.9 Review Questions

Q08.01 Create a program to ask a user for a temperature. If the temperature the user enters is below 50, print back the user "It is cold outside". Hint: remember to convert the user's input to a number before comparing the user's input to 50.

Q08.02 Create a program that asks the user for their temperature. If the user enters a temperature above 98.6, print back to the user "You have a fever".

Q08.03 Create a program that chooses a random number number between 1 and 5. Ask the user for a number between 1 and 5. Compare the user's number to the random number. If the user guessed the random number print "you guessed it!", if the user did not guess the random number print back to the user "try again". You can use the code below to choose a random number n between 1 and 5.

```
import random

n = random.randint(0,5)
```

Q08.04 Create a program that asks a user for two numbers, x and y. If the x is greater than y, print back to the user "x>y". If x is less than y, print back to the user "x<y". If x is equal to y, print back to the user "x=y".

Q08.05 Create a program that asks a user for one of three trig functions: sine, cosine or tangent. Calculate the sine, cosine or tangent of $\pi/4$ depending on the user's input and print the result of the calculation back to the user.

Q08.06 Create a program that asks the user for two numbers (use two different input lines). If the second number the user enters is zero, print back to the user "can't divide by zero", otherwise divide the user's first number by the user's second number and print the result to the user.

Q08.07 The table below shows a couple fruits and their associated color

fruit	color
banana	yellow
apple	red
lemon	yellow
lime	green
orange	orange

Create a program that asks a user to choose from a list of fruit. Print back to the user the color of the fruit they chose.

Q08.08 The average size of a US congressional district is about 700,000 people. Ask the user for a state population and print back to the user the number of congress members in the state. For example, a state with 1.4 million people is represented by 2 members of congress. Each state has at least one member of congress by default. If the user enters a population less than $700,000$, tell the user their state only has 1 member of congress.

Q08.09 In a college engineering class, final grades are related to percentages as follows:

percentage range	grade
90 - 100	A
80 - 89	B
70 - 79	C
65 - 69	D
0 - 64	F

Build a program that asks a user for a final score (in percent) and prints back to the user their letter grade.

Q08.10 Write a function called r() that takes in a single variable x (a numeric value) and outputs a single variable y (a numeric value). y should be 1 of 3 values (1, 2, or 3) depending on which range x is in.

range 1: x is less than -10

range 2: x is equal to or greater than -10 and less than 200

range 3: x is 200 or greater

8.9. REVIEW QUESTIONS

Errors, Explanations, and Solutions

Run the following code snippets. Explain the error in your own words. Then rewrite the code snippet and run the code error-free.

Q08.80
```
a = 1
if a = 0:
    print('zero')
else if a = 1:
    print('one')
```

Q08.81
```
a = 1
if a == 0:
    print('zero')

else print('one')
```

Q08.82
```
n = input('Enter a number')

if n > 0:
    print('positive')
```

Chapter 9

Loops

9.1 Introduction

Repetition structures allow the same piece of code to run multiple times. Two repetion structures in Python are for loops and while loops. For loops run a set number of times. While loops run as long as a specific logical condition is true.

By the end of this chapter you will be able to:

- use a while loop
- use a for loop
- use the break statement
- use the continue statement
- construct flowcharts that describe programs with loops

9.2 For Loops

In this chapter, you will learn about two kinds of *repetition structures* in Python: *for loops* and *while loops*. This section describes for loops.

For Loops are a component of many programming languages. A *for loop* is a repetition structure where a section of code runs a specified number of times.

Say we want to print out the statements:

```
Problem solving in teams
Problem solving in teams
Problem solving in teams
```

One way to accomplish this task is by coding three print statements in a row:

```
In [1]: print('Problem solving in teams')
        print('Problem solving in teams')
        print('Problem solving in teams')
```

Another way to accomplish the same task is to use a for loop. The basic structure of a for loop in Python is below:

```
for <var> in range(<num>):
    <code>
```

Where `<var>` can be any variable, `range(<num>)` is the number of times the for loop runs and `<code>` are the lines of code that execute each time the for loop runs.

Note the for loop starts with the keyword `for` and includes a colon `:`. Both `for` and the colon `:` are required. Also, note `<code>` is indented. Each line of code that runs as part of the for loop needs to be indented the same number of spaces. Standard indentation in Python is four spaces.

The example above can be rewritten using a for loop:

```
In [2]: for i in range(3):
            print('Problem solving in teams')
```

Python's `range()` function

Python's `range()` function returns an iterable list of values starting at zero and ending at n-1. For example, when `range(3)` is called, the values 0, 1, 2 are returned. 3 is not part of the output, even though the function input was `range(3)`. We can be confirm the behavior of `range()` with a for loop:

```
In [3]: for i in range(3):
            print(i)
```

Remember Python counting starts at 0 and ends at n-1.

9.2. FOR LOOPS

Customizing range()

Python's range() function can be customized by supplying up to three arguments. The general format of the range function is below:

```
range(start,stop,step)
```

When range(3) is called, it produces the same output as range(0,3,1) (start=0,stop=3,step=1). Remember Python counting starts at 0 and ends at n-1. If only two arguments are supplied, as in range(0,3), a step=1 is assumed.

The table below includes examples of the Python's range() function and the associated output.

range() function	output
range(3)	0, 1, 2
range(0,3)	0, 1, 2
range(0,3,1)	0, 1, 2
range(2,7,2)	2, 4, 6
range(0,-5,-1)	0, -1, -2, -3, -4
range(2,-3,1)	(no output)

A code section that uses a for loop and range() with three arguments is below:

```
In [4]: for i in range(5,9,1):
            print(i)
```

For loops with lists

For loops can also be run using Python lists. If a list is used, the loop will run as many times as there are items in the list. The general syntax is:

```
for <var> in <list>:
    <code>
```

Where <var> is a variable name assigned to the item in the list and <list> is the list object. Remember to include a colon : after the list. <code> is the programming code that runs for each item in the list.

An example of a list in a for loop is below:

```
In [5]: my_list = ['electrical','civil','mechanical']
        for item in my_list:
            print(item)
```

The loop ran three times because there are three items in my_list. Each time through the loop, the variable item is set to one of the items in the list.

- first time through the loop, item='electrical'
- second time through the loop item='mechanical'
- third time through the loop item='civil'.

For loops with strings

For loops can also be run using strings. In Python, strings can be indexed just like lists. A loop defined by a string runs as many times as there are characters in the string. The general structure a for loop using a string is:

```
for <char> in <string>:
    <code>
```

Where `<char>` is one of the characters in the string `<string>`. Just like for loops with `range()` and for loops with lists, make sure to include a colon : after the list. `<code>` is the programming code that runs for each character in the string. `<code>` needs to be indented

An example of a string in a for loop is below:

```
In [6]: for letter in "Gabby":
            print(f"looping over letters in name: {letter}")

looping over letters in name: G
looping over letters in name: a
looping over letters in name: b
looping over letters in name: b
looping over letters in name: y
```

9.3 While Loops

A *while loop* is a type of loop that runs as long as a logical condition is `True`. When the logical condition becomes `False`, the loop stops running. The general form of a while loop in Python is below:

```
while <logical_condition>:
    <code>
```

The keyword `while` must be included, as well as a `<logical_condition>` which can be evaluated as True or False. The `<code>` after the while statement must be indented. Each line of code runs in the while loop needs to be indented the same number of spaces. (Many code editors, including Jupyter notebooks, auto-indent after a `while` statement) If you add indentation manually, four space spaces is the Python standard.

An example of a while loop is below:

```
In [1]: i = 0
        while i<4:
            print(i)
            i = i+1
```

The first line `i=0` creates the variable `i` and assigns it the value 0. The next line declares the logical condition needed to keep the loop running. The statement `i<4` is `True` or `False` depending on the variable `i`. Since `i=0`, the statement `i<4` is `True` and the while loop starts to run. The code inside while the loop prints the value of `i` then increases `i` by 1. When `i=4`, the statement `i<4` is `False` and the while loop ends.

Using a while loop to validate user input

While loops can be used to validate user input. Say you want to insist that a user inputs positive number. You can code this into a while loop that keeps repeating `'Enter a positive number: '` until the user enters valid input.

The code below continues to ask a user for a positive number until a positive number is entered.

```
In [ ]: num_input = -1
        while num_input < 0:
            str_input = input('Enter a positive number: ')
            num_input = float(str_input)
```

In the section of code above, it is important to initialize the variable `num_input` with a value that causes the statement `num_input < 0` to evaluate as `True`. `num_input = -1` causes the statement `num_input < 0` to evaluate as `True`. Besides `num_input = -1`, any other negative number would have worked.

If the while statement can't be evaluated as `True` or `False`, Python throws an error. Therefore, it is necessary to convert the user's input from a string to a float. The statement `'5' < 0` does not evaluate to `True` or `False`, because the string `'5'` can't be compared to the number 0.

9.4 Break and Continue

Break and *continue* are two ways to modify the behavior of for loops and while loops.

Break

In Python, the keyword `break` causes the program to exit a loop early. `break` causes the program to jump out of for loops even if the for loop hasn't run the specified number of times. `break` causes the program to jump out of while loops even if the logical condition that defines the loop is still `True`.

An example using `break` in a for loop is below.

```
In [1]: for i in range(100):
            print(i)
            if i == 3:
                break
        print('Loop exited')
```

When the loop hits `i=3`, `break` is encountered and the program exits the loop.

An example using `break` in a while loop is below.

```
In [ ]: while True:
            out = input('type q to exit the loop: ')
            if out == 'q':
                break
        print('Loop exited')
```

Continue

In Python, the keyword continue causes the program to stop running code in a loop and start back at the top of the loop. Remember the keyword break cause the program to *exit* a loop. continue is similar, but continue causes the program to stop the *current iteration* of the loop and *start the next iteration at the top* of the loop.

A code section that uses continue in a for loop is below.

```
In [ ]: for i in range(4):
            if i==2:
                continue
            print(i)
```

When the code section is run, the number 2 is not printed. This is because when i=2 the program hits the continue statement. Therefore, the line print(i) isn't run when i=2. Then the program starts back up at the start of the loop with the next number i=3.

9.5 Flowcharts Describing Loops

Flowcharts show the flow of a program graphically. Flow charts were introduced in the previous chapter to describe how a programs that include *if* statements are illustrated graphically.

This chapter is about *loops*. Flowcharts can also be used to describe programs which contain *for loops* and *while loops*.

Basic Flow Chart Shapes

Let's review the four basic flowchart shapes. Each shape represents a different type of operation.

- oval: start and end
- parallelogram: input and output
- rectangle: calculations
- diamond: selection structures

The basic shapes in a flowchart are connected by arrows. The shapes and arrows in a flowchart represent the flow of a program from start to end.

Flowchart of a program that contains a for loop

Below is the description of a program that can be coded with a for loop:

> The program starts. The program prints the word "looping" 10 times. Finally, the program ends.

A flowchart that describes this program is shown.

The Python code that corresponds to this flowchart is below:

9.5. FLOWCHARTS DESCRIBING LOOPS

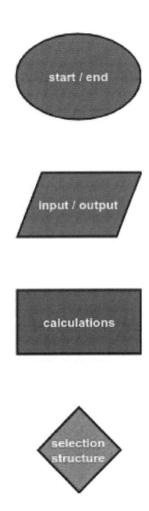

Figure 9.1. Four the four flowchart shapes: oval, parallelogram, rectangle, and diamond

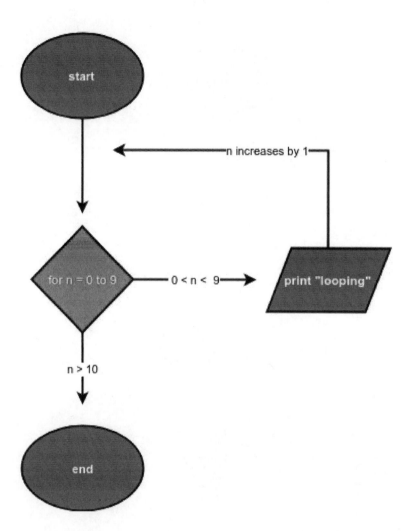

Figure 9.2. Flowchart of a program that contains a for loop

9.5. FLOWCHARTS DESCRIBING LOOPS

```
# start
for i in range(10):
    print("looping")
# end
```

Flowchart of a program that contains a while loop

Below is the description of a program which can be coded with a while loop:

> The program starts. The program asks the user for a positive number. If the number is negative, the program asks the user for a positive number again. If the number is positive, the program prints "positive". Finally, the program ends.

A flowchart that describes this program is shown.

The Python code that corresponds to this flow chart is:

```
# start
num = -1
while num < 0:
    num = input("Enter a positive number: ")
    num = float(num)
print("positive")
# end
```

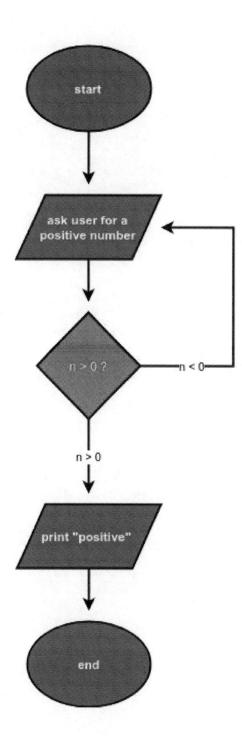

Figure 9.3. Flow chart of a program that contains a for loop

9.6 Summary

Repetition structures allow the same piece of code to run multiple times.

In this chapter, you learned how to write for loops and while loops in Python. For loops run a block of code a definite number of times. You learned how to use Python's range() function in a for loops and how to use a list or string in a for loop. A while loop runs a block of code as long as a logical condition is true. The keywords break and continue cause for and while loops to exit early.

At the end of the chapter, you learned how to build flowcharts that describe programs with for loops and while loops.

Key Terms and Concpets

repetition structure	for loop	continue
loop	iterate	infinite loop
while loop	break	flowchart

9.7 Review Questions

For Loops

Q09.01 Create a for loops to print out the numbers 1 to 10.

Q09.02 Create a for loop to print out the number -1 to -10 starting at -1 and ending at -10.

Q09.03 Create a for loop to print out all the letters in the word `'love'`

Q09.04 Use a for loop to sum the elements in the list [1,3,5,8,12]. Print the sum to the user.

Q09.05 The first 10 terms of the Fibonacci sequence are below:

$$1, 1, 2, 3, 5, 8, 13, 21, 34, 55 \ldots$$

Create the Fibonacci sequence using a for loop. Print out the first 20 terms of the Fibonacci sequence on one line.

Q09.06 This problem is about *Fizz Buzz*, a programming task that is sometimes used in interviews.

(a) Use a for loop to print out the numbers 1 to 30

(b) Use a for loop to print out all the numbers 1 to 30, but leave out any number which is divisible by 3, such as 3, 6 and 9.

(c) Use a for loop to print out all the numbers 1 to 30, but leave out any number which is divisible by 5, such as 5, 10 and 15.

(d) Use a for loop to print out all the numbers 1 to 30, but insert the word `fizz` for any number that is divisible by 3, insert the word `buzz` for any number that is divisible by 5 and insert the word `fizz buzz` for any numbers that are both divisible by 3 and 5, like 15.

Q09.07 Imagine you can see the future of investing and over the next four years, the interest rate of return on investments is going to be 0.02, 0.03, 0.015, 0.06. Prompt the user for an initial investment with Python's input(_) function and use the formula below to calculate how much the investment will be worth after four years.

new balance = old balance + old balance × interest rate

Note the first "old balance" is the person's initial investment.

Q09.08 A geometric series is a series that has a common ratio between the terms. The sum of the geometric series that starts at $\frac{1}{2}$ and has a common ratio of $\frac{1}{2}$ approaches the value 1.

The formula that shows the sum of a geometric series which approaches 1 is below.

$$1 = \frac{1}{2} + \frac{1}{4} + \frac{1}{8} + \frac{1}{16} + ...$$

Use the geometric series above to approximate the value of 1 after 10 terms are added. Print out how far off the geometric series approximation is to 1.

Q09.09 A Taylor Series is an infinite series of mathematical terms when summed together approximate a mathematical function. A Taylor Series can be used to approximate the mathematical functions e^x, *sine*, and *cosine*.

Taylor Series expansion for the function e^x is below:

$$e^x = \sum_{n=0}^{\infty} \frac{x^n}{n!} = 1 + x + \frac{x^2}{2!} + \frac{x^3}{3!} + \frac{x^4}{4!} + ...$$

Write a program that asks a user for a number x, then calculates e^x using the Taylor Series expansion. Calculate 20 terms.

Q09.10 Write a function called lt100() that accepts 1 variable as input: a 1D NumPy array. The output of lt100() will be a single 1D NumPy array.

Use a for loop to go through the input NumPy array 1 element at a time starting with element 0 going upward. If the element's value is less than 100, put the element into the output 1D NumPy array. If a value of nan (Python's not a number) is encountered, stop adding elements to the output variable, but do not raise an exception. If nan appears in the first element, the function should return an empty 1D NumPy array, not the None object.

Researching the numpy.append() function will help. Use np.nan for testing your code with a nan value.

Q09.11 Write a function called get_bigger() that accepts two 1D NumPy arrays for input: A and B. A and B will contain the same number of elements. Use a for loop to iterate through both A and B one element at a time. If A's current element is greater than B's, put A's element into the output 1D NumPy array variable C. Otherwise, put the sum of the 2 elements into C. C will have the same number of elements as both A and B.

For example, if A contains [5, -10, 1] and B contains [2, -10, 8], then C should contain [5, -20, 9].

Q09.12 Write a function called str_add() that accepts 1 variable as its input: a list of strings. Use a for loop to add the character 'G' to the end of each string in the list. Return the list of altered strings as the only output.

9.7. REVIEW QUESTIONS

For example, if the list ['hello', 'bye'] was passed into your function, the output should be ['helloG', 'byeG'].

Q09.13 Write a loop that prints out your name 20 times. Each time your name is printed, it should be on a new line.

Q09.14 Write a loops that prints out "around and" 20 times. Each time "around and" is printed, it should be on the same line. As in around and around and around and around and around ....

Q09.15 The Appendix contains a section on ASCII character codes. Use code similar to the code shown in the Appendix to print out the ASCII character code and resulting character for just the letters a to z, A to Z, and 0 to 9.

Q09.16 Use a for loop to print out the days of the week. Print each day of the week on its own line.

Q09.17 Use a for loop to print out the spelling of the word mississippi with one letter on each line.

Q09.18 An employee starts with an annual salary of 58 thousand dollars. Print out the employees salary each year for five years if the employee receives a 2.5 percent (0.02) raise each year.

Q09.19 The factorial function is the product of integers between 1 and n. The formula for factorial is below:

$$n! = 1 \times 2 \times 3 \times 4 \times 5 \times \ldots \times n$$

Write a Python function that contains a for loop to find 5 factorial (5!) and 20 factorial (20!)

Q09.20 Create a for loop that prints out all of the even numbers between 1 and 100.

Q09.21 Use Python's input() function to ask a user for an integer between 1 and 10. Then use a for loop to print out all of the multiples of that number between 1 and 100. Use your program to print out all of the multiples of 9 between 1 and 100.

Q09.22 The Leibniz approximation for the value of π is below.

$$\frac{\pi}{4} = \frac{1}{1} - \frac{1}{3} + \frac{1}{5} - \frac{1}{7} + \frac{1}{9} - \ldots$$

Use 15 terms in the Leibniz approximation to calculate the value of π. Compute the error of the Leibniz approximation with 15 terms compared to Pythons math.pi function. Hint: $(-1)^i$ will alternate in sign as i steps through integers.

Q09.23 Use a for loop to print two columns on each line. In each line, give an SI prefix, then show which power the prefix corresponds to. Start with "nano" and "10^-9" and end on "giga" and "10^9". An example of the table is below.

```
nano      10^-9
micro     10^-6
milli     10^-3
 ...       ...
mega      10^6
giga      10^9
```

Q09.24 Python's bin() function converts an integer into its binary representation (a number represented as 1's and 0's). Use the bin() function to build a table of values from 1 to 10 showing the binary representation of each number. Hint: use `bin(i)[2:]` to remove `0b` from the output of the `bin()` function. An example of the table is below.

0	0
1	1
2	10
3	11
4	100
...	...

Q09.25 Iodine-131 is a radioactive isotope of iodine that has a half-life of about 8 days. This means that after 8 days 100g of iodine-131 will decay to 100g/2 = 50g, and after 16 days, 100g of iodine-131 will decay to (100g/2)/2 = 25g. Use a for loop to calculate the mass of 100g of Iodine-131 left after 1 year of radioactive decay.

Q09.26 Use a for loop to ask a user for five numbers. Use another for loop to print out the largest of the five numbers back to the user.

Q09.27 Use a for loop to ask a user for three exam grades. Print back to the user the average of the three grades.

Q09.28 Use a for loop to ask a user for 10 numbers. Print back the the user the mean, median and mode of the numbers. Hint: Python's `statistics` module is part of the Standard Library. `statistics.mean()`, `statistics.median()` and `statistics.mode()` are three functions present in the `statistics` module.

Q09.29 Write a program that requests a word from a user and then counts the number of vowels in the word. The English vowels are a, e, i, o, u, y. Hint: the code `'a' in ['a','e','i','o','u','y']` and `'a' in 'aeiouy'` both return True.

While Loops

Q09.40 Use a while loop to sum the elements in the list `[1,3,5,8,12]`. Print the sum to the user.

Q09.41 Use a while loop to print out the numbers between 1 and 100 that have whole number square roots.

Q08.42 Create a program that prompts a user for test scores. Continue to prompt the user for additional test scores until the user types `'q'`. When the user types `'q'`, the program stops asking the user for test scores and prints out the following statistics about the test scores the user entered:

- mean
- median
- standard deviation

Q09.43 Use a while loop to validate user input. Ask the user to enter a value between 0 and 1. Print back to the user "Try again" if the user's input is invalid. Print "Your number works!" when the user enters valid input.

Q09.44 Use a while loop to validate user input. Ask the user to enter a day of the week. Keep asking the user for a day of the week until they enter one. When the user enters a day of the week, print "Yup, it's <day of the week>".

Q09.45 Write a program to play the game higher/lower. Tell the user you have picked a random integer between 1 and 20.

9.7. REVIEW QUESTIONS

The code below creates a random integer n between 1 and 20:

```
from random import randint
n = (randint(1, 20))
```

(a) Ask the user to enter a number (one time) and tell the user if the random number is higher or lower. Print higher if the random number is higher than the user's guess, print lower if the random number is lower than the user's guess. Print You guessed it: <random number> if the user guesses the random number.

(b) Modify your program so that the program keeps printing higher or lower after each guess until the user guesses the random number. When the user guesses the random number print You guessed it: <random number>.

(c) Extend your higher/lower game to record the number of guesses the user enters to guess the random number. Then the user guesses the random number print You guessed: <random number> in <number of tries>.

Q09.46 A Taylor Series is an infinite series of mathematical terms that when summed together approximate a mathematical function. A Taylor Series can be used to approximate e^x, sine, and cosine.

Taylor Series expansion for the function e^x is below:

$$e^x = \sum_{n=0}^{\infty} \frac{x^n}{n!} = 1 + x + \frac{x^2}{2!} + \frac{x^3}{3!} + \frac{x^4}{4!} + ...$$

Write a program that asks a user for a number x, then calculates e^x using the Taylor Series expansion. Continue to add terms to the Taylor Series until the result from the Taylor series is less than 0.001 off the value of e^x calculated with Python's math.exp() function.

Errors, Explanations, and Solutions

Run the following code snippets. Explain the error in your own words. Then rewrite the code snippet to solve the error.

Q09.80

```
n = [1 2 3]
for n[1] == 2:
    n = n + 1
end
```

Q09.81

```
while x in [1, 2, 3]:
    print(x)
```

Q09.82

```
n = 1
while 1 == n
    print('valid')
    n = n +1
```

Q09.83

```
for i in range(3):
print(i)
```

Q09.84

```
for i in range(5,1):
    print(i)
```

Chapter 10

Symbolic Math

10.1 Introduction

By the end of this chapter you will be able to:

- Define Python variables as symbolic math variables
- Define mathematical expressions and equations using symbolic math variables
- Solve for symbolic math variables in terms of other symbolic math variables
- Derive numerical solutions using symbolic math variable substitution
- Solve linear and quadratic equations using symbolic math
- Solve systems of equations using symbolic math

10.2 SymPy

SymPy http://www.sympy.org is a Python library for *symbolic math*.

In symbolic math, symbols are used to represent mathematical expressions. An example of a symbolic math expression is below.

$$x^2 + y^2 = z$$

The expression contains the symbols x, y, and z.

If we define a second symbolic math expression:

$$x = a + b$$

then we can substitue in $a + b$ for x.

The result is the expression:

$$(a + b)^2 + y^2 = z$$

$$a^2 + 2ab + b^2 + y^2 = z$$

Solving for y in terms of a, b and z results in:

$$y = \sqrt{z - a^2 - 2ab - b^2}$$

In the symbolic math substitution above, symbolic math variables were rearranged, grouped and inserted. None of the variables were equal to a specific number, like 5 or 0.001, but we can still solve for one variable in terms on the other variables when we use symbolic math.

If we have numerical values for z, a and b, we can use Python to calculate the value of y.

But if we don't have numerical values for z, a and b, Python and the SymPy package can be used to rearrange terms and solve for one variable in terms of the other.

Working with mathematical symbols in a programmatic way instead of working with numerical values in a programmatic way is called *symbolic math*.

10.3 Installing SymPy

To work with symbolic math in Python, the SymPy library needs to be installed. SymPy comes pre-installed with the Anaconda distribution of Python.

If you are not using the Anaconda distribution of Python, SymPy can be installed with the **Anaconda Prompt**. Use the command:

```
> conda install sympy
```

Alternatively, you can install SymPy using the Python package manager **pip**. The command below installs SymPy into the current environment.

10.4. DEFINING VARIABLES

```
$ pip install sympy
```

You can confirm your SymPy installation by opening up the Python REPL and typing the two commands below.

```
>>> import sympy
>>> sympy.__version__
'1.4'
```

The ouput above shows SymPy version '1.4' is installed.

10.4 Defining Variables

Before we can construct symbolic math expressions or symbolic math equations with SymPy, first we need to create symbolic math variables, also called symbolic math *symbols*.

To define symbolic math variables with SymPy, first import the `symbols()` function from the SymPy module:

```
In [1]: from sympy import symbols
```

Symbolic math symbols are declared using SymPy's `symbols()` function. Pass a string surrounded by quotes to the `symbols()` function as an input argument. The the output of the `symbols()` function is assigned to a SymPy symbols object (not a string, no quotes).

```
In [2]: x = symbols('x')
        y = symbols('y')
```

SymPy's `symbols()` function can define multiple symbols in the same line of code. Note the input arguments passed to the `symbols()` function is a string, entries separated by a space (no comma) and surrounded by quotes. The output of the `symbols()` function are SymPy symbol objects. Commas separate these output objects (no quotation marks).

```
In [3]: x, y = symbols('x y')
```

10.5 Expressions and Substitutions

Symbolic math variables can be combined into symbolic math expressions. Once in an expression, symbolic math variables can be exchanged with substituion.

Expressions

A symbolic math expression is a combination of symbolic math variables with numbers and mathematical operators such as +, -, / and *. The standard Python rules for calculating numbers apply in SymPy symbolic math expressions.

After the symbols x and y are created, a symbolic math expression using x and y can be defined.

```
In [1]: from sympy import symbols

        x, y = symbols('x y')
        expr = 2*x + y
```

Substitution

Use SymPy's .subs() method to insert a numerical value into a symbolic math expression. The first argument of the .subs() method is the mathematical symbol and the second argument is the numerical value. In the expression above:

$$2x + y$$

If we substitute

$$x = 2$$

The resulting expression should be

$$2(2) + y$$

$$4 + y$$

We can code this substitution above using the code below.

```
In [2]: expr.subs(x, 2)
```

Out[2]:

$y + 4$

The .subs() method does not replace variables in place, .subs() only completes a one-time substitution. If expr is called after the .subs() method is applied, the original expr expression is returned.

```
In [3]: expr
```

Out[3]:

$2x + y$

To make the substitution permanent, a new expression object needs to be assigned to the output of the .subs() method.

```
In [4]: expr = 2*x + y
        expr2 = expr.subs(x, 2)
        expr2
```

10.5. EXPRESSIONS AND SUBSTITUTIONS

Out[4]:

$y + 4$

SymPy variables can also be substituted into SymPy expressions. In the code section below, the symbol z is substituted for the symbol x (z replaces x).

```
In [5]: x, y, z = symbols('x y z')
        expr = 2*x + y
        expr2 = expr.subs(x, z)
        expr2
```

Out[5]:

$y + 2z$

Expressions can also be substituted into other expressions. Consider the following:

$$y + 2x^2 + z^{-3}$$

substitute in

$$y = 2x$$

results in

$$2x + 2x^2 + z^{-3}$$

```
In [6]: x, y, z = symbols('x y z')
        expr = y + 2*x**2 + z**(-3)
        expr2 = expr.subs(y, 2*x)
        expr2
```

Out[6]:

$2x^2 + 2x + \dfrac{1}{z^3}$

A practical example involving symbolic math variables, expressions and substitutions could include a large expression and several replacements.

$$n_0 e^{-Q_v/RT}$$

$$n_0 = 3.48 \times 10^{-6}$$

$$Q_v = 12,700$$

$$R = 8.31$$

$$T = 1000 + 273$$

We can create four symbolic math variables and combine the variables into an expression with the code below.

```
In [7]: from sympy import symbols, exp
        n0, Qv, R, T = symbols('n0 Qv R T')
        expr = n0*exp(-Qv/(R*T))
```

Multiply SymPy subs() methods can be chained together to substitute multiple variables in one line of code.

```
In [8]: expr.subs(n0, 3.48e-6).subs(Qv,12700).subs(R, 8031).subs(T, 1000+273)
```

Out[8]:

$$\frac{3.48 \cdot 10^{-6}}{e^{\frac{12700}{10223463}}}$$

To evaluate an expression as a floating point number, use SymPy's .evalf() method.

```
In [9]: expr2 = expr.subs(n0, 3.48e-6).subs(Qv,12700).subs(R, 8031).subs(T, 1000+273)
```

```
In [10]: expr2.evalf()
```

Out[10]:

$3.47567968697765 \cdot 10^{-6}$

You can control the number of digits the .evalf() method outputs by passing a number as an argument.

```
In [11]: expr2.evalf(4)
```

Out[11]:

$3.476 \cdot 10^{-6}$

Summary

The SymPy functions and methods used in this section are summarized in the table below.

SymPy function or method	Description	Example
symbols()	create symbolic math variables	x, y = symbols('x y')
.subs()	substitute a value into a symbolic math expression	expr.subs(x,2)
.evalf()	evaluate a symbolic math expression as a floating point number	expr.evalf()

10.6 Equations

You can define equations in Python using SymPy and symbolic math variables. *Equations* in SymPy are different than *expressions*. An expression does not have equality. An expression is a collection of symbols and operators, but expressions are not equal to anything. Equations have equality. An equation can be thought of as an expression equal to something else.

A code section that defines the equation $4x + 2 = 0$ is below. Note all equations defined in SymPy are assumed to equal zero.

```
In [1]: from sympy import symbols, Eq

        x = symbols('x')

        eq1 = Eq(4*x + 2)
```

If you want to define the equation $2y - x = 5$, which is not equal to zero, you just have to subtract the right hand side of the equation from the left hand side of the equation first.

$$2y - x = 5$$

$$2y - x - 5 = 0$$

```
In [2]: x, y = symbols('x y')

        eq2 = Eq(2*y - x - 5)
```

Alternatively, an equation can be defined with a left hand side and a right hand side passed as separate arguments.

```
In [3]: x, y = symbols('x y')

        eq2 = Eq(2*y - x, 5)
```

Substitutions in Equations

Symbols and expressions can be substituted into equations. In the code section below, the variable z is substituted in for the variable x (z replaces x).

```
In [4]: x, y, z = symbols('x y z')

        eq2 = Eq(2*y - x - 5)
        eq3 = eq2.subs(x,z)
        eq3

Out[4]: Eq(2*y - z - 5, 0)
```

10.7 Solving Equations

SymPy's `solve()` function can be used to solve equations and expressions that contain symbolic math variables.

Equations with one solution

A simple equation that contains one variable like $x - 4 - 2 = 0$ can be solved using the SymPy's `solve()` function. When only one value is part of the solution, the solution is in the form of a list.

The code section below demonstrates SymPy's `solve()` function when an expression is defined with symbolic math variables.

```
In [1]: from sympy import symbols, solve

        x = symbols('x')
        expr = x-4-2

        sol = solve(expr)

        sol

Out[1]: [6]
```

To pull the value out of the solution list `sol`, regular list indexing can be used.

```
In [2]: num = sol[0]

        num

Out[2]: 6
```

The code section below demonstrates SymPy's solve() function when an equation is defined with symbolic math variables.

```
In [3]: from sympy import symbols, Eq, solve

        y = symbols('y')
        eq1 = Eq(y + 3 + 8)

        sol = solve(eq1)
        sol

Out[3]: [-11]
```

Equations with two solutions

Quadratic equations, like $x^2 - 5x + 6 = 0$, have two solutions. SymPy's solve() function can be used to solve an equation with two solutions. When an equation has two solutions, SymPy's solve() function outputs a list. The elements in the list are the two solutions.

The code section below shows how an equation with two solutions is solved with SymPy's solve() function.

```
In [4]: from sympy import symbols, Eq, solve

        y = symbols('x')
        eq1 = Eq(x**2 -5*x + 6)

        sol = solve(eq1)
        sol

Out[4]: [2, 3]
```

If you specify the keyword argument dict=True to SymPy's solve() function, the output is still a list, but inside the list is a dictionary that shows which variable was solved for.

```
In [5]: from sympy import symbols, Eq, solve

        y = symbols('x')
        eq1 = Eq(x**2 -5*x + 6)

        sol = solve(eq1, dict=True)
        sol

Out[5]: [{x: 2}, {x: 3}]

In [6]: sol[0]

Out[6]: {x: 2}

In [7]: sol[1]

Out[7]: {x: 3}
```

10.8 Solving Two Equations for Two Unknows

Solving two equations for two unknown can be accomplished using SymPy. Consider the following set of two equations with two variables:

$$x + y - 5 = 0$$

$$x - y + 3 = 0$$

To solve this system of two equations for the two unknowns, x and y, first import the SymPy package. From the SymPy package, the functions symbols, Eq and solve are needed.

In [1]: `from sympy import symbols, Eq, solve`

Next, create two SymPy symbols objects, x and y. As shown in a previous section, the string passed as an input argument to the symbols() function, 'x y', does not have any commas. The outputs of the symbols() function are the two symbol objects x and y. These outputs must be separated by a comma and are not surrounded by quotes.

In [2]: `x, y = symbols('x y')`

Now define the two equations as SymPy equation objects.

In [3]:
```
eq1 = Eq(x + y - 5)
eq2 = Eq(x - y + 3)
```

We can use SymPy's solve() function to compute the value of x and y. The first argument passed to the solve() function is a tuple of the two equations (eq1, eq2). The second argument passed to the solve() function is a tuple of the variables we want to solve for (x, y).

In [4]: `solve((eq1,eq2), (x, y))`

Out[4]: `{x: 1, y: 4}`

The solution is in the form of a Python dictionary. The dictionary keys are the variables and the dictionary values are the numerical solutions.

We can access the solution out of the solution dictionary using regular dictionary indexing.

In [5]:
```
sol_dict = solve((eq1,eq2), (x, y))
print(f'x = {sol_dict[x]}')
print(f'y = {sol_dict[y]}')
```

```
x = 1
y = 4
```

Solve a statics problem with SymPy

Consider the following engineering statics problem which can be solved with symbolic math and SymPy.

10.8. SOLVING TWO EQUATIONS FOR TWO UNKNOWS

GIVEN:

A weight of 22 lbs is hung from a ring. The ring is supported by two cords. The first cord, cord CE, is 30 degrees above the horizontal and to the right. The second cord, cord BD, is 45 degrees to the left and above the horizontal.

$w = 22$ lb

T_{CE} @ +30 degrees CCW relative to +x-axis

T_{BD} @ +45 degress CW relative to -x-axis

FIND:

The magnitude of T_{CE} and T_{BD}

SOLUTION:

To solve for the magnitude of T_{CE} and T_{BD}, we need to solve to two equations for two unknowns.

To accomplish this with Python, first import NumPy and SymPy. The SymPy functions `symbols`, `Eq` and `solve` are needed. We will also use NumPy's trig functions to solve this problem.

```
In [6]: import numpy as np
        from sympy import symbols, Eq, solve
```

Next, define the symbolic math variables. Multiple symbolic math variables can be defined at the same time. Remember the argument names (on the right-hand side of the assignment operator =) need to be enclosed in quotes' ' and separated by spaces, no commas. The object names (on the left-hand side of the assignment operator =) are separated with commas, no quotes.

```
In [7]: Tce, Tbd = symbols('Tce Tbd')
```

Two equations based on the sum of the forces need to be defined.

Assuming the ring is in static equilibrium:

$$\Sigma \vec{F} = 0$$

$$\Sigma F_x = 0$$

$$\Sigma F_y = 0$$

The three forces opperating on the ring are defined as:

$$T_{ce} = \text{tension in cable CE}$$

$$\vec{T_{ce}} = T_{ce}cos(30)\hat{i} + T_{ce}sin(30)\hat{j}$$

T_{bd} = tension in cable BD

$$\vec{T}_{bd} = -T_{bd}\cos(45)\hat{i} + T_{bd}\sin(45)\hat{j}$$

$$\vec{w} = 0\hat{i} - 22\hat{j}$$

Taking $\Sigma F_x = 0$ (sum of the $\hat{i}$ terms):

$$T_{ce}\cos(30) - T_{bd}\cos(45) + 0 = 0$$

Taking $\Sigma F_y = 0$ (sum of the $\hat{j}$ terms):

$$T_{ce}\sin(30) + T_{bd}\sin(45) - 22 = 0$$

The first equation, based on the sum of the forces in the x-direction (the $\hat{i}$ terms) is:

$$T_{ce}\cos(30) - T_{bd}\cos(45) + 0 = 0$$

This equation can be represented as a SymPy equation object. Note the right-hand side of the equation is 0. SymPy equation objects are instantiated with expressions equal to zero. If the expression was not equal to zero, simply subtract both sides by the term on the right-hand side of the equals sign and use the resulting expression (equal to zero) to create the SymPy equation object.

A detail in the code section below is that NumPy's np.cos() function accepts an angle in radians, so we need to convert our angles from degrees to radians using NumPy's np.radians() function.

```
In [8]: eq1=Eq(Tce * np.cos(np.radians(30)) - Tbd * np.cos(np.radians(45)))
        print(eq1)
```

Eq(-0.707106781186548*Tbd + 0.866025403784439*Tce, 0)

The second equation, based on the sum of the forces in the y-direction is:

$$T_{ce}\sin(30) + T_{bd}\sin(45) - 22 = 0$$

Define this equation as a SymPy equation object as well:

```
In [9]: eq2=Eq(Tce * np.sin(np.radians(30)) + Tbd * np.sin(np.radians(45))-22)
        print(eq2)
```

Eq(0.707106781186548*Tbd + 0.5*Tce - 22, 0)

10.8. SOLVING TWO EQUATIONS FOR TWO UNKNOWS

Now solve the two equations for T_{ce} and T_{bd} with SymPy's `solve()` function. The first argument passed to the `solve()` function is a tuple of equations to solve, the second argument passed to the `solve()` function is a tuple of the variables to solve for.

```
In [10]: solve((eq1,eq2),(Tce, Tbd))

Out[10]: {Tbd: 19.7246603876972, Tce: 16.1051177665153}
```

The solution is saved in a Python dictionary. The dictionary keys are the variable names Tbd and Tce and the dictionary values are the numerical solutions.

The numerical solutions can be pulled out of the dictionary using regular Python dictionary access. Note Tce and Tbd are SymPy symbols objects, not strings.

```
In [11]: sol_dict = solve((eq1,eq2),(Tce, Tbd))
         print(f'Tce = {sol_dict[Tce]}')
         print(f'Tce = {sol_dict[Tbd]}')

Tce = 16.1051177665153
Tce = 19.7246603876972
```

The same problem can be solved again, but with w kept as a variable.

```
In [12]: w, Tce, Tbd = symbols('w, Tab, Tac')

         eq1=Eq(Tce * np.cos(np.radians(30)) - Tbd * np.cos(np.radians(45)))
         eq2=Eq(Tce * np.sin(np.radians(30)) + Tbd * np.sin(np.radians(45))-w)

         solve((eq1,eq2),(Tce,Tbd))

Out[12]: {Tab: 0.732050807568877*w, Tac: 0.896575472168053*w}
```

The result is a solution is in terms of the variable w.

10.9 Summary

In this chapter, you learned about symbolic math and how to complete symbolic math calculations with Python the SymPy package. Symbolic math treats variables as mathematical symbols rather than defining variables as numbers.

At the start of the chapter, you learned how to create symbolic math variables with SymPy's `symbols()` function.

Symbolic math variables can be combined into symbolic math expressions and symbolic math equations. You learned how to substitute variables and numbers into symbolic math expressions and equations.

At the end of the chapter, you learned how to solve linear and quadratic equations with SymPy.

The final example in the chapter was a multi-variable statics problem where two equations were solved for two unknowns.

Key Terms and Concepts

symbolic math	systems of equations	evaluate
symbolic variable	expression	linear equation
object	equation	quadratic equation
numerical calculation	substitution	

SymPy Functions and Methods

SymPy Function	Description	Example
`symbols()`	Define a symbolic math variable	`x, y = symbols('x y')`
`.subs()`	Substitute a variable or value	`expr.subs(x, 2)`
`Eq()`	Define a SymPy equation	`eq1 = Eq(4*x + 2)`
`solve()`	Solve a SymPy expression or equation	`solve((eq1,eq2), (x, y))`

10.10 Review Questions

Creating Expressions Equations

Q10.01 Create the symbolic math variables a, b, c and x. Use these variables to define the symbolic math expressions:

$$ax^2 + bx + c$$

$$sin(ax) + cos(bx) + tan(cx)$$

10.10. REVIEW QUESTIONS

Q10.02 Create the symbolic math variables a, b, c and x. Use these variables to define the symbolic math equations:

$$ax^2 + bx = c$$

$$\frac{\sin(ax)}{\cos(bx)} = \tan(cx)$$

Q10.03 Create the symbolic math variables a, b, c, x, and y. Use these variables to define the symbolic math expression:

$$ax^2 + bx + c$$

Substitute the variable y in for the variable c.

Substitute the value 5 in for the variable y.

Q10.04 Create the symbolic math variables E, A, d, P, L, and F. Use these variables to define the symbolic math equation:

$$d = \frac{PL}{AE}$$

Substitute the value 29×10^6 for E

Substitute $F/2$ for the variable P

Q10.05 Create the symbolic math variables t, T, c, and J. Use these variables to define the symbolic math equation:

$$t = \frac{Tc}{J}$$

Substitute the $J = \frac{\pi}{2}c^4$ into the equation

Substitute $T = 9.0$ and $c = 4.5$. Print out the resulting value of t.

Q10.06 Mohr's circle is used in mechanical engineering to calculate the shear and normal stress. Given the height of Mohr's circle τ_{max} is equal to the expression below:

$$\tau_{max} = \sqrt{(\sigma_x - \sigma_y)/2)^2 + \tau_{xy}}$$

Use SymPy expressions or equations to calculate τ if $\sigma_x = 90$, $\sigma_y = 60$ and $\tau_{xy} = 20$.

Solving Equations

Q10.20 Use SymPy to solve for x if $x - 4 = 2$

Q10.21 Use SymPy to solve for the roots of the quadratic equation $2x^2 - 4x + 1.5 = 0$

Q10.22 Create the symbolic math variable b and define the equation below:

$$\frac{1}{\sqrt{2}}(b-6) = -1$$

Find the numeric value of b to three decimal places

Q10.30 Use SymPy to solve the system of linear equations below for the variables x and y:

$$-3x - 2y + 7 = 0$$

$$5x - 3y - 6 = 0$$

Q10.31 Use SymPy to solve the system of linear equations below for the variables x, y, and z:

$$2x + 4y - z = -0.6$$

$$-x - 3y + 2z = 2.2$$

$$\frac{1}{2}x + 6y - 3z = -6.8$$

Q10.32 A set of five equations is below:

$$-5x_1 - 4x_2 - 2x_3 + 2x_4 + 3x_5 = 10$$

$$9x_1 + 3x_2 + 4x_3 + 10x_4 + 5x_5 = -5$$

$$2x_1 + 4x_2 + 3x_3 + 2x_4 + x_5 = 12$$

$$5x_1 - 4x_2 + 3x_3 - 2x_4 + 2x_5 = 32$$

$$x_1 - x_2 + 2x_3 + 4x_4 + 3x_5 = 42$$

Use symbolic math variables and equations to solve for x_1, x_2, x_3, x_4 and x_5.

Q10.33 An equation in terms of the variables L and x is defined below.

$$\frac{1}{6}L^3x^2 - \frac{1}{6}Lx^3 + \frac{1}{24}x^4 - \frac{1}{45}L^4 = 0$$

Solve the equation for x in terms of the variable L. Note their will be more than one solution.

Q10.50 Use SymPy to solve the system of non-linear equations below for the variables x and y:

$$3x^2 + 2y^3 = -\frac{17}{4}$$

10.10. REVIEW QUESTIONS

$$\frac{-x^3}{2} - 8y^2 + \frac{127}{2} = 0$$

Chapter 11

Python and External Hardware

11.1 Introduction

By the end of this chapter you will be able to:

- Connect external hardware to a computer running Python
- Install the PySerial library
- Read data over a serial connection using Python
- Save data coming in over a serial connection using Python
- Write data to a serial line using Python
- Read data from a sensor using Python
- Control an LED using Python

11.2 PySerial

PySerial is a Python package that facilitates serial communication. A computer running Python with the PySerial package installed can communicate with external hardware. PySerial is a useful package for problem solvers because it allows us to exchange data between computers and pieces of external hardware such as voltmeters, oscilloscopes, strain gauges, flow meters, actuators, and lights.

PySerial provides an interface to communicate over the *serial* communication protocol. Serial communication is one of the oldest computer communication protocols. Serial communication protocol predates the USB specification used by computers and other pieces of hardware like mice, keyboards, and webcams. USB stands for Universal Serial Bus. USB and is built upon and extends the original serial communication interface.

Installing PySerial

To use the PySerial package with Python, PySerial first needs to be installed. If you installed the full Anaconda distribution of Python, PySerial comes pre-installed. If you do have the full Anaconda distribution of Python installed, PySerial can be installed using the **Anaconda Prompt**.

```
> conda install pyserial
```

Alternatively, PySerial can be installed on the command line using **pip**:

```
$ pip install pyserial
```

After PySerial is installed, the installation can be confirmed at the Python REPL:

```
In [1]: >>> import serial
        >>> print(serial.__version__)
```

3.4

NOTE: Even though the command to install PySerial was `> conda install pyserial`, **the PySerial module is imported with the line** `import serial`.

11.3 Bytes and Unicode Strings

Before using PySerial to communicate with external hardware over the serial interface, it is import to understand the difference between *bytes* and *unicode strings* in Python.

The distinction between bytes and Unicode strings is important because strings in Python are *Unicode* by default. However, external hardware like Arduino's, oscilloscopes and voltmeters transmit characters as *bytes*.

Unicode Strings

In Python, the syntax to define a new string is:

11.3. BYTES AND UNICODE STRINGS

```
In [1]: ustring = 'A unicode string'
```

Use Python's built-in `type()` function to determine the data type of the `ustring` variable:

```
In [2]: print(type(ustring))
```

```
<class 'str'>
```

When the Python interpreter declares the variable `ustring` is of `<class 'str'>`, it indicates `ustring` is a *Unicode string*.

In Python 3, all strings are *Unicode strings* by defaut.

Unicode strings are useful because there are many letters and letter-like characters that are not part of the set of letters, numbers, and symbols on a regular computer keyboard. For example in Spanish, the accent character is used over certain vowels. Letters with accents cannot be represented by the letters on a standard English keyboard. However, letters with accents are part of a set of letters, numbers, and symbols in *unicode strings*.

Byte Strings

Another way that characters such as letters, numbers, and punctuation can be stored is as *bytes*. A *byte* is a unit of computer information that has a fixed width (one byte long). Because of this fixed width, one *byte* only has a small number of unique combinations. This limits *byte strings* to only the letters, numbers and punctuation marks on a computer keyboard (plus a couple extra). This limited set of characters is called the ASCII (pronounced *ask-ee two*) character set. A table of ASCII character codes is in the appendix. For instance, the ASCII character code 49 corresponds to the number one 1.

Machines speak bytes.

However, external hardware such as Arduinos, oscilloscopes, and voltmeters speak *byte strings* by default. Almost all machines speak *byte strings* by default, including the servers that bring Netflix to your laptop.

To define a *byte string* in Python, the letter b is placed before the quotation marks b' ' when a string is created.

```
In [3]: bstring = b'bstring'
```

We can view the data type of the `bstring` variable using the `type()` function.

```
In [4]: print(type(bstring))
```

```
<class 'bytes'>
```

Convert between Unicode strings and byte strings

In order for a Python program to communicate with external hardware, it needs to be able to convert between *Unicode strings* and *byte strings*. This conversion is completed with the `.encode()` and `.decode()` methods.

The `.encode()` method "encodes" a Unicode string into a byte string.

```
<byte string> = <unicode string>.encode()
```

The `.decode()` method "decodes" a byte string into a unicode string.

```
<unicode string> = <byte string>.decode
```

Remember: Machines speak bytes, Python strings are Unicode by default.

A Python script must decode what machines transmit before further processing. Python defaults to Unicode (and machines do not), so within a script's Python code, remember to *encode* Unicode strings so machines can understand them.

```
In [5]: ustring = 'A unicode string'
        new_bstring = ustring.encode()
        type(new_bstring)

Out[5]: bytes

In [6]: bstring = b'bstring'
        new_ustring = bstring.decode()
        type(new_ustring)

Out[6]: str
```

When a command from a Python program (a Unicode string) is sent to a piece of external hardware (that reads bytes):

The `.encode()` method is applied to the Unicode string (to convert the Unicode string to a byte string) before the command is sent to the piece of external hardware.

When a chunk of data comes in from a piece of external hardware (a byte string) and is read by a Python script (which speaks Unicode by the default):

The `.decode()` method is applied to the byte string (to convert the byte string to a Unicode string) before it is processed further by Python program.

11.4 Controlling an LED with Python

In this section, you will learn how to control an LED connected to an external piece of hardware (an Arduino) using Python. To accomplish this task, the following hardware is required:

- A computer running Python
- An Arduino
- An LED

11.4. CONTROLLING AN LED WITH PYTHON

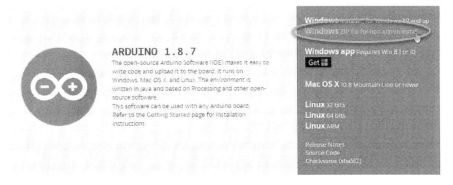

Figure 11.1. Arduino IDE Download Page

- Wires, a resistor and a breadboard to connect the LED to the Arduino
- A USB cable to connect the Arduino to the computer

You will also need to download the Arduino IDE (Integrated Development Environment). Download the Arduino IDE using the following link:

```
https://www.arduino.cc/en/Main/Software
```

If you are working on a computer that you don't have administrator privileges to install software on, be sure to select: [Windows ZIP for non-admin install].

Wire the LED to the Arduino

Connect the LED to the Arduino using a resistor, wires and a breadboard. Note the short leg of the LED is connected to ground, and the long leg of the resistor is connected through a resistor to PIN 13. A resistor is needed to prevent too much current from flowing through the LED. This type of resistor is called a *pull up resistor*.

Upload code to the Arduino

Upload the following code to the Arduino using the Arduino IDE. The code is same as in the example sketch called `Physical Pixel`. The `Physical Pixel` sketch is found in the Arduino IDE under File –> Examples –> 04.Communication –> PhysicalPixel

The code for the Physical Pixel Sketch is shown below.

```
// Arduino IDE:
// File -> Examples -> 04.Communication -> PhysicalPixel

const int ledPin = 13; // pin the LED is attached to
int incomingByte;      // variable stores  serial data
```

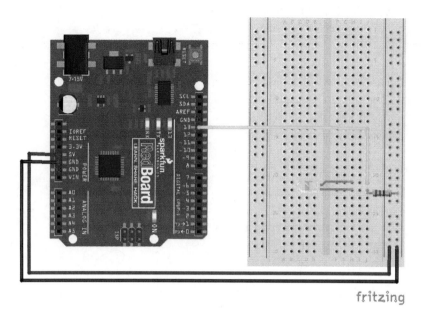

Figure 11.2. Arduino with LED

Figure 11.3. Physical Pixel Example Sketch in the Arduino IDE

11.4. CONTROLLING AN LED WITH PYTHON

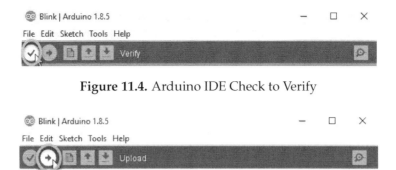

Figure 11.4. Arduino IDE Check to Verify

Figure 11.5. Arduino IDE Arrow to Upload

```
void setup() {
  // initialize serial communication:
  Serial.begin(9600);
  // initialize the LED pin as an output:
  pinMode(ledPin, OUTPUT);
}

void loop() {
  // see if there's incoming serial data:
  if (Serial.available() > 0) {
    // read the oldest byte in the serial buffer:
    incomingByte = Serial.read();
    // if it's a capital H (ASCII 72), turn on the LED:
    if (incomingByte == 'H') {
      digitalWrite(ledPin, HIGH);
    }
    // if it's an L (ASCII 76) turn off the LED:
    if (incomingByte == 'L') {
      digitalWrite(ledPin, LOW);
    }
  }
}
```

Connect the Arduino to the Computer

Connect the Arduino to the computer using a USB cable. Ensure two settings in the Arduino IDE are set correctly.

- Make sure the Port is selected properly in the Arduino IDE under Tools –> Port.
- Make sure the Board is selected in the Arduino IDE under Tools –> Board –> Arduino/Genuino Uno

In the Arduino IDE, click the [checkmark] to verify and the [arrow] to upload. If the sketch does not upload, check which COM port is selected in Tools –> Port.

Figure 11.6. Arduino Serial Monitor

Turn the LED on and off with the Arduino Serial Monitor

Open the Arduino Serial Monitor using Tools –> Serial Monitor. In the Serial Monitor type L or H and click [Send]. Observe the LED turn on and off. Send H to turn the LED on. Send L to turn the LED off.

Use the Python REPL to turn the Arduino LED on and off

Next, use the Python REPL to turn the Arduino on and off. (You can open the Python REPL by typing > python at the **Anaconda Prompt**) At the Python REPL, type the following commands. If a REPL prompt >>> precedes the command, type the command into the REPL. If the line does not start with a REPL prompt, the line represents expected output.

When you type the command: ser = serial.Serial('COM4', 9800, timeout=1), ensure the 'COM#' corresponds to the port that worked with the Arduino IDE in Tools –> Port.

```
>>> import serial
>>> import time

>>> ser = serial.Serial('COM4', 9600)   # open serial port
>>> time.sleep(2)                        # wait 2 seconds
>>> ser.name()
'COM4'

>>> ser.write(b'H')
# LED turns on

>>> ser.write(b'L')
# LED turns off

>>> ser.write(b'H')
# LED turns on
```

11.4. CONTROLLING AN LED WITH PYTHON

```
>>> ser.write(b'L')
# LED turns off

>>> ser.close()
>>> exit()
```

Ensure the command `ser.close()` is issued before exiting the Python REPL.

Write a Python Script to turn the LED on and off

After the LED turns on and off based on sending H and L with the Arduino Serial Monitor and you can turn the LED on and off with the Python REPL, it's time to write a Python script to turn the LED on and off. Again, the serial communication between the Python script and the Arduino is facilitated by the PySerial package. Ensure PySerial is installed before running the Python script.

At the top of the Python script, import the PySerial package. Note that even though the package is called PySerial, the line `import serial` is used. Python's built-in `time` module is also imported as the `time.sleep()` function will be used in the script.

```
# blink.py

import serial
import time
```

In the next part of the Python script, connect to the Arduino over the serial port. In the line `ser = serial.Serial('COM4', 9800, timeout=1)`, ensure the `'COM#'` corresponds to the port that worked with the Arduino IDE. Then create a loop that blinks the Arduino LED on and off for about 5 seconds. Notice the byte string `b'H'` is sent to the Arduino, not the Unicode string `'H'`. The Unicode string `'H'` is prepended with the letter b in the line `ser.writelines(b'H')`. This line of code turns the Unicode string into a byte string before it is sent to the Arduino.

```
ser = serial.Serial('COM4', 9800, timeout=1)
time.sleep(2)

for i in range(10):
    ser.writelines(b'H')    # send a byte
    time.sleep(0.5)         # wait 0.5 seconds
    ser.writelines(b'L')    # send a byte
    time.sleep(0.5)

ser.close()
```

Run the entire Python script and watch the Arduino LED blink ten times. A common problem is the serial port was not closed before the script starts. Make sure the Arduino Serial Monitor is closed and try running `>>> ser.close()` at the Python REPL.

Write a Python script to allow a user to turn the LED on and off

Once the LED blinks on and off successfully using a for loop in a Python script, you can write a new Python script that allows a user to turn the LED on and off. At the top of the new Python script import the **PySerial** package and built-in `time` module.

```
import serial
import time
```

Next, give the user instructions. If the user types H, the LED turns on. If the user types L the LED turns off. If the user types q, the program terminates.

```
print('This program allows a user to turn an LED on and off')
print('type H to turn the LED on')
print('type L to turn the LED off')
print('type q to quit')
```

Finally, the script needs a while loop to ask the user to enter the letter H, L or q. Once the user enters the letter, the letter is converted to a byte string. Next, the byte string is sent over the serial line to the Arduino. A delay is added so that the Arduino can process the command before reading with the next one.

```
ser = serial.Serial('COM4', 9800, timeout=1)
time.sleep(2)

user_input = 'L'
while user_input != 'q':
    user_input = input('H = on, L = off, q = quit' : )
    byte_command = encode(user_input)
    ser.writelines(byte_command)   # send a byte
    time.sleep(0.5) # wait 0.5 seconds

print('q entered. Exiting the program')
ser.close()
```

Run the Python script. Type H and L and observe the LED turn on and off. Type q to end the program.

11.5 Reading a Sensor with Python

In this section, you will learn how to read a sensor connected to an external piece of hardware (an Arduino) with Python. To accomplish this, the following hardware is required:

- A computer running Python
- An Arduino
- A potentiometer (the sensor)
- wires, a resistor, an LED, and a breadboard to connect the sensor to the Arduino
- A USB cable to connect the Arduino to the computer

You will also need to download the Arduino IDE (the Arduino Integrated Development Environment) using the following link as shown in the previous section:

https://www.arduino.cc/en/Main/Software

11.5. READING A SENSOR WITH PYTHON

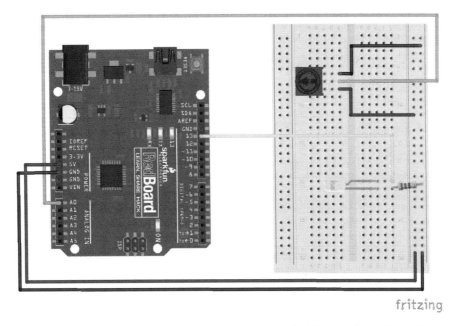

Figure 11.7. Arduino with potentiometer and LED on a breadboard

Wire the sensor to the Arduino

Connect the potentiometer sensor to the Arduino using a resistor, wires and a breadboard. The middle pin of the potentiometer is connected to pin A0 on the Arduino (green wire). Connect the LED to the Arduino. Note the long lead of the LED is connected to PIN13 on the Arduino (yellow wire) and the short lead of the LED is connected through a resistor to ground (black wire). If the LED is wired backward, the LED will not turn on.

In the hardware schematic, the blue square with an arrow on it is a potentiometer. The user knows when the sensor signal changes because the user manually turns the potentiometer dial.

The hardware schematic describes how to the Arduino, LED, resistor, and potentiometer are connected with jumper wires and a breadboard.

Upload code to the Arduino

Once the LED and potentiometer are hooked up the Arduino, upload the following code to the Arduino using the Arduino IDE. Note that Arduinos don't use the Python programming language. The programming language used by Arduinos is a variant of the C programming language.

The Arduino sketch below (an Arduino program is called a sketch) accomplishes a couple things. First, the Arduino reads the potentiometer sensor value and stores the sensor value in the variable `sensorValue`. Next, the Arduino sends the sensor value over the serial line (as a byte string). Finally, `sensorValue` is compared to 500. If `sensorValue` is less than 500, the LED stays off. If `sensorValue` is greater than 500, the LED turn on. The read-send-compare process repeats in a loop.

```
// potentiometer_read.ino
// reads a potentiometer and sends value over serial
```

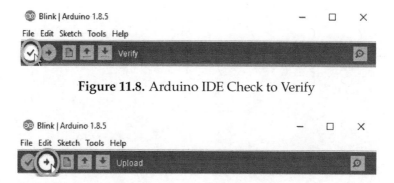

Figure 11.8. Arduino IDE Check to Verify

Figure 11.9. Arduino IDE Arrow to Upload

```
int sensorPin = A0;   // The potentiometer on pin 0
int ledPin = 13;      // The LED is connected on pin 13
int sensorValue;      // variable to stores data

void setup() // runs once when the sketch starts
{
  // make the LED pin (pin 13) an output pin
  pinMode(ledPin, OUTPUT);

  // initialize serial communication
  Serial.begin(9600);
}

void loop() // runs repeatedly after setup() finishes
{
  sensorValue = analogRead(sensorPin);   // read pin A0
  Serial.println(sensorValue);           // send data to serial

  if (sensorValue < 500) {               // less than 500?
    digitalWrite(ledPin, LOW); }         // Turn the LED off

  else {                                 // greater than 500?
    digitalWrite(ledPin, HIGH); }        // Keep the LED on

  delay(100);             // Pause 100 milliseconds
}
```

Connect the Arduino to the computer and Upload the Sketch

Connect the Arduino to the computer with a USB cable. In the Arduino IDE select Tools –> Board –> Arduino/Genuino Uno. Upload the sketch to the Arduino. In the Arduino IDE, click the [check mark] to verify and the [arrow] to upload. If the sketch does not upload, check which COM port is selected in the Arduino IDE under Tools –> Ports.

11.5. READING A SENSOR WITH PYTHON

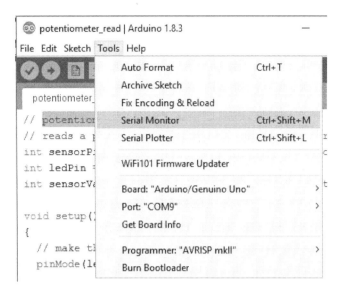

Figure 11.10. Select the Arduino Serial Monitor from the Tools Menus

Check the Sensor Signal

To verify the Arduino sketch is working correctly, the sensor signal can be checked in three ways:

- The LED turns on and off as the potentiometer dial is rotated
- In the Arudino **Serial Monitor**, numbers change as the potentiometer dial is rotated
- In the Arduino **Seral Plotter**, the line moves as the potentiometer dial is rotated

LED turns ON and OFF

The LED should turn on and off as the potentiometer is rotated. If the LED does not turn on and off when the potentiometer is rotated, make sure the potentiometer is turned back and forth through it's full range of rotation. Also, ensure the USB cable is plugged into both the Arduino and the computer.

Arudino Serial Monitor

Access the Arduino **Serial Monitor** using Tools –> Serial Monitor.

If the Arduino sketch is working correctly, a running list of numbers is shown in the Arduino **Serial Monitor**. When the potentiometer is dialed back and forth, the numbers streaming down the **Serial Monitor** should change. The output in the Serial Monitor should be a running list of numbers between 0 and 1024.

If a running list of numbers can't be seen in the Arduino **Serial Monitor**, ensure [Auto Scroll], [Both NL & CR] and [9600 baud] are selected. Also, make sure the Port is set correctly in the Arduino IDE under Tools –> Port.

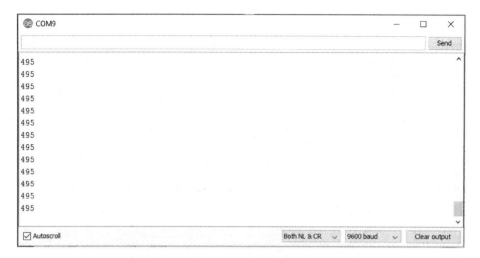

Figure 11.11. Arduino Serial Monitor Ouput

Arduino Serial Plotter

To access the Arduino Serial Plotter, select Tools –> Serial Monitor in the Arduino IDE. Note the Arduino Serial Monitor needs to be closed before the Arduino Serial Plotter can be opened. If the sketch is working correctly, potentiometer rotation produces a moving line on the Arduino Serial Plotter.

The output of the Arduino Serial Plotter should be a running line graph. The height of the line on the graph should change as the potentiometer is dialed back and forth. If the Arduino Serial Plotter is blank, make sure [9600 baud] is selected in the lower right corner of the Serial Plotter. Also, make sure the `Port` has been set correctly in the Arduino IDE in Tools –> Port.

Use the Python REPL to read the potentiometer data

At the Python REPL, type the following commands. If the REPL prompt >>> precedes the command, type the command into the REPL. If the line does not start with a REPL prompt, this line represents expected output.

```
# serial read using the Python REPL

>>> import serial
>>> import time
>>> ser = serial.Serial('COM4',9600)
>>> time.sleep(2)
>>> b = ser.readline()
>>> b
b'409\r\n'
>>> type(b)
<class 'bytes'>
>>> str_rn = b.decode()
>>> str_rn
'409\r\n'
```

11.5. READING A SENSOR WITH PYTHON

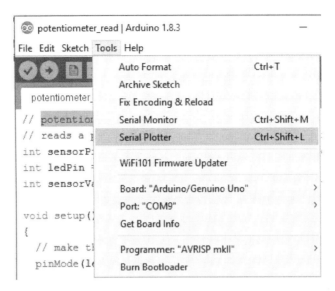

Figure 11.12. Arduino Serial Plotter Menu

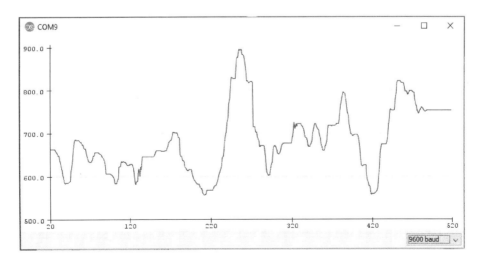

Figure 11.13. Arudino Serial Plotter

```
>>> str = str_rn.rstrip()
>>> str
'409'
>>> type(str)
<class 'str'>
>>> f = float(str)
>>> f
409.0
>>> type(f)
<class 'float'>
>>> ser.close()
>>> exit()
```

Write a Python script to read the sensor

After the hardware is connected and the Arduino sketch is working correctly, you can construct a Python script to read the sensor value.

Communication between the Python script and the Arduino is accomplished using the PySerial package. Make sure PySerial is installed before the script is run. See a previous section in this chapter on how to install the PySerial package.

At the top of the Python script, import the PySerial module. Note that although the package is called PySerial, use the line `import serial` to import the package.

```
import serial
import time
```

Next, set up the serial communication line with the Arduino. Ensure the port specified in the command `ser = serial.Serial('COM4', 9600)` is the same COM# that was used in the Arduino IDE.

```
# set up the serial line
ser = serial.Serial('COM4', 9600)
time.sleep(2)
```

Next, code a loop runs for about 5 seconds while data is collected from the sensor. If it seems like the loop is stuck, press [Ctrl] + [c].

```
# Read and record the data
data =[]                                 # empty list to store the data
for i in range(50):
    b = ser.readline()                   # read a byte string
        string_n = b.decode()            # decode byte string into Unicode
    string = string_n.rstrip()           # remove \n and \r
    flt = float(string)                  # convert string to float
    print(flt)
    data.append(flt)                     # add to the end of data list
    time.sleep(0.1)                      # wait (sleep) 0.1 seconds

ser.close()
```

11.5. READING A SENSOR WITH PYTHON

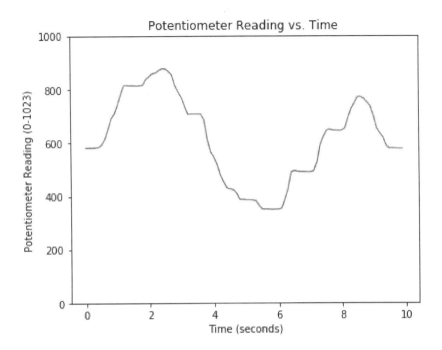

Figure 11.14. Matplotlib plot of potentiometer readings recorded with an Arduino and PySerial

After the data is collected, the data can be displayed with the Python's `print()` function and a `for` loop. The output looks like the numbers in the Arduino **Serial Monitor**.

```
# show the data

for line in data:
    print(line)
```

The data can also be plotted with Matplotlib. The resulting plot looks like the line plot in the Arduino **Serial Plotter**.

```
import matplotlib.pyplot as plt
# if using a Jupyter notebook include
%matplotlib inline

plt.plot(data)
plt.xlabel('Time (seconds)')
plt.ylabel('Potentiometer Reading')
plt.title('Potentiometer Reading vs. Time')
plt.show()
```

Run the entire script and twist the potentiometer. You should see the potentiometer values running by in the Python REPL command window.

After all the data is collected, you will see a plot like the one below.

11.6 Summary

In this chapter, you learned how to use Python to interact with external hardware. In particular, you learned how to use Python and the PySerial package to communicate with an Arduino.

The chapter began with a discussion of Unicode strings and byte strings. In Python, all strings are Unicode by default, but machines speak in bytes. To create a byte string in Python, prepend a string with the letter b as in b'my string'. Python's .encode() and .decode() methods convert between Unicode strings and byte strings.

In the first project of the chapter, you learned how to use Python and the PySerial package to control an LED attached to an Arduino. The general steps were:

- download and install the Arduino IDE
- wire a LED to an Arduino
- connect the Arduino the computer and upload code
- blink the LED with the Arduino Serial Monitor
- blink the LED with the Python REPL
- blink the LED with a Python script
- run a Python script to have a user turn the LED on and off

The second project of the chapter involved reading a sensor connected to an Arduino with Python and PySerial. To complete this project, the general steps were:

- download and install the Arduino IDE
- wire a potentiometer sensor and LED to the Arduino
- connect the Arduino the computer and upload an Arduino sketch
- check the sensor signal with the LED, Arduino Serial Monitor and Arduino Serial Plotter
- use the Python REPL to read the potentiometer sensor
- run a Python script to collect the potentiometer sensor data and plot the data using Matplotlib

Key Terms and Concepts

External Hardware	serial line	.ino-file
Sensor	USB	C programming language
LEDArduino	Unicode	baud
IDE	Unicode string	newline character
serial	byte string	
serial communication	port	

Additional Resources

The official documentation for the PySerial Package is found here: https://docs.pyserial.com

The Arduino project has a great set of tutorials found here:https://Arduino.com/tutorials

SparkFun has a great overview of wiring an LED to an Arduino here: and a great overview of writing a potentiometer to an Arduino here:

11.7 Project Ideas

P11.01 Use Python and PySerial measure light levels using a photoresistor connected to an Arduino.

P11.02 Use Python and PySerial to control a relay connected to an Arduino

P11.03 Use Python and PySerial to read a pH sensor connected to an Arduino

P11.04 Use Python and PySerial to read a photosensor connected to an Arduino and turn on and off an LED based on light level.

P11.05 Use Python and PySerial to read a temperature connected to an Arduino and send temperature measurements up to an IoT cloud server, like io.adafruit.com using the Requests package.

P11.06 Use Python and PySerial to turn on and off an LED connected to an Arduino based on values stored on an IoT cloud server, like io.adafruit.com, using the Requests package.

Chapter 12

MicroPython

12.1 Introduction

By the end of this chapter you will be able to:

- Install MicroPython on a microcontroller
- Run Python commands on a microcontroller using the MicroPython REPL
- Save module files and run Python scripts on a microcontroller
- Use MicroPython to read data off a sensor
- Use MicroPython to switch on and off a light

12.2 What is MicroPython?

What is MicroPython?

MicroPython is a port, or version of Python designed to run on small, inexpensive, low-power microcontrollers. Examples of microcontrollers that Micropython can run on includes the pyboard, the WiPy and ESP8266-based boards like the Adafruit Feather Huzzah and ESP8266 NodeMCU.

Traditionally, Python runs on desktop or laptop computers and cloud servers. Compared to a desktop or laptop, microcontrollers are much smaller, cheaper and less powerful. A "regular" version of Python can't run on small, cheap microcontrollers because Python is too resource intensive. Regular Python takes up too much hard disk space, runs on too much RAM and requires a more powerful processor than microcontrollers have.

It is pretty amazing that a version of Python (MicroPython) runs on these small, cheap microcontrollers like the ESP8266. To get MicroPython to run at all on these little low-cost boards, MicroPython only contains a subset of all the Standard Library modules included with "regular" Python. Some of the libraries that are included with MicroPython don't have the full set of functions and classes that come with the full version of Python. By not including the full functionality of "regular" Python, MicroPython is compact (around 600 kB for the ESP8266 port), and MicroPython only uses a small amount of RAM (down to 16k according to the Micropython main page.)

You can try using MicroPython online with a browser-based MicroPython online emulator. The emulator allows you to run commands at a MicroPython Prompt and see the result on a virtual pyboard.

What is MicroPython used for?

MicroPython can be installed on small, cheap microcontrollers like the ESP8266. Anything these small microcontrollers can do, MicroPython can do. A microcontroller running MicroPython can read a remote sensor to measure things like temperature, humidity and light level. MicroPython can also be used to blink LED's, control arrays of LED's, or run small displays. MicroPython can control servo motors, stepper motors, and solenoids. Civil Engineers could use MicroPython to monitor water levels. Mechanical Engineers could use MicroPython to drive robots. Electrical Engineers could use MicroPython to measure voltage levels in embedded systems.

By the end of this chapter, you will learn how to use MicroPython, running on a small cheap ESP8266 board, to turn on and off a light and read a sensor.

Why should problem solvers learn MircoPython?

Python is used to solve problems such as calculations, statistics, modeling, and visualization. But Python on its own is relatively limited in controlling devices outside the computer it's running on. You don't want to leave a laptop in a remote estuary to measure water temperature, but you could leave a little microcontroller and low-cost temperature sensor in a remote location. A small robot can't carry around a heavy laptop, but a small, light, low-power board could run a simple robot. You don't want to use a computer for every small electrical measurement or embedded system control, but a $2 WiFi module would work.

Besides, learning how to use MicroPython on small, cheap microcontroller can help problem

12.3 Installing MicroPython

MicroPython is a port of the Python programming language that runs on small, inexpensive microcontrollers. In this section, you will learn how to install MicroPython on an ESP8266-based microcontroller such as the Adafruit Feather Huzzah ESP8266 and the ESP8266 NodeMCU using Python and a package called **esptool**. In subsequent sections, you will learn how to control an LED and read a sensor using MicroPython.

The following hardware is needed to install MicroPython on an ESP8266-based microcontroller:

Hardware	Purpose
A laptop or desktop computer	install MicroPython on the microcontroller
Adafruit Feather Huzzah ESP8266	microcontroller running MicroPython
micro USB cable	connect the microcontroller to computer

The following software is used to install MicroPython on an ESP8266-based microcontroller:

Software	Purpose
Anaconda distribution of Python	run **esptool** that installs MicroPython
Anaconda Prompt	Install **esptool** package with **pip**
esptool	A **pip** installable package used to install MicroPython
firmware *.bin* file	Version of MicroPython run on the microcontroller

Summary of Steps:

1. Install the Anaconda distribution of Python
2. Create a new conda environment and `pip install esptool`
3. Download the latest MicroPython .bin firmware file
4. Install the SiLabs driver for the Adafruit Feather Huzzah ESP8266
5. Connect the ESP8266-based microcontroller board to the laptop using a micro USB cable
6. Determine which serial port the microcontroller is connected to
7. Run the **esptool** to upload the *.bin* firmware file to the microcontroller
8. Download and install PuTTY, a serial monitor
9. Use PuTTY to connect to the microcontroller and run commands at the MicroPython REPL

Install the Anaconda distribution of Python

If you don't have the Anaconda distribution of Python installed already, go to Anaconda.com/download to download and install the latest version.

Create a new conda environment and install esptool

To install MicroPython on the ESP8266-based microcontroller, we will start by creating a *virtual environment*. A virtual environment is an isolated Python interpreter and a set of packages that are separate from the base version of Python running on your computer. We'll create a new virtual environment with the **Anaconda Prompt** and the conda command line tool.

Open the **Anaconda Prompt** and create a new virtual environment named micropython. Activate the environment with the command conda activate. After activating the virtual environment, you should see the virtual environment name (micropython) before the > Prompt. Once inside the virtual environment, use pip to install esptool. esptool will be used to upload the MicroPython *.bin* firmware file onto the ESP8266-based microcontroller. Confirm that esptool is installed in the (micropython) virtual environment by running the command conda list. The list of commands below also creates a new directory in the Documents folder called micropython to store all the project files.

```
> conda create -n micropython python=3.6
> conda activate micropython
(micropython) > pip install esptool
(micropython) > conda list
(micropython) > cd Documents
(micropython) > mkdir micropthon
(micropython) > cd micropython
```

Download the latest MicroPython firmware .bin file

Go to GitHub.com and download the latest *.bin* firmware file at micropython.org/download#esp8266. Move the *.bin* firmware file to a new micropython directory. The *.bin* firmware file is the version of MicroPython that runs on the ESP8266 microcontroller. Straight from the manufacturer, the ESP8266 microcontroller probably does not have MicroPyton installed, so we need to install MicroPython ourselves. After installing the Micropython *.bin* firmware file onto the board, we will be able to bring up the MicroPython REPL prompt, type commands into the Micropython REPL and run Micropython *.py* scripts on the board.

Install the SiLabs driver for the ESP8266-based microcontroller

Before we connect the ESP8266-based microcontroller such as an Adafruit Feather Huzzah ESP8266 or ESP8266 NodeMCU to the computer, a specific driver needs to be installed. For Windows 10 laptop to see the board, the CP210x USB to UART Bridge VCP driver needs to be downloaded from SiLabs and installed. The driver download and installation is quick and easy but does require administrator privileges.

12.3. INSTALLING MICROPYTHON

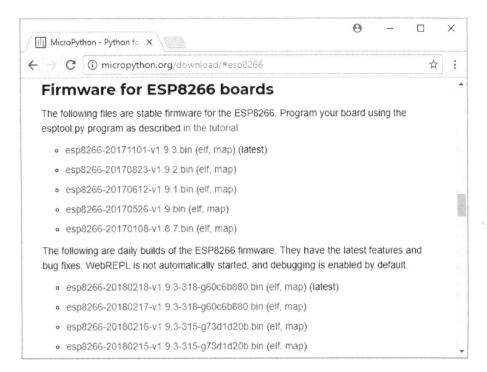

Figure 12.1. MicroPython Firmware

Figure 12.2. SiLabs Driver Download Page

Connect the ESP8266-based microcontroller to the computer

Use a microUSB cable (the same kind of cable that charges many mobile phones) to connect the ESP8266-based microcontroller to the computer. Make sure the microUSB cable is a full **USB data cable** and not just a power only cable. If you have trouble getting the microcontroller to work, one reason might be the micoUSB cable you are using is only a charging cable and can not transfer data.

Determine which serial port the ESP8266-based microcontroller is connected to

Use the Windows Device Manager to determine which serial port the ESP8266-based microcontroller is connected to is connected to. The serial port is one of the parameters which needs to be defined when the *.bin* firmware file is upload on the board.

Look for something like **Silicon Labs CP210x USB to UART Bridge (COM4)** in the **Ports (COM & LPT)** menu of the Windows Device Manager. TCP210x USB to UART Bridge refers to the chip that handles serial communication on the board, not the ESP8266 chip itself. Make a note of the number after **(COM)**. The serial port number often comes up as **(COM4)** but it may be different on your computer.

Run esptool to upload the .bin file to the ESP8266-based microcontroller

Open the Anaconda Prompt with the Windows Start Menu and cd(change directory) into the `micropython` directory which contains the *.bin* file. Use the `dir` command to see the `micropython` directory contents. Make sure the *.bin* firmware file is in the directory. The *.bin* firmware file is named something like esp8266-20171101-v1.9.3.bin. Activate the micropython virtual environment with the command `conda activate micropython`. Run `esptool --help` to ensure **esptool** is installed properly. Note there is no **.py** extension after `esptool`. On Windows , the command `esptool` works, but the command `esptool.py` may not. (Note this behavior is different than the commands shown on the MicroPython docs). If you try to run `esptool` and you are not in the (micropython) virtual environment, an error is returned.

```
> cd Documents
> cd micropython
> pwd
Documents/micropython
> dir
> conda activate micropython
(micropython) > esptool --help
```

Before uploading the *.bin* firmware file to the ESP8266-based microcontroller, it is best practice to first erase the flash memory on the board using the command `esptool erase_flash`. Make sure to specify the `--port`. The argument after `--port` is the COM port assigned to the ESP8266 board shown in the Windows Device Manager. This port often comes up as COM4.

```
(micropython) > esptool --port COM4 erase_flash
```

Now you can finally write the *.bin* firmware file to the flash memory on the microcontroller using the `esptool write_flash` command. Make sure to use the exact firmware file name you see sitting in the `micropython` directory. The port needs to be set corresponding to the port you found in the Windows Device Manager. ---baud is the baud rate or upload speed. I found that --baud 460800

12.3. INSTALLING MICROPYTHON

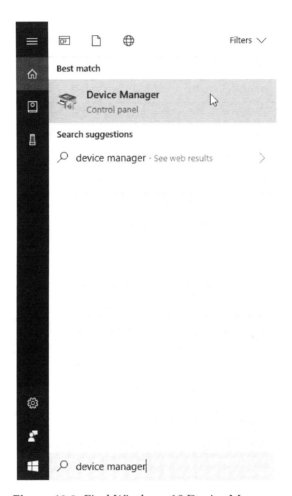

Figure 12.3. Find Windows 10 Device Manager

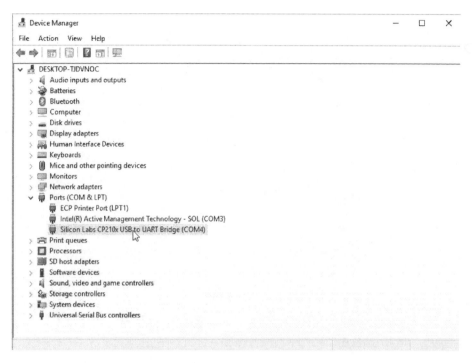

Figure 12.4. Windows 10 Device Manager Menu

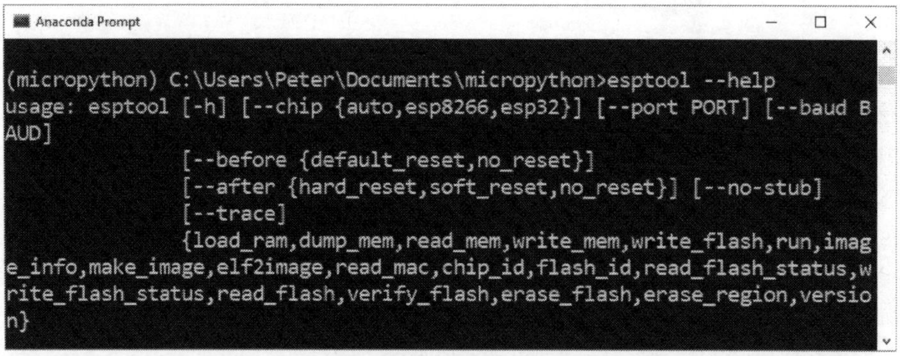

Figure 12.5. Anaconda Prompt: Result of esptool –help command

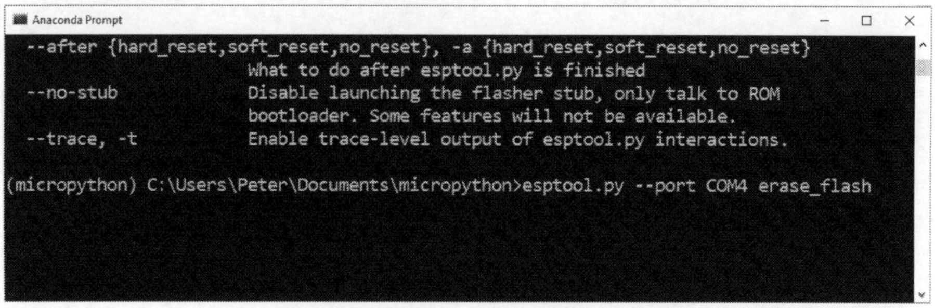

Figure 12.6. Anaconda Prompt: esptool erase_flash command

12.3. INSTALLING MICROPYTHON

Figure 12.7. Anaconda Prompt: esptool upload command

Figure 12.8. PuTTY Downloads Page

worked, but you could also specify --baud 115200 which is slower. The upload time was a matter of seconds with either baud rate. The 0 after --flash_size=dectect means the firmware is written at the start of the flash memory (the 0th position) on the board. Again, make sure the *.bin* firmware file name is correct. The long file name is easy to mistype.

```
(micropython) > esptool --port COM4 --baud 115200 write_flash \
--flash_size=detect 0 esp8266-20171101-v1.9.3.bin
```

Download and install PuTTY, a serial monitor

Now that MicroPython is installed on the ESP8266-based microcontroller, we can communicate with our board over a serial connection. However, Windows doesn't have a built-in serial monitor (like **screen** on MacOS and Linux). Therefore, if you are using the Windows operating system, you need to download and install a serial communication tool like **PuTTY**.

PuTTY is a lightweight serial and SSH client for Windows. PuTTY provides an interface to communicate with the ESP8266-based microcontroller. PuTTY can be downloaded here. PuTTY is pretty small, and the download and installation are quick.

Connect to the ESP8266-based Microcontroller with PuTTY

Ensure the ESP8266-based microcontroller is connected to the computer with a USB cable and ensure the board is visible in the Windows Device Manager. Then use PuTTY to connect to the board over serial. Make sure to specify the correct serial port in the **Serial line** box and set **115200** baud in the Speed box. **Micropython is set to run at 115200 baud**, other baud rates will lead to junk characters in the serial monitor. Make sure to select the **Serial** radio button below the header **Connection type:** near the top of the PuTTY window. Overlooking this detail is easy.

If you see >>> the MicroPython REPL (the MicroPython prompt), MicroPython is successfully installed on your ESP8266-based microcontroller.

Figure 12.9. PuTTY in Windows 10 Start Menu

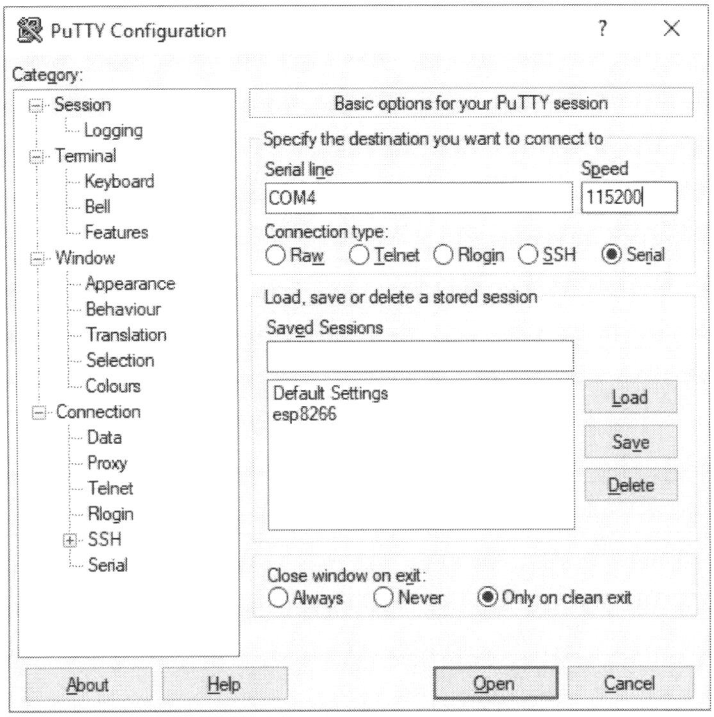

12.3. INSTALLING MICROPYTHON

Figure 12.10. PuTTY Configuration

Sometimes, you may need to type [Enter] or Ctrl-D to bring up the >>> REPL prompt. If the >>> REPL prompt is not displayed in your PuTTY window, try to close PuTTY, unplug then replug the board and open PuTTY again. Most ESP8266-based microcontrollers also have a tiny little black RESET button that can be pressed to restart the board.

At the >>> MicroPython REPL prompt try the following commands:

```
>>> print('Problem Solving with MicroPython!')
Problem Solving with MicroPython!

>>> import sys
>>> sys.platform
'esp8266'
```

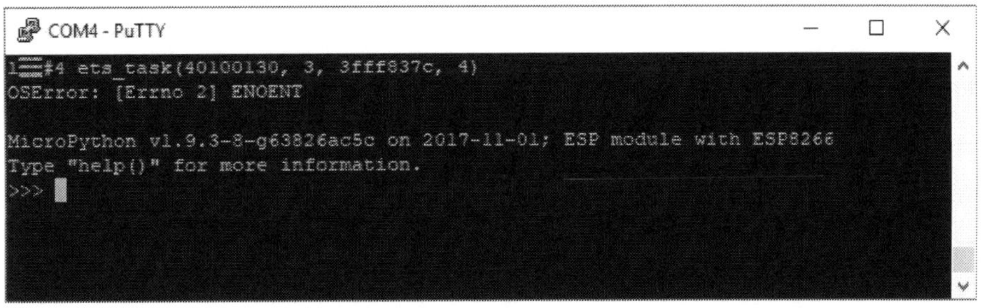

Figure 12.11. The MicroPython REPL Prompt

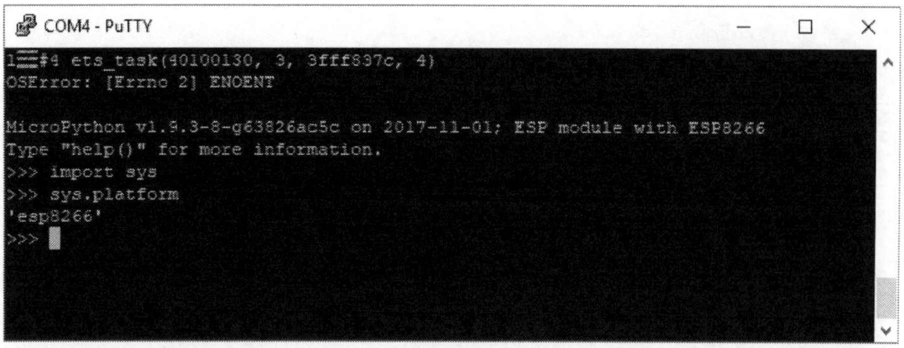

Figure 12.12. Results of commands typed in the MicroPython REPL

12.4 The MicroPython REPL

The last section detailed the installation of MicroPython on an ESP8266-based microcontroller using Python and a package called **esptool**. In this section, you will learn how to write commands to the MicroPython REPL (the Micropython prompt) to turn an LED on and off.

Before you can use the MicroPython REPL (the MicroPython prompt) running on a microcontroller, MicroPython needs to be installed on the board. A serial communication tool, like PuTTY, also needs to be installed on your computer to communicate with the microcontroller over a serial line. The previous section detailed how to install MicroPython on an ESP8266-based microcontroller and how to install PuTTY on Windows.

Summary of Steps

1. Connect the ESP8266-based microcontroller to your computer with a USB cable
2. Determine which COM port the microcontroller is connected to using the Windows Device Manager
3. Open PuTTY and connect to the ESP8266-based microcontroller
4. Run commands at the MicroPython REPL

Connect the ESP8266-based microcontroller to your computer with a USB cable

Use a microUSB cable to connect the microcontroller to the computer. Make sure that the microUSB cable is a full USB data cable and not just a simple power cable. Cables that are just used to charge phones may only be power cables and may not be capable of transmitting data.

Determine which COM port the microcontroller is connected to using the Windows Device Manager

Use the Windows Device Manager to determine which serial port the microcontroller is connected to. On Windows, the microcontroller usually comes up as COM4. You can find the serial port by looking in the Ports (COM & LPT) category of the Windows Device Manager. Look for something

12.4. THE MICROPYTHON REPL

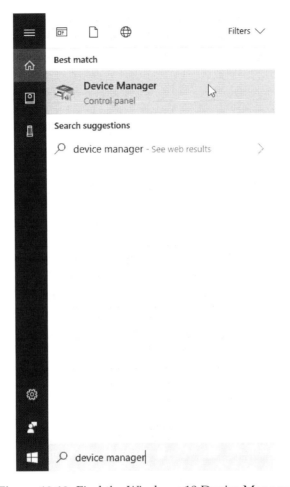

Figure 12.13. Find the Windows 10 Device Manager

like **Silicon Labs CP210x USB to UART Bridge (COM4)** in the **Ports (COM & LPT)** menu. It is the **COM#** that's needed to connect to the board.

Open PuTTY and connect to the ESP8266-based microcontroller

Ensure the microcontroller is connected to your computer with a USB cable. Then initialize serial communication between the microcontroller and your computer with PuTTY. In PuTTY set the proper serial port (COM#) and 115200 baud. Remember to use the **[Serial[** radio button under **[Connection Type:]** to select serial communication or PuTTY will attempt to communicate with the microcontroller over SSH which won't work.

In PuTTY, click **[Open]** to bring up the MicroPython REPL prompt >>>. If you can't see the >>> prompt, try typing [Enter], [Ctrl]-[D], pushing the RESET button on the microcontroller or unplugging then replugging the USB cable.

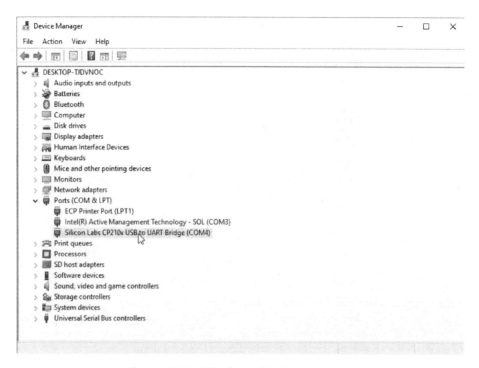

Figure 12.14. Windows Device Manager

Run commands at the MicroPython REPL

At the MicroPython REPL (the MicroPython command prompt >>>) try the following commands:

```
>>> print('MicroPython for Engineers!')
MicroPython for Engineers
```

If you import the sys module, you can see the MicroPython implementation and platform.

```
>>> import sys
>>> sys.implementation
(name='micropython', version=(1, 9, 3))
>>> sys.platform
'esp8266'
```

If you see similar output, that means MicroPython is working on the ESP8266-based microcontroller. You can also view the flash memory size of your microcontroller and the size of the MicroPython firmware you installed. Try the command below at the MicroPython prompt:

```
>>> import port_diag
```

In the results above, you can see the flash memory size is 4 MB. Below the label `Firmware checksum:` you can see a line for `size: 600872`. `size: 600872` means the size of the Micropythpon installation is about 600 KB or about 0.6 MB. Just over half a megabyte on the microcontroller and you are running a working version of Python!

Now try a simple for loop. When you initiate a loop, the MicroPython REPL automatically indents the next line. A tab is not needed on code lines below a loop statement. To run the loop, type

12.4. THE MICROPYTHON REPL

Figure 12.15. PuTTY in Windows 10 start menu

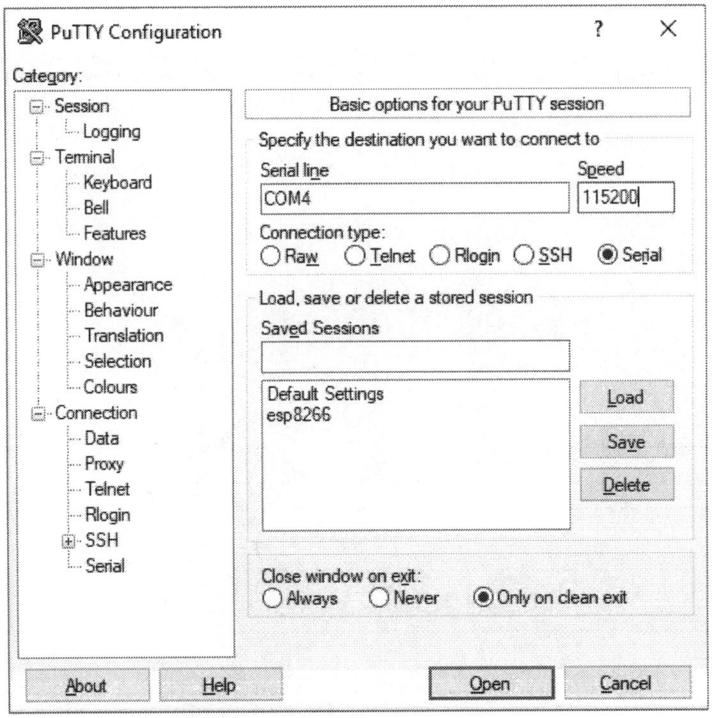

Figure 12.16. PuTTY configuration

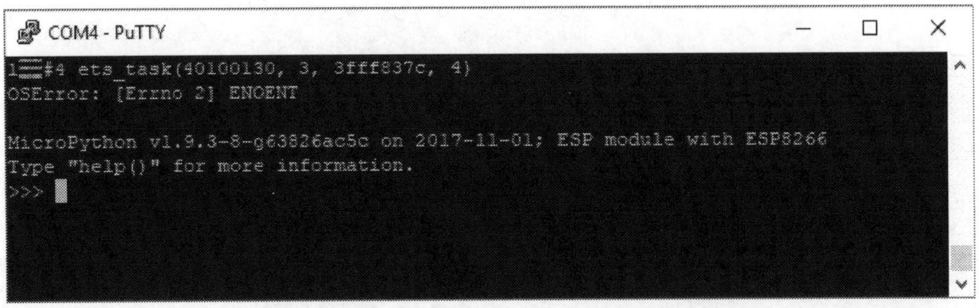

Figure 12.17. MicroPython REPL prompt

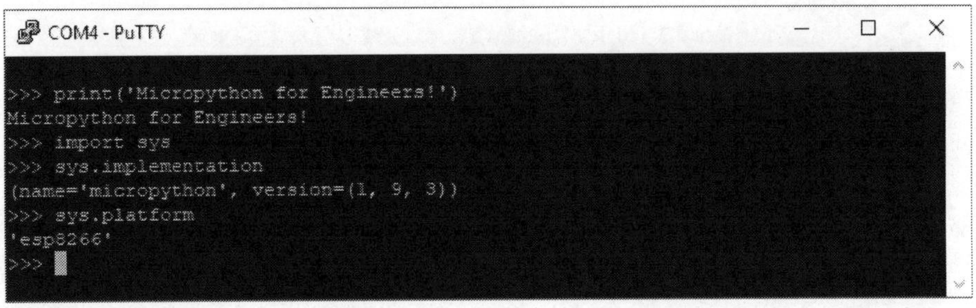

Figure 12.18. Results of running sys commands at the MicroPython REPL prompt

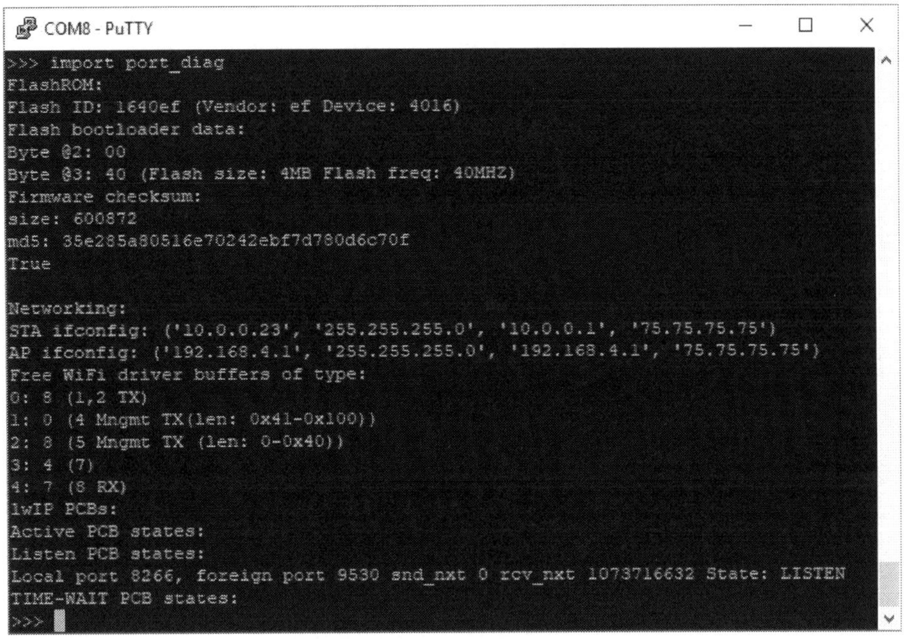

12.5. BLINKING A LED

Figure 12.19. Results of running import port_diag at the MicroPython REPL prompt

backspace on an empty line (to backspace away from an indented line) and hit [Enter].

```
>>> for i in range(5):
...     print("Problem Solving with MicroPython!")
...
Problem Solving with MicroPython!
Problem Solving with MicroPython!
Problem Solving with MicroPython!
Problem Solving with MicroPython!
Problem Solving with MicroPython!
```

12.5 Blinking a LED

In this section, you will learn how to blink the built-in LED on ESP8266-based microcontroller using the MicroPython REPL.

Before the LED on the ESP8266-based microcontroller can be blinked, MicroPython needs to be installed on the microcontroller and PuTTY needs to be installed on your computer. PuTTY facilitates interaction between a computer and the microcontroller using the serial communication protocol. An alternative to PuTTY is a MacOS or Linux terminal and the **screen** utility. The **screen** utility can also be used for serial communication.

Most ESP8266-based microcontrollers (such as the Adafruit Feather Huzzah ESP8266) have a built-in LED mounted on the board. On many boards, the built-in LED is connected to Pin 0. You can control the board's built-in LED with MicroPython's `machine` module.

Figure 12.20. PuTTY in the Windows 10 Start Menu

Connect the ESP8266-based Microcontroller to the computer and bring up the MicroPython REPL

Connect the ESP8266-based microcontroller to the computer with a microUSB cable. Ensure the microUSB cable is a USB data cable, not just a charging cable. Open PuTTY and connect to the microcontroller using the proper serial port (COM#) and 115200 baud. (Remember to use the **Serial** radio button under **Connection Type:**)

Clicking [Open] will bring up the MicroPython REPL prompt >>>. If you can't see the >>> prompt, try typing [Enter] or [Ctrl]+[D] or push the RESET button on the microcontroller. If none of these methods work, try closing PuTTY and unplugging then replugging in the microUSB cable that connects the board to the computer.

Use the MicroPython REPL to turn the microcontroller's LED on and off

Test to see if the MicroPython REPL is functioning correctly with a basic *Hello World* program. Type the following into the PuTTY window:

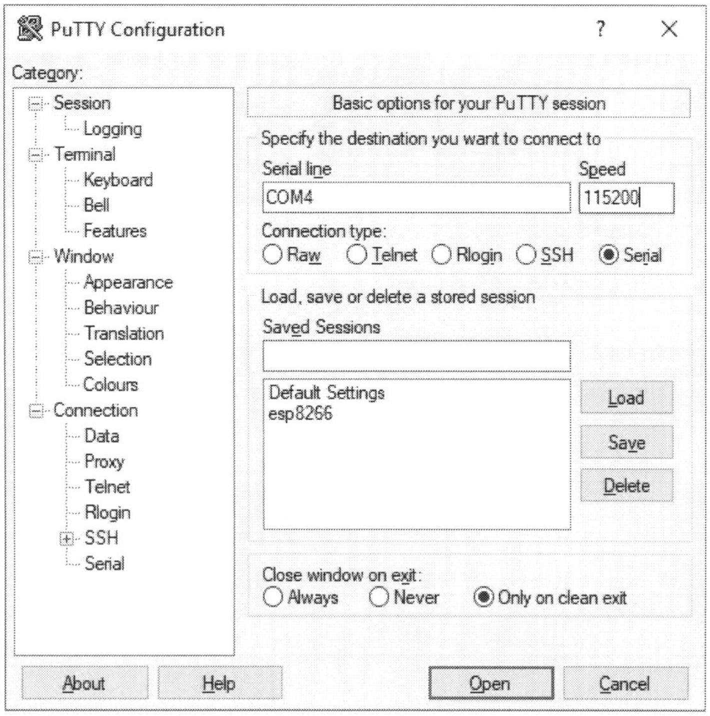

12.5. BLINKING A LED

Figure 12.21. PuTTY Configuration

```
>>> print("Hello World")
Hello World
```

Next, try to turn the microcontroller's built-in LED on and off. Most ESP8266-based microcontrollers (such as the Adafruit Feather Huzzah ESP8266) have a built-in LED connected to Pin 0. If you control the voltage going to Pin 0, you control if the built-in LED on the microcontroller is on or off. To control a Pin on a microcontroller with MicroPython, you first need to import the **machine** module. The **machine** module is built into MicroPython, but absent from "regular" Python. Next, a Pin object needs to be created. The integer passed into machine.Pin() determines the pin number assigned to the Pin object.

```
>>> import machine
>>> pin = machine.Pin(0)
```

The value of Pin0 (on or off) is determined with the command below.

```
>>> pin.value
1
```

In or assign a value to Pin 0, the Pin object must be assigned as an *output* pin. An output pin is a pin where a program or user determines the pin output. An input pin is a pin set up to read input, like the input from a sensor. In this case, you want to assign Pin 0 as an output pin.

```
>>> pin = machine.Pin(0, machine.Pin.OUT)

# turn the LED on
```

```
>>> pin.value(0)

# turn the LED off
>>> pin.value(1)
```

Run code at the MicroPython REPL to blink the LED

Now let's make the microcontroller's built-in LED blink. Blinking the LED can be accomplished with a simple for loop. At the MicroPython REPL, initiating a loop automatically indents the next line, so a tab is not needed before the pin.on() statement. To run the loop, type backspace on an empty line (to backspace from an indented line) and hit [Enter].

```
>>> import machine
>>> import time
>>> pin = machine.Pin(0, machine.Pin.OUT)
>>> for i in range(10):
...     pin.on()
...     time.sleep(0.5)
...     pin.off()
...     time.sleep(0.5)
...
```

The microcontroller's built-in LED turns on and off for a total of about 10 seconds.

12.6 Reading a Sensor

In this section, you will learn how to connect a temperature sensor to an ESP8266-based microcontroller and use the MicroPython REPL to read the temperature. This section includes specifics for the Adafruit Feather Huzzah ESP8266 microcontroller and the MCP9808 temperature sensor. Other ESP8266-based microcontrollers and temperature sensors could be used instead, but the specifics of the procedure may be different from what's shown in this section.

Before you can use MicroPython to read a temperature sensor, MicroPython needs to be installed on the board, and PuTTY needs to be installed on your computer (on MacOS and Linux, use a terminal and screen) to communicate with the board over serial.

Summary of Steps

1. Connect the MCP9808 temperature sensor to the Adafruit Feather Huzzah ESP8266 microcontroller
2. Connect the Adafruit Feather Huzzah ESP8266 microcontroller to the computer with a USB cable and bring up the MicroPython REPL with PuTTY
3. Run code at the MicroPython REPL to measure the temperature

12.6. READING A SENSOR

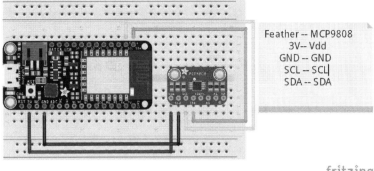

Figure 12.22. MCP9808 temperature sensor connected to an Adafruit Feather Huzzah ESP8266

Connect the MCP9808 temperature sensor to the Adafruit Feather Huzzah ESP8266 microcontroller

Connect the MCP9808 temperature sensor breakout board to the Adafruit Feather Huzzah ESP8266 microcontroller with jumper wires. There are four connections: A 3V power line from the Feather Huzzah to the MCP9808 Vdd pin, GND connected between both boards, and the I2C data and clock lines connected between the two boards. On the Feather Huzzah ESP8266, the I2C data line is SDA (pin 4) and the I2C clock line is SCL (pin 5). These pins on the microcontroller connect with the MPC9808 I2C data line SDA and the MPC9808 I2C clock line SCL. Unlike serial communication where RX connects to TX, in I2C communication SDA connects to SDA and SCL connects to SCL.

Feather Huzzah	wire	MCP9808
3V	red	Vdd
GND	black	GND
SDA (pin 4)	green	SDA
SCL (pin 5)	yellow	SCL

Connect the Adafruit Feather Huzzah ESP8266 microcontroller to the computer with a USB cable and bring up the MicroPython REPL with PuTTY

Connect the Adafruit Feather Huzzah ESP8266 to the computer with a microUSB cable. Ensure the cable is a USB data cable, not just a power cable. Open PuTTY and connect to the Feather Huzzah using the proper serial port (COM#) and 115200 baud. (Remember to use the **Serial** radio button under **Connection Type:**)

Clicking [Open] will bring up the MicroPython REPL prompt >>>. If you can't see the >>> prompt, try typing [Enter] or [Ctrl]+[D] or push the RESET button on the Feather Huzzah. If none of these methods work, try closing PuTTY and unplugging then replugging in the USB cable then reopen PuTTY.

Figure 12.23. PuTTY in the Windows 10 Start Menu

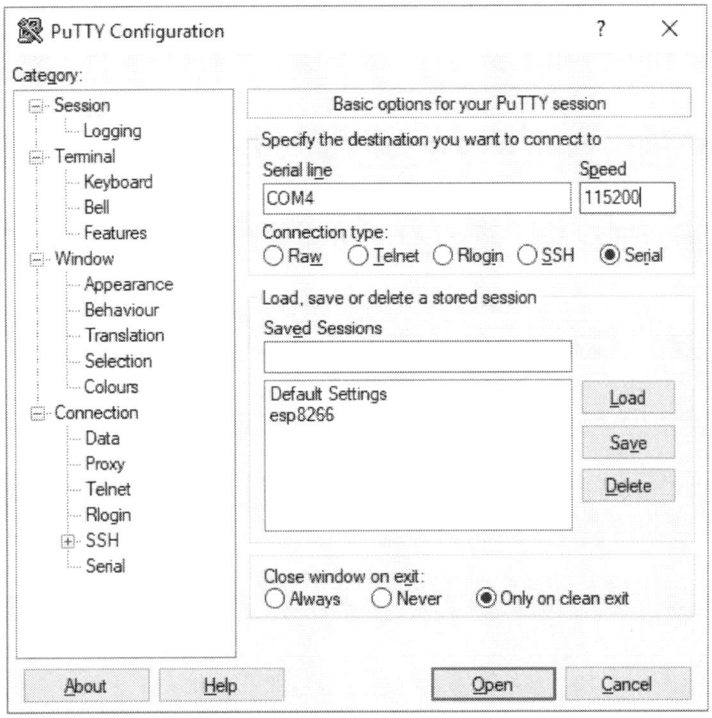

12.6. READING A SENSOR

Figure 12.24. PuTTY Configuration

Run code at the MicroPython REPL to measure the temperature

At the MicroPython REPL, import the `machine` module and then create an instance of the `machine.I2C` class. Set the `scl` and `sda` parameters as `scl=machine.Pin(5)` and `sda=machine.Pin(4)`. Next, create an empty bytearray to store the data coming in from the MCP9808 temperature sensor. As strings in Micropython are UTF-8 encoded by default (like in Python 3), a *bytearray* needs to be used to read the raw output from the MCP9808 chip registers. The command `i2c.readfrom_mem_into()` reads the data from the sensor and saves it to the `byte_data` variable. The arguments inside the `i2c.readfrom_mem_into()` method 24 and 5 correspond to the I2C memory address and registry address of the temperature data stored in the MCP9808 temperature sensor.

```
>>> import machine
>>> i2c = machine.I2C(scl=machine.Pin(5), sda=machine.Pin(4))
>>> byte_data = bytearray(2)
>>> i2c.readfrom_mem_into(24, 5, byte_data)
>>> value = byte_data[0] << 8 | byte_data[1]
>>> temp = (value & 0xFFF) / 16.0
>>> if value & 0x1000:
...     temp -= 256.0
.....   print(temp)
```

12.7 Uploading Code

In this section, you will learn how to upload code to an ESP8266-based microcontroller with a tool called **ampy**. The code in this section was written to turn the ESP8266-based microcontroller in a scrolling thermometer. The same upload method shown in this section can be used to upload MicroPython code you write to a ESP8266-based microcontroller.

Before MicroPython code is uploaded on the ESP8266-based microcontroller, MicroPython needs to be installed on the board. PuTTY also needs to be installed on you computer in order for the computer to communicate with the microcontroller over a serial connection.

A previous section in this chapter detailed how to install MicroPython on an ESP9266 microcontroller and how to install PuTTY on a Windows. The procedures in this section are specific to the Adafruit Feather Huzzah ESP8266 microcontroller and the MCP9808 temperature sensor, both of which were used in a previous section. Other ESP8266-based microcontrollers and I2C sensors could be used instead, but the specifics of the procedure may be different from what's shown in this section.

Summary of Steps

1. Install **ampy** with **pip**
2. Write MicroPython code
3. Upload the MicroPython on code on the microcontroller with **ampy**
4. Unplug and then power up the Feather Huzzah and watch the temperature scroll by

Install ampy with pip

Ampy is a Python package developed by Adafruit, a company that makes MicroPython compatible hardware. **Ampy** is used to push code stored on a computer onto a microcontroller running MicroPython. **Ampy** can be installed using the **Anaconda Prompt**. Alternatively, a terminal can be used to install **ampy**. If you are using a virtual environment, active the virtual environment first then proceed with **ampy** package installation.

```
> conda activate micropython
(micropython) > pip install adafruit-ampy
(micropython) > ampy --help
```

Write MicroPython Code

Now write the MicroPython code which you will uploaded on the microcontroller. The Adafruit Feather Huzzah ESP8266 microcontroller contains two main Python files: *boot.py* and *main.py*. But additional files can also be uploaded to the microcontroller. *boot.py* is the file that runs first when the board is powered up. First *boot.py* runs, then **main.py** runs. An additional *.py* file can be added to the board to provide *main.py* with a function to run.

Two different *.py* files will be constructed in this section. One *.py* file contains a function that reads the temperature off the temperature sensor. A second *.py* file calls the function in the first *.py* file and prints the temperature to the terminal window with a loop.

12.7. UPLOADING CODE

The first *MCP9808.py* file includes one function called `readtemp()`. The `readtemp()` function reads temperature recorded by the MCP9808 temperature sensor. The `readtemp()` function parses out the temperature data from the I2C bus on the MCP9808 temperature sensor and outputs the temperature in degrees C as a float.

At the top of *MCP9808.py* we need to import the `machine` module to use the I2C bus. The `machine` module provides a class to create a new I2C object.

When the I2C object is instantiated, the `scl` and `sda` pins that the MCP9808 temperature sensor is connected to need to be specified. `scl` is the I2C clock line and `sda` is the I2C data line. `scl` and `sda` are pin 5 and pin 4 on the Adafruit Feather Huzzah ESP8266.

The next part of the `readtemp()` function creates a byte array. Data from the MCP9808 temperature sensor will be stored in the byte array.

The next part of the `readtemp()` function in the *MCP9808.py* file uses the `i2c.readfrom_mem_into()` method to read the temperature off the sensor. The first argument passed to the `i2c.readfrom_mem_into()` method is the I2C bus address of the sensor. On the MCP9808 temperature sensor, the I2C bus address is 24(if you type the line >>> `i2c.scan()` into the MicroPython REPL, the I2C bus address is returned). The next parameter passed to the `i2c.readfrom_mem_into()` method is the register on the MCP9808 temperature sensor where the measured temperature is stored. On the MCP9808, the temperature is stored in register 5. The third parameter passed to the `i2c.readfrom_mem_into()` method is the variable we want to store the temperature data in. The `i2c.readfrom_mem_into()` method *changes* the variable passed into the method as the third argument. Most Python methods modify the object the method operates on, but MicroPython's `i2c.readfrom_mem_into()` method changes the third variable passed to it, in our case the variable `byte_data`. That's why we created the `byte_data` variable before we called the `i2c.readfrom_mem_into()` method.

The last part of the `readtemp()` function includes post-processing needed to convert the byte array into a temperature in degrees C. The final temperature in degrees C is a float

The entire contents of the *MCP9808.py* file are below:

```
# MCP9808.py

# Functions for the  MCP9808 temperature sensor
# learn.adafruit.com/micropython-hardware-i2c-devices/i2c-master

def readtemp():
    import machine
    i2c = machine.I2C(scl=machine.Pin(5), sda=machine.Pin(4))
    byte_data = bytearray(2)
    i2c.readfrom_mem_into(24, 5, byte_data)
    value = byte_data[0] << 8 | byte_data[1]
    temp = (value & 0xFFF) / 16.0
    if value & 0x1000:
        temp -= 256.0
    return temp
```

Now construct a MicroPython script called *main.py* which will use the function `readtemp()` stored in *MCP9808.py*.

The *main.py* script will import the *MCP9808.py* module and use the `readtemp()` function to read the temperature from the MCP9808 temperature sensor.

Inside *main.py* will be a loop that runs for a total of 120 seconds. Each second the temperature is recorded. Inside the loop, the temperature is read off the MCP9808 temperature sensing using the `MCP9808.readtemp()` function. `time.sleep(1)` is inserted into the loop to wait one second between each measurement.

The complete *main.py* file is below.

```
# main.py

import MCP9808
import time

time.sleep(2)

for i in range(120):
    data = MCP9808.readtemp()
    print(data)
    time.sleep(1)
```

Upload MicroPython Code to the ESP8266 Microcontroller with ampy

Once the *MCP9808.py* file and the *main.py* files are saved, both files can be uploaded on the Adafruit Feather Huzzah ESP8266 microcontroller.

Ensure the microcontroller is connected with a USB cable, and be aware of which serial port the microcontroller is connected to.

Upload the *MCP9808.py* file and the *main.py* file to the board using **ampy**. Make sure you are in the directory with the *.py* files and that you are working in a virtual environment that has ampy installed in it. In the example code below, the (micropython) virtual environment is active. The command `ampy --port COM4 ls` lists the files stored on the microcontroller.

```
(micropython) > ampy --port COM4 put MCP9808.py
(micropython) > ampy --port COM4 put main.py
(micropython) > ampy --port COM4 ls
boot.py
MCP9808.py
main.py
```

Unplug and then power up the Feather Huzzah and watch the temperature scroll by

The Feather Huzzah needs to be restarted to run the *main.py* file uploaded with **ampy**.

To restart the board, unplug and then replug in the board's power (the USB cable). Once power is restored, the board will run through the *boot.py* script then start the *main.py* script. When the board runs the *main.py* script, the board will read the temperature from the MCP9808 temperature sensor then print the temperature out to the terminal. After two minutes the program should end.

The output below demonstrates the results shown in a terminal window.

12.7. UPLOADING CODE

```
...
25.6875
25.75
25.6875
25.6875
25.75
25.6875
25.75
25.75
25.75
25.75
25.75
25.8125
25.8125
25.8125
25.75
25.75
25.8125
>>>
```

12.8 Summary

In this chapter, you learned about MicroPython. MicroPython is a small slimed down port of the Python programming language designed to run on small cheap microcontrollers. The first part of the chapter introduced MicroPython. "Regular" Python consumes to much hard disk space and RAM to be run installed on a microcontroller. But MicroPython is very small for a programming language. It only takes up less than 1MB on a microcontroller.

The next section of the chapter involved how to install MicroPython on a microcontroller. To install MicroPython on a microcontroller, use a package called **esptool** and upload a .bin firmware file to the board.

The rest of the chapter involved two projects. Blinking an LED with MicroPython and reading a sensor with MicroPython.

To blink an LED on a microcontroller, you need to connect to the microcontroller with a program called PuTTY. Through a PuTTY terminal, you can use MicroPython's `machine` module to write high and low values to the pins on the microcontroller.

An MCP9808 temperature sensor was read using MicroPython in the second project. The sensor first needed to be wired up to the microcontroller, and then the MicroPython's `ic2` class was used to read data off the sensor. At the end of the project, a Python package called **ampy** was used to upload a *.py* file to the microcontroller.

Key Terms and Concepts

MicroPython	pyboard	USB data cable
microcontroller	ESP8266	PuTTY
MicroPython REPL	resource intensive	MCP9808 temperature sensor
REPL prompt	esptool	ampy
baud rate	.bin firmware file	Hello World
port	driver	

12.9 Project Ideas

P12.01 Use MicroPython and a microcontroller to read a potentiometer and print the results to the screen of a computer.

P12.02 Use MicroPython, a microcontroller, and a light sensor to measure light level. Light up different numbers of LED's based on the measured light level.

P12.03 Use MicroPython and a microcontroller to read a potentiometer and print the results to the screen of a computer.

P12.04 Use MicroPython to turn on and off an LED based on a value stored on an IoT cloud server, like io.adafruit.com.

P12.05 Use MicorPython and a temperature sensor connected to a microcontroller to measure the temperature and send the temperature to a computer running Python and PySerial. Use Matplotlib

12.9. PROJECT IDEAS

on the computer to plot the temperature.

P12.06 Use MicroPython and uRequests package to send temperature sensor measurements up to an IoT cloud server, like io.adafruit.com.

Appendix

Appendix A Contents

The following is detailed in the appendix:

- Reserved and Key Words in Python
- ASCII Character Codes
- Virtual Environments
- NumPy Math Functions
- Git and GitHub
- LaTeX Math
- Problem Solving with Python 3.7 Edition Book Construction
- Contributions
- Cover Artwork
- About the author

Appendix B Reserved and Keywords in Python

The following are reserved and keywords in Python. These words should not be used as the names for user-defined variables, functions, classes, methods or modules. Python's keywords can be accessed with the following code:

```
import keyword
print(f'There are {len(keyword.kwlist)} key words')
for keywrd in keyword.kwlist:
    print(keywrd)

There are 33 key words
False
None
True
and
as
...
```

Logical Keywords

True	and	None
False	or	in
not	is	

Control Flow Key Words

if	break	finally
else	continue	raise
elif	pass	return
for	try	yield
while	except	

Definition Key Words

def	class	assert
global	lambda	del
nonlocal	with	

Module Keywords

```
import              from              as
```

Appendix C ASCII Character Codes

A listing of ASCII character codes is below. ASCII character codes character codes can be accessed using the following code:

```
In [1]: for n in range(32, 127):
            print(f'ASCII code: {n}    Character: {chr(n)}')

ASCII code: 32      Character:
ASCII code: 33      Character: !
ASCII code: 34      Character: "
ASCII code: 35      Character: #
ASCII code: 36      Character: $
ASCII code: 37      Character: %
ASCII code: 38      Character: &
ASCII code: 39      Character: '
ASCII code: 40      Character: (
ASCII code: 41      Character: )
ASCII code: 42      Character: *
ASCII code: 43      Character: +
ASCII code: 44      Character: ,
ASCII code: 45      Character: -
ASCII code: 46      Character: .
ASCII code: 47      Character: /
ASCII code: 48      Character: 0
ASCII code: 49      Character: 1
ASCII code: 50      Character: 2
ASCII code: 51      Character: 3
ASCII code: 52      Character: 4
ASCII code: 53      Character: 5
ASCII code: 54      Character: 6
ASCII code: 55      Character: 7
ASCII code: 56      Character: 8
ASCII code: 57      Character: 9
ASCII code: 58      Character: :
ASCII code: 59      Character: ;
ASCII code: 60      Character: <
ASCII code: 61      Character: =
ASCII code: 62      Character: >
ASCII code: 63      Character: ?
ASCII code: 64      Character: @
ASCII code: 65      Character: A
ASCII code: 66      Character: B
ASCII code: 67      Character: C
ASCII code: 68      Character: D
```

```
ASCII code: 69         Character: E
ASCII code: 70         Character: F
ASCII code: 71         Character: G
ASCII code: 72         Character: H
ASCII code: 73         Character: I
ASCII code: 74         Character: J
ASCII code: 75         Character: K
ASCII code: 76         Character: L
ASCII code: 77         Character: M
ASCII code: 78         Character: N
ASCII code: 79         Character: O
ASCII code: 80         Character: P
ASCII code: 81         Character: Q
ASCII code: 82         Character: R
ASCII code: 83         Character: S
ASCII code: 84         Character: T
ASCII code: 85         Character: U
ASCII code: 86         Character: V
ASCII code: 87         Character: W
ASCII code: 88         Character: X
ASCII code: 89         Character: Y
ASCII code: 90         Character: Z
ASCII code: 91         Character: [
ASCII code: 92         Character: \
ASCII code: 93         Character: ]
ASCII code: 94         Character: ^
ASCII code: 95         Character: _
ASCII code: 96         Character: `
ASCII code: 97         Character: a
ASCII code: 98         Character: b
ASCII code: 99         Character: c
ASCII code: 100        Character: d
ASCII code: 101        Character: e
ASCII code: 102        Character: f
ASCII code: 103        Character: g
ASCII code: 104        Character: h
ASCII code: 105        Character: i
ASCII code: 106        Character: j
ASCII code: 107        Character: k
ASCII code: 108        Character: l
ASCII code: 109        Character: m
ASCII code: 110        Character: n
ASCII code: 111        Character: o
ASCII code: 112        Character: p
ASCII code: 113        Character: q
ASCII code: 114        Character: r
ASCII code: 115        Character: s
ASCII code: 116        Character: t
ASCII code: 117        Character: u
```

```
ASCII code: 118        Character: v
ASCII code: 119        Character: w
ASCII code: 120        Character: x
ASCII code: 121        Character: y
ASCII code: 122        Character: z
ASCII code: 123        Character: {
ASCII code: 124        Character: |
ASCII code: 125        Character: }
ASCII code: 126        Character: ~
```

Appendix D Virtual Environments

Using *virtual environments* is standard practice in Python. A virtual environment is an isolated installation of Python with associated packages. When you use virtual environments, one project can have a separate version of Python and packages. Another project can use a different virtual environment and therefore have a different version of Python and a different set of packages.

Two projects on the same computer can use different versions of Python and different versions of packages if virtual environments are used.

Create a virtual environment with the Anaconda Prompt

To create the new virtual environment, open the **Anaconda Prompt** and issue the command:

```
> conda create --name env_name python=3.7
```

The `conda create` command builds the new virtual environment. The `--name env_name` flag gives the new virtual environment the name `env_name`. Including `python=3.7` ensures the virtual environment has a current version of Python.

The following output or something similar results:

```
The following NEW packages will be INSTALLED:

    ca-certificates    ca-certificates-2019.5.15-0
    certifi            certifi-2019.6.16-py37_0
    openssl            openssl-1.1.1c-he774522_1
    pip                pip-19.1.1-py37_0
    python             python-3.7.3-h8c8aaf0_1
    setuptools         setuptools-41.0.1-py37_0
    sqlite             sqlite-3.28.0-he774522_0
    vc                 vc-14.1-h0510ff6_4
    vs2015_runtime     vs2015_runtime-14.15.26706-h3a45250_4
    wheel              wheel-0.33.4-py37_0
    wincertstore       wincertstore-0.2-py37_0
```

Type y to confirm and create the new virtual environment.

Activate a virtual environment

To use the new virtual environment env_name, the virtual environment needs to be *activated*. To activate the environment env_name, issue the command:

```
> conda activate env_name
```

The virtual environment is active when you see (env_name) > in parenthesis at the start of the prompt.

```
(env_name) >
```

Install packages in a virtual environment

When a new virtual environment is created, no packages are installed by default. If you use the Anaconda distribution of Python, the base environment contains about 600 packages that come with Anaconda. But a fresh new virtual environment will just have Python installed, no other packages.

To install a package into the virtual environment env_name, first make sure the environment is active ((env_name) before the prompt). Then package installation is accomplished with the conda install command followed by the package name. To install Matplotlib into a virtual environment type:

```
(env_name) > conda install matplotlib
```

Multiple packages can be installed with the same command. To install both NumPy and Jupyter at the same time use:

```
(env_name) > conda install numpy jupyter
```

Deactivate a virtual environment

To deactivate an active environment, run the command:

```
(env_name) > conda deactivate
>
```

When the virtual environment is deactivated, the prompt looks normal (just >), with no environment name in parenthesis before it.

List your virtual environments

View a list of your virtual environments using the command conda info --envs or conda env list.

```
> conda activate env_name
(env_name) > conda info --envs

# conda environments:
#
```

APPENDIX D. VIRTUAL ENVIRONMENTS

```
base                        /home/tribilium/anaconda3
env_name                  * /home/tribilium/anaconda3/envs/env_name
matplotlib                  /home/tribilium/anaconda3/envs/matplotlib
```

Notice the * asterisk on the line with env_name. The virtual environment with the * is currently active.

To exit the virtual environment, use the command conda deactivate.

```
(env_name) > conda deactive
```

If you run conda info --envs again, there is no * in front of env_name. That's because the env_name virtual environment is no longer active.

```
> conda info --envs

# conda environments:
#
base                      * /home/tribilium/anaconda3
env_name                    /home/tribilium/anaconda3/envs/env_name
matplotlib                  /home/tribilium/anaconda3/envs/matplotlib
```

Remove a virtual environment

Remove a virtual environment with the command conda remove --name env_name --all. You need to exit out of the environment before you remove it.

Check to see if the virtual environment you want to remove is present:

```
> conda info --envs

# conda environments:
#
base                      * /home/tribilium/anaconda3
env_name                    /home/tribilium/anaconda3/envs/env_name
matplotlib                  /home/tribilium/anaconda3/envs/matplotlib
```

Remove the virtual environment called env_name using the command.

```
> conda remove --name env_name --all

Proceed ([y]/n)?
```

Type [y] to remove the environment. Now view a list of your virtual environments again. Note that env_name is no longer in the list.

```
> conda info --envs

# conda environments:
#
base                      * /home/tribilium/anaconda3
matplotlib                  /home/tribilium/anaconda3/envs/matplotlib
```

Appendix E NumPy Math Functions

The code below prints out all NumPy functions and methods:

```
import numpy as np
for func in dir(np):
    print(func)
```

NumPy Array Creation and Manipulation Functions and Methods

np.array	np.matrix	np.meshgrid
np.arange	np.traspose	np.dot
np.ndarray	np.size	np.cross
np.zeros	np.shape	np.asmatrix
np.ones	np.reshape	np.asarray

NumPy Exponential and Logarithmic Functions and Methods

np.log	np.logaddexp	np.sqrt
np.log10	np.logaddexp2	np.power
np.log1p	np.exp	np.e
np.log2	np.exp2	

NumPy Trigonometric Functions and Methods

np.pi	np.arcsinh	np.radians
np.sin	np.arccosh	np.sinc
np.cos	np.arctanh	np.sinh
np.tan	np.arctan2	np.tanh
np.arcsin	np.radians	np.angle
np.arccos	np.rad2deg	
np.arctan	np.deg2rad	

NumPy Statistics Functions and Methods

np.mean	np.var	np.amax
np.average	np.correlate	np.ptp
np.median	np.histogram	np.percentile
np.std	np.amin	

Appendix F Git and GitHub

Git is one of the standard *version control* systems used by developers to save code and work on code collaboratively as a team. **Git** is a program run on the command line or **Anaconda Prompt**. If you use Windows, the **gitbash** program can be downloaded at git-scm.com/downloads. **Git** was created by Linus Torvalds, who also designed the Linux operating system.

GitHub.com (now owned by Microsoft) is a website and service used by programmers and open source projects to share code and allow contributors to propose changes to existing code. Other services such as BitBucket.org can be integrated with **git** too.

Both **git** and GitHub.com are useful for problem solvers working in teams.

Before using **git** and GitHub.com, it is helpful to understand a couple of terms:

- **git** - a command line program used to track file changes and collaborate on code with others.
- **repo** - short name for "repository". A repo is a directory and its contents.
- **local repo** - a directory and its contents on your computer that **git** knows about.
- **remote repo** - a directory and its contents stored in the cloud that **git** knows about.

Useful **git** commands are summarized below:

- `git clone https://github.com/user/repo.git` copy a remote repo from GitHub.com into a local directory
- `git init` create a new local repo in the current folder
- `git remote add origin https://github.com/user/repo.git` link a local repo to a remote repo on GitHub.com
- `git add .` add all files and changes to the local repo
- `git commit -m "commit message"` commit the changes in the local repo with the message `"commit message"`
- `git push origin master` push local changes up to the remote repo
- `git pull origin master` pull down the version in the remote repo into the local repo

Cloning a repo

One common operation to complete with **git** is to clone a repo from GitHub.com and save it locally. This means you copy all the files stored in the remote repo on GitHub.com onto your local computer. Cloning a repo from Github.com is accomplished with:

```
$ git clone https://github.com/user/repo.git
```

This command copies the repo named `repo` from the user named `user` to a local computer. To clone the repo for MicroPython, use:

```
$ git clone https://github.com/micropython/micropython.git
```

Creating and synching a remote repo on GitHub.com with a local repo

Another common task to complete with **git** is to synch a remote repo on GitHub.com with a local repo on your local computer. This is useful when you want to keep the files in a particular project synched across multiple computers. Synched remote and local repos are also useful for a group of problem solvers working on the same project. Each team member has access to the same remote repo on GitHub.com and each team member has the same local repo on their computer.

Create a remote repo on GitHub.com

First, go to GitHub.com/join and create a new account. Log in and create a new repo. It is a good idea to include a license and a *.gitignore* file. For a Python project, the *.gitignore* file for Python is a good start. Two common licenses for open source projects (projects you are willing to share with others) are the *GNU General Public License v3.0* and the *MIT License*.

Make a new local repo and link the local repo to the remote repo on GitHub.com

Second, create a local directory and `cd` into it. Initialize a git repo locally in that directory. Then synch the local folder with the remote repo on GitHub.com.

```
$ mkdir newproject
$ cd newproject
$ git init
$ git remote add origin https://github.com/user/repo.git
$ git pull origin master
```

Add, commit and push changes up to Github.com

Third, work on the project locally. For example, you could edit one of the files in the directory `newproject` or create a new file in the directory `newproject`.

Finally, save your work and commit the changes you made with **git**. Push those changes up to the remote repo on GitHub.com

```
$ git add .
$ git commit -m "commit message"
$ git push origin master
```

Pull the most recent version from GitHub.com before each work session

If using **git** and GitHub.com, remember to pull the most recent version of the repo down from GitHub.com before you make any changes locally. If changes are made locally before the version of the repo on GitHub.com is synched, the local repo and remote repo will be out of synch.

```
$ git pull origin master
```

After local changes are made, save the changes and push to GitHub.com

```
$ git add .
$ git commit -m "commit message"
$ git push orign master
```

Appendix G   LaTeX Math

LaTeX math can be included in Jupyter notebook markdown cells. LaTeX math can also be included in parts of Matplotlib plots like axis labels and text fields.

Inline LaTeX math commands need to be enclosed by the dollar signs.

```
The angle is $2\pi$ radians
```

The markup above is rendered as:

The angle is 2π radians

A table of useful LaTeX commands and the associated output is below. Note curly braces { } are used to surround LaTeX math elements and a backslash \ is used before LaTeX commands.

LaTeX Command	Output
2^{3}	2^3
H_{2}	H_2
\frac{3}{4}	$\frac{3}{4}$
\pi	π
\Delta	Δ
\epsilon	ϵ
\sigma	σ
2 \times 3	2×3
\int_{a}^{b} x^2 dx	$\int_a^b x^2 dx$
\sum	$\sum$
\vec{F}	$\vec{F}$
\hat{k}	$\hat{k}$
\bar{x}	$\bar{x}$
15 \%	15%

Appendix H   Problem Solving with Python Book Construction

Jupyter Notebooks

This book was constructed using Jupyter notebooks. The GitHub.com repo for the book can be found at:

   github.com/ProfessorKazarinoff/Problem-Solving-with-Python-37-Edition

The directory structure of the GitHub repo contains all the Jupyter notebooks used the write the book. The repo also contains a set of custom conversion scripts and templates which convert the Jupyuter notebooks into *.html* and *.tex* files.

```
Problem-Solving-with-Python-37-Edition/
|-- conversion_tools/
|-- notebooks/
|-- LICENSE
|-- notebooks/
|-- pdf/
|-- README.md
|-- website/
```

The notebooks directory contains a directory for each chapter of the book:

```
notebooks/
|-- 00-Preface/
|-- 01-Orientation/
|-- 02-Jupyter-Notebooks/
|-- 03-The-Python-REPL/
|-- 04-Data-Types-and-Variables/
|-- 05-Matrices-and-Arrays/
|-- 06-Plotting-with-Matplotlib/
|-- 07-Functions-and-Modules/
|-- 08-If-Else-Try-Except/
|-- 09-Loops/
|-- 10-Symbolic-Math/
|-- 11-Python-and-External-Hardware/
|-- 12-MicroPython/
|-- 99-Appendix/
`-- figures/
```

There is a Jupyter notebook for each section of the book within each chapter directory. Each chapter directory contains an images directory for any images used in the markdown cells of the notebooks.

```
01-Orientation/
|-- 01.00-Welcome.ipynb
|-- 01.01-Why-Python.ipynb
|-- 01.02-The-Anaconda-Distribution-of-Python.ipynb
|-- 01.03-Installing-Anaconda-on-Windows.ipynb
|-- 01.04-Installing-Anaconda-on-MacOS.ipynb
|-- 01.05-Installing-Anaconda-on-Linux.ipynb
|-- 01.06-Installing-Python-from-Python-dot-org.ipynb
|-- 01.07-Summary.ipynb
|-- 01.08-Review-Questions.ipynb
`-- images/
```

Website

The website for this book was constructed using **Mkdocs** (https://www.mkdocs.org) and the **Material for MkDocs** (https://squidfunk.github.io/mkdocs-material/) theme. Jupyter noteboks were exported to *.html* files with markdown cells unformatted using a custom script and **nbconvert**.

Hardcopy

The hard copy of the book was constructed using LaTeX, **nbconvert** and a set of custom scripts and templates. One conversion script combined all of the notebooks into one BIG notebook. The BIG notebook was then converted into LaTeX using **nbconvert** and a custom template. Outside of the Python ecosystem, a separate installation of TeXworks compiled the LaTeX *.tex* file to a *.pdf* document.

Appendix I   Contributions

Any corrections, typos or suggestions to improve the text can be emailed to:

```
errata@problemsolvingwithpython.com
```

Please include the chapter number and section number in your email. Include in your email if you would like to remain anonymous or have your name recognized in the contributor list. Thank-you in advance for improving the text for others.

Contributor List

- Levi, Blessing, and Ngan helped improve some review questions

Appendix J   Cover Artwork

Mike Schultz is a printmaker and illustrator who has taught art to Burmese migrant youth on the Thailand-Burma border. He currently lives and works in Portland, Oregon with his cat, Siam.

Instagram: `@mike_schultz_studio`

Website: mikeschultzstudio.com

Appendix K   About the Author

Peter D. Kazarinoff, PhD is a full-time faculty member in Engineering and Engineering Technology at Portland Community College in Portland, Oregon. Peter earned a PhD in Materials Science and Engineering from the University of Washington and a BA from Cornell University. He teaches courses in Engineering Programming, Materials Science, Manufacturing and others at Portland Community College.

He blogs at: pythonforundergradengineers.com

Peter lives in beautiful Portland, Oregon with his wife and two kids.

Made in the USA
Coppell, TX
29 August 2020